Adventure Guide™ *to*

Michigan

Kevin & Laurie Hillstrom

HUNTER

Hunter Publishing, Inc.
130 Campus Drive, Edison NJ 08818
(732) 225 1900, (800) 255 0343, Fax (732) 417 0482
e-mail: hunterpub@emi.net

In Canada
1220 Nicholson Rd., Newmarket, Ontario
Canada L3Y 7V1, (800) 399 6858

In the UK
Windsor Books International
The Boundary, Wheatley Road
Garsington, Oxford OX44 9EJ
England, 01865 361122, Fax 01865 361133

ISBN 1-55650-820-4

© 1998 Hunter Publishing, Inc.

Maps by Kim André & Lissa Dailey
(© 1998 Hunter Publishing, Inc.)

Photos:
Lake Richie, Isle Royale, John & Ann Mahan (front cover);
Pictured Rocks, Stan Chladex (back cover)

About the Authors

Kevin Hillstrom and Laurie Collier Hillstrom have backpacked or paddled throughout the Upper and Lower Peninsulas of Michigan, their long-time home. In addition, their adventure travels have taken them to some of North America's most spectacular wilderness areas, including Alaska's Gates of the Arctic and Lake Clark National Park, Arizona's Grand Canyon, the Canadian Rockies, Olympic National Park, and various other destinations throughout the Pacific Northwest and High Southwest.

The Hillstroms are also partners in Northern Lights Writers Group, an editorial services firm. They are the authors of several books, including the award-winning *Biography Today, Environmental Leaders* and *The Vietnam Experience: A Concise Encyclopedia of American Literature, Songs, and Films.*

Acknowledgments

During the course of writing this book, we drew upon the knowledge and experience of a wide range of people, including an array of outfitters, dive shop and canoe livery operators, and bike shop owners; rangers and other staffers who protect Michigan's parks and forests; and a wide circle of friends who share our enthusiasm for exploring the state's rivers, lakes, and woodlands. We thank all of these folks for their help.

www.hunterpubling.com

Our Web site features an in-depth sysnopsis of each Hunter travel guide (we have several hundred different titles), including the latest arrivals hot off the press! Comments from book reviewers are quoted, along with price, page count, ISBN and even an author profile. Quick-loading cover images show you every title.

Secure online ordering is available with payment by credit card or check. Commercial customers may also use the Web site to place their orders.

Contents

■ Maps

Adventure Guides

Adventure travel is a way to experience places at a slower pace – on foot, on a bike, in a canoe, on horseback.

The focus of Adventure Guides is on outdoor activities – everything from hiking to scuba diving, fishing to sailing. The best local outfitters are listed, with contact numbers, prices, and all the details you need. The guides also cover the basic needs of **all** travelers, with full information on accommodations, restaurants, shopping, getting around, historical background and sightseeing.

(ISBN prefix 1-55650)

Alaska Highway 824-7 $15.95

Arizona 725-9 $12.95

Atlantic Canada 819-0 $16.95

Barbados 707-0 $15.95

Belize 785-2 $16.95

Bermuda 706-2 $12.95

Cayman Islands 786-0 $16.95

Colorado 724-0 $15.95

Costa Rica 722-4 $16.95

Dominican Republic 814-X $15.95

Florida Keys/Everglades 745-3 $14.95

Florida's West Coast 787-9 $14.95

Georgia 782-8 $15.95

Georgia/Carolina Coasts 747-X $15.95

Great Smokies 720-8 $15.95

High Southwest 723-2 $15.95

Idaho 789-5 $16.95

Jamaica 748-8 $16.95

Leeward Islands 788-7 $15.95

New Hampshire 822-0 $15.95

New Mexico 727-5 $12.95

Northern California 821-2 $15.95

Northern Florida 769-0 $15,95

Orlando/Ctrl Florida 825-0 $15.95

Puerto Rico 749-6 $15.95

Southeast Florida 811-5 $15.95

Southern California 791-7 $16.95

Tennessee 745-7 $13.95

Texas 812-3 $15.95

Utah 726-7 $12.95

Vermont 773-9 $15.95

Virginia 816-6 $15.95

Virgin Islands 746-1 $16.95

The Yucatán 792-5 $15.95

These and other Hunter travel guides are available nationwide in bookstores or from the publisher at Hunter Publishing, 130 Campus Drive, Edison NJ 08818. ☎ (800) 255 0343, (732) 225 1900. Or order through our Web site at www.hunterpublishing.com.

Introduction

Blessed with more than 11,000 inland lakes, more miles of freshwater shoreline than any other state, several national wild and scenic rivers, four national forests, six major state forests, two national lakeshores, an extensive state park system, and one glorious national park, Michigan promises myriad pleasures for outdoorsy natives and visitors. The state also is home to a multitude of other attractive destinations, from the quaint, 19th-century atmosphere of Mackinac Island to the neon nightlife and cultural attractions of Metropolitan Detroit and other cities. These varied charms make the Great Lakes State one of the most popular vacation destinations.

History

Native Americans

Native American Indians were the first inhabitants of Michigan. In fact, evidence suggests that Indian tribes mined copper out of the Upper Peninsula and Isle Royale more than 3,000 years ago, indicating that they may have been the first fabricators of metal in the western hemisphere. By the early 17th century, when white men took their first footsteps in the region, half a dozen different tribes made their homes in present-day Michigan. The most important of these Algonquin tribes were the **Potawatomi** people, who lived in southern Michigan; the **Ottawa**, who resided in the western reaches of the Lower Peninsula; and the **Chippewa**, who roamed the forests of the northeast.

European Exploration

The first European to explore Michigan soil was probably **Étienne Brulé**, a colorful fellow with a thirst for wilderness and the unknown. He and subsequent French explorers discovered and began mapping Lakes Michigan and Superior in an effort to find the fabled water passage to the Pacific Ocean and the Orient. French explorer Jean Nicolet, who traversed the Great Lakes in the 1630s, reportedly was so convinced that he had found the Northwest Passage upon crossing Lake Michigan that he garbed himself in mandarin's robes when he went ashore at Green Bay.

The French

Thirty-some years later, in 1668, French missionary **Jacques Marquette** founded Michigan's first permanent white settlement at Sault Ste. Marie. He and other Jesuit priests of the era were pivotal in settling Michigan, not only because they established missions that became the cornerstones of future cities, but because of their passion for exploring the strange and vast wilderness that surrounded them. "Long before the crown's representatives in the east knew how the land lay or how the rivers ran in the high country, the Jesuits were finding out, joining a passion for saving lost souls to a deep and abiding curiosity about the geography of the region where the lost souls were temporarily in residence," wrote historian Bruce Catton in *Michigan: A Bicentennial History.* "Along with everything else, they were matchless explorers, and they left their mark on the land in a way the king's men never did."

During much of the 17th century, France attached value to Michigan only because of the rising volume of valuable furs that came from the region. A network of missions, trading posts, and forts subsequently materialized, but it is fair to say that France never fully appreciated what it had in its grasp. Some of the Crown's representatives – most notably Antoine de la Mothe Cadillac, who in 1701 built Fort Ponchartrain and founded the city of Detroit – tried to convince France that it should "stop treating this country as a mere outpost [and] plant a genuine colony here." Cadillac argued that "this country [is] so temperate, so fertile, and so beautiful that it may justly be called the earthly paradise of North America," and that it could be a dazzling addition to the Crown's holdings if France would expend some effort to make it so. But French support for settlement of the region was fitful; it remained preoccupied, to the exclusion of all else, with the wealth that lay in the sleek coats of Michigan's wildlife.

But even though France's efforts at colonization were sporadic, the feverish fur trade took its toll on the tribes that had long roamed the territory's deep forests. Prior to the arrival of the Europeans, the Indians had been content with their lifestyles. But when they saw how the Europeans compensated them for the furs that they brought in to the wilderness trading posts, a fundamental shift took place in Indian society. The daily lives of the Indians became increasingly driven by the need to gather furs, and other aspects of their society began to fall into disrepair. The Indian, wrote Catton, "was no longer independent, and although he tried desperately to cling to his old culture it had been cut loose from its roots.... The Indian was beginning to live in a new cultural atmosphere that he had not bargained for and in which he could not be happy. His society was no longer primeval; it lived in the shadow of a society richer, stronger, and infinitely more complex; and as the years went on, the Indian's society grew weaker and duller."

The British

In 1760, after defeating France in the French and Indian War, the British took over Michigan and its lucrative fur trade. This control was further cemented with the signing of the 1763 Treaty of Paris, which gave Britain dominion over Canada and the Great Lakes region. But the territory proved a difficult one to maintain, for the Indians of the region were decidedly unhappy with the turn of events. In 1763 the Ottawa chieftain Pontiac led an uprising that laid siege to Detroit for five months. This revolt ultimately failed, but the British triumph proved short-lived. The Union Jack would fly over Michigan for only a few more years. The American Revolution triggered another change of ownership, and in 1783 Britain was forced to hand the territory over to the fledgling United States. But like boorish tenants refusing to heed an eviction notice, the British continued to control the forts at Detroit and Michilimackinac, determined to milk every last drop of wealth out of the fur business. They finally left in 1796.

The Territory of Michigan

On July 1, 1805, the territory of Michigan was created. Detroit was named the capital, and Revolutionary War soldier William Hull became the region's first governor. Hull's tenure proved a bumpy one, though. Most of Detroit was destroyed by fire shortly after his arrival, and rapidly deteriorating relations with the region's Indians retarded economic and population growth. Hull's less than glorious stewardship of the territory ended with the onset of the War of 1812, during which he surrendered the capital to the British and their Indian allies after frittering away a significant portion of his men and resources on an unsuccessful invasion of Canada.

In 1813 the United States brought Michigan back under its control and, under the guidance of its new governor, Lewis Cass, the territory finally began to grow. Cass, wrote Catton, was "wholly dedicated to the idea that Michigan Territory must be developed, populated, and made prosperous. He undertook to get the Indians to surrender title to the land, saw to it that the land thus acquired was properly surveyed so that people could buy farms and building lots, and then made certain that the restless folk in the east and beyond the Atlantic who wanted to get homesteads in the virgin west knew about Michigan and directed their footsteps toward it. He was fantastically successful in all three ventures."

During the 1820s and 1830s, as settlers poured into the territory, the woodland fur trade peaked and then began its slow decline, weakened by growing agricultural pressure and decades of feverish trapping activity. This decline marked the end of an era for the Michigan Territory. "On close examination the fur trade does not seem to have been exactly golden," mused Catton. "It was as ugly and vicious as unbridled greed, and a good many of its practitioners were lawless thugs who defied the authorities, debased the Indians, and murdered each other with total absence of restraint. Yet the whole thing did have color and excitement, and when all is said and done, it must be admitted that it was never dull. Lawless men have always captivated Americans, and what they did in Michigan was at least done against a backdrop of enchanting scenery."

By the mid-1830s, a **state government** had been formed, and the southern part of the Lower Peninsula was gaining an increasing reputation as a fertile area for agricultural endeavors. Many settlers from the eastern states and immigrants from Europe were bowled over by what lay arrayed before them upon their arrival. "I have left [England] and am in a country where all is life and animation, where I hear on every side the sound of exultation, where everyone speaks of the past with triumph, the present with delight, the future with growing confidence and anticipation," marveled one English settler. "Is not this a community in which one may rejoice to live?"

But even as Michigan's southern reaches blossomed with rolling pastureland and fields of corn and wheat, Michigan's attempts to gain entrance into the Union were stalled by a bitter dispute with Ohio over ownership of the town of Toledo. Indeed, Michigan and Ohio nearly came to blows over the issue. As time passed, however, it became clear that Michigan's hopes for statehood were predicated on relinquishing its claims on the town. It did so, albeit reluctantly, and was welcomed into the Union in 1837. The state was given the Upper Peninsula as compensation for the loss of Toledo, but most of its citizens were dismissive of the parcel. The area, sneered critics, was a cold, unfriendly wilderness of little economic value.

Mining

Attitudes rapidly changed, though, with the discovery of major copper and iron deposits in the Upper Peninsula in the 1840s. Mining companies quickly descended on the region, but the dearth of transportation options triggered a good deal of teeth gnashing, and a great hue and cry went up to build a canal on the St. Mary's River so that the iron and copper could be more easily delivered to the east. The **Sault Ste. Marie Canal** was thrown open for service in 1855, and the Upper Peninsula mining industry promptly exploded. "What was done at the Soo (as the Sault Ste. Marie Canal was commonly known) pulled the ores out of the Upper Peninsula rocks like a gigantic magnet – at exactly the moment when the country's manifold necessities demanded more and ever more things made of iron and steel," said Catton.

Timber

A similar explosion of activity was taking place in the Lower Peninsula, as the timber industry gobbled up Michigan's vast woodlands with incredible speed. Lumbering in Michigan had initially been little more than an effort to clear land for farming, but by the mid-19th century, people had figured out that there was money to be made. As demand for Michigan lumber grew, state timber companies rushed to meet the call. Sawmill towns sprung up overnight, and the state's riverways became clogged with logs. The timber industry also was a major factor in the development of the state's railroad system, as the lumber companies called for an infrastructure that would enable them to transport their logs more easily. As a result, an ever-growing network of little railroad tracks began to snake their way into the heart of Michigan's North Country. The Michigan timber industry took off in 1847, and for the next 50 years the state's woodland resources were harvested with amazing zeal. "By 1897 the sawmills of Michigan... processed 160 billion board feet of white pine and left no more than six billion standing in the whole state," wrote Wallace Stegner in *A Short History of Conservation*. "It was a feeding frenzy of sharks."

Post-Civil War

After the Civil War – in which Michigan lined up as a staunch ally of the Union – the state continued to enjoy sustained economic development, in large part because of its timber and mineral resources. "Suddenly that fatal Michigan word – *inexhaustible* – began to be heard," noted Catton. "The copper was inexhaustible, and so was the iron, and so of course was the timber, and it was time for everybody to step up to the Lord's table and eat his fill, no matter how great his appetite." Farming, however, remained the cornerstone of the state's economy. During the last quarter of the 19th century, Michigan farming families generally did well for themselves, and the state's agricultural base enabled it to survive when its timber and mining industries began to decline. But life was not always rosy in Michigan's farm country, either. Many farming communities resented the excessive influence that railroad and other business interests wielded over the state legislature, and periodic flare-ups between Michigan's farming and business communities created a sometimes unstable political environment.

The Automobile

In 1896 Detroiter Henry Ford rolled out the **world's first automobile**. This vehicle ushered in a new era for Michigan and the world. The invention proved immensely popular and, bolstered by the introduction of a flurry of performance improvements and mass production methods, Detroit emerged as the center of world automobile production by the early 1920s.

Around this same time, the state's timber industry began a fast fade, a victim of its own appetites. Many little logging towns slowly dried up and blew away in a manner that must have been exceedingly painful for their inhabitants. Ill-advised efforts to farm the cleared land often fared poorly, and abandoned farms and ghost towns became commonplace in Michigan's North Country. Ironically, however, the economic downturn allowed the wilderness to make a comeback of sorts, and as the region's woodlands began to fill in again, a corresponding increase in Michigan wildlife could be seen.

The Depression

The Great Depression of the early 1930s devastated Michigan. The state's all-important auto industry staggered as car purchases plummeted across the nation. By 1933 nearly half of Michigan's factory workers were without work, and social unrest intensified throughout the state. Riots erupted in Southeast Michigan, and the state was shaken by discovery of the Black Legion, a secret right-wing terrorist organization. Meanwhile, in Royal Oak, a suburb of Detroit, Father Charles E. Coughlin's anti-Semitic, pro-Nazi tirades reached a radio audience of millions in the late 1930s (he was finally reined in by his superiors in the early 1940s).

The Arsenal of Democracy

During World War II, Detroit and other state industrial centers emerged as the so-called "arsenal of democracy," as Michigan factories operated full-bore to produce trucks, tanks, armaments, and other materials for the war effort. This industrial expansion created a great need for labor, and Southern blacks and whites rushed to fill the void. Racial tensions soon cast a shadow over Michigan's factories, and in 1943 a clash between whites and blacks resulted in the deaths of 34 people.

The Peace Dividend

After the war, Michigan was one of the main recipients of the "peace dividend." Its economy flourished, as 1950s-era prosperity created an unprecedented demand for automobiles and other consumer products in which the state was heavily involved. The 1940s and 1950s also saw a fundamental change in worker-management relations. Many factory workers had labored for years under grim circumstances, with low wages and poor working conditions the norm. The rise of labor unions in the state's factories and assembly lines changed all that. Once unions established themselves in the auto industry, the state became a strongly pro-union one, and workers saw a dramatic upturn in their economic fortunes.

The 1960s

This era was a period of turmoil in Michigan, just as elsewhere in the country. Festering social and economic problems triggered a conflagration of violence in 1967, when Detroit erupted in several days of violence that took 43 lives. Social unrest continued into the 1970s, as the state grappled with issues like school desegregation, unemployment, the oil "crisis," and the Big Three's dangerously slow reaction to changing consumer demands. But the 1970s also saw the state make some noteworthy advances. It emerged as a national leader on environmental issues, adopting a number of strong laws to protect its natural resources. One of the most noteworthy of the state's environmental actions was its 1970 decision to ban the pesticide DDT (Michigan was the first state to do so).

The 1980s

During the 1980s, unemployment remained high, and Detroit and some other major metropolitan areas continued to stagger under the weight of a whole slew of urban problems, including "white flight," poverty, crime, drugs, and government neglect. But the all-important auto industry began to rebound from its woeful late 1970s-early 1980s performance, and the state continued to nourish its fast-growing tourism industry.

The 1990s

The 1990s has been a good decade for Michigan. Carried along by the national economic upturn of the mid-1990s, many of its key industries have enjoyed immensely profitable operations in the last few years, and unemployment reached record low levels in 1997. Some of its most troubled cities, most notably Detroit, appear to be on the rebound as well, and the state's bountiful natural attractions continue to make it a most appealing destination for vacationers throughout the year. Of course, concerns still remain: the state government's lackluster management of its natural resources in recent years is a major concern among Michigan conservationists and sportsmen, and Southeast Michigan's continued reliance on the automotive industry, despite increased economic diversification, makes it particularly vulnerable to national economic downturns. But as Michigan sits poised on the cusp of the 21st century, it is an undeniably prosperous state, and one that looks to the future with confidence.

Geography/Land

Michigan's total area of more than 58,500 square miles (including nearly 1,600 square miles of inland water) is divided into upper and lower peninsulas. The **Lower Peninsula**, a mitten-shaped block of land that accounts for about 70% of the state's total area, extends northward from Indiana and Ohio. It is bordered on the west by Lake Michigan and on the east by Lakes Huron and Erie and their connecting waterways (the St. Clair River, Lake St. Clair, and the Detroit River). Similarly, a good portion of the **Upper Peninsula** is bracketed by the Great Lakes. Though its western side shares a border with northern Wisconsin, the peninsula's remaining flanks look out on steel-grey waters. Lake Superior guards its northern shores, while Lakes Michigan and Huron stand sentinel over its southern and eastern ramparts.

The western half of the Upper Peninsula is a part of the **Laurentian Shield** (also known as the Canadian Shield), a massive rock formation that is the most dominant feature of eastern and central Canada. Composed of crystalline rocks and granites, the shield was North America's earliest land mass. The Upper Peninsula's eastern region and the entire Lower Peninsula have far heavier concentrations of shale, sandstone, and limestone, with iron and copper deposits. Both of these sections lie in a geographic region known as the **Great Lakes Plain of the Central Lowlands**.

Just as ancient glaciers carved out the mighty Great Lakes as they advanced and retreated, so too did they create the valleys, ridges, rivers, and coastlines that comprise present-day Michigan. In addition to shaping the topography, ice-age glacial movements determined the quality of soil in various portions of the state. Advancing glaciers scoured the Laurentian Shield, lifting its soil and depositing it further south, where it combined with earth created by the erosion of sandstone and shale to create a tremendously fertile belt of land. This long-ago glacial movement accounts not only for southern Michigan's agricultural past and present, but for the lack of same in much of the state's northern reaches. Still, even though the Upper Peninsula got the short end of the stick in terms of good farming soil, it received compensation in the form of rich mineral deposits.

The Terrain

Today, the central and southern counties of Michigan's Lower Peninsula are composed of primarily flat or gently rolling terrain, large expanses of which were cleared of forest back in the 18th and 19th centuries so that fields could be planted. Further north, the land is hillier and more rugged, and the landscape more closely resembles its heavily wooded appearance prior to the arrival of European settlers. The largest of the state's 11,000 lakes – Houghton, Burt, Charlevoix, Mullett, and Torch – are within the Lower Peninsula.

The Upper Peninsula's eastern sections are level for the most part, with a preponderance of marshy lands, but the peninsula's western reaches offer considerably more challenging terrain, as craggy valleys mix with the state's most formidable mountainous ridges. Indeed, the state's highest elevations can be found in the Porcupine Mountains (Ontonagon County) and the Huron Mountains (Marquette County, Baraga County), both of which run along Lake Superior's southern shoreline, and the Keweenaw Peninsula's Copper Range, which owes its name to the vast copper deposits found in the region.

The Rivers

Both the Upper and Lower Peninsulas feature many scenic rivers in addition to thousands of pretty lakes. Most UP rivers are of modest length, but a number of them have a wild temperament, with rapids and waterfalls dotting their lengths. The Escanaba, which originates in Marquette County and empties into Lake Michigan's Green Bay, is the longest of the UP rivers. The Lower Peninsula's rivers are generally longer and milder, and are vital in draining Lower Peninsula watersheds. The Muskegon River is the longest river in the entire state, while the Saginaw River and its tributaries (the Shiawassee, Tittabawassee, and Cass), which drain water from the Saginaw Valley into Lake Huron, comprise the state's largest river system.

Climate

Michigan sees dramatic changes in weather over the course of the year. This is true of both the Upper and Lower Peninsulas, but it is worth noting that these two regions often experience significantly different weather. Indeed, throughout the year there tends to be a temperature difference of 10-12° between the extreme northern and southern parts of the state, and during the winter, the northern counties of the UP receive an exceptional amount of snowfall (20 feet or more in some years), many times what typically falls on Detroit and other southeastern Michigan communities. Rainfall is moderate throughout the state.

In the Lower Peninsula, summer days are hot (90° temperatures are not uncommon) and often humid, while winter temperatures typically hover in the 15-30° range for much of the season. The western side of the Lower Peninsula receives significantly more snow accumulation than the eastern side because of lake-effect snow. Spring and autumn are often glorious, with sunny days giving way to cool evenings. Fall is a particularly beautiful time to roam Michigan's trails and roadways, as its bristling hardwood forests erupt with color.

Up in the UP, the summer season is significantly shorter (patches of snow can still be found in deep woods around Memorial Day), with spring arriving later and fall rolling in earlier than they do in lower Michigan. As with the Lower Peninsula, spring and fall often provide some of the year's most pleasant weather.

Flora & Fauna

Michigan contains a fantastic array of wildlife, including black bear, deer, elk, moose, wolf, coyote, rabbit, beaver, skunk, weasel, marten, mink, otter, raccoon, badger, porcupine, bobcat, and red fox. Many of these species make their home in the forests of the state's northern Lower Peninsula and Upper Peninsula, which also contain a wide variety of birds, including hundreds of species of songbirds (including the rare Kirtland's warbler). Many of these, from the acadian flycatcher to the yellow-throated vireo, are migratory. Michigan also supports a multitude of raptors (eagles, peregrine falcons, ospreys, owls) and many types of game birds (pheasants, partridges, wild turkeys, grouse, and a variety of ducks and geese).

The state also has a tremendous variety of plant species. Many different kinds of hardwoods and conifers can be found in the forestlands. In its southern counties, hardwoods such as maple, elm, oak, and hickory predominate, while conifers become an integral feature in the woodlands of the Upper Peninsula and the northern part of the Lower Peninsula. Indeed, the state's northern realms feature a stunning blend of pine, spruce, aspen, white birch, maple, oak, beech, and other species. The state's moderate rainfall, vast forest canopies, and sunny meadows combine to create good growing conditions for hundreds of plant species, from wild flowering plants (bloodroot, dicentra, cress, asters, buttercups, trillium, mandrake, blue lupine, arbutus, goldenrod, iris, orange milkweed, shooting stars, violets, daisies, sunflowers, tiger lilies, asters) to fruit-bearing plants (blackberry, raspberry, blueberry). Fern species are plentiful as well.

Government & Economy

The Constitution

Michigan's current constitution went into effect on January 1, 1964. This was the fourth state constitution that was approved; previous constitutions were adopted in 1835 (two years before the state was admitted to the Union), 1850, and 1908. The 1964 constitution has been amended on several occasions since it was passed, and it includes a provision that calls for Michigan voters to decide every 16 years whether to call a convention for the purpose of undertaking a general revision of the constitution.

The primary sections of the constitution are a general declaration of rights; an allocation of duties, responsibilities, and powers among the state's executive, legislative, and judicial branches; and guidelines regarding local government, taxation, finance, and education. In the executive branch, the state's governor, lieutenant governor, secretary of state, and attorney general are elected by Michigan citizens to four-year terms. Other key government officials in such areas as natural resource management, finance, transportation, and education are appointed by the governor. The state legislature is composed of a house of representatives of 110 members, who are elected to two-year terms, and a state senate of 38 members, elected to four-year terms. Michigan, which has 18 electoral votes, sends two senators and 16 representatives to the US Congress.

Politics

Historically, Michigan's political leanings have undergone a couple of significant changes since it joined the Union. A Republican stronghold during the late 19th and early 20th centuries, the state switched allegiances to the Democratic side for much of the mid-20th century, at least on the national level (the state sided with the Democratic candidate in presidential elections from 1932 to 1968). Neither party has assumed a commanding presence on the state level. Although Republicans have held the governorship for a good portion of the last 35 years, the state legislature during that time has often been controlled by the Democrats.

Manufacturing

Economically, Michigan's star has been hitched to manufacturing and, more specifically, the automotive industry for most of this century. Indeed, Detroit's status as the home of America's "Big Three" automotive empires – Ford, General Motors, and Chrysler – has historically meant that the state's economic fortunes have closely paralleled those of the auto industry. But while the health of the industry remains very important to the state, and especially to the communities of southeast Michigan, numerous other industries also have a significant impact. Over on the southwestern side of the state, cereal and office furniture are king. Battle Creek is home to the Kellogg's cereal company, the largest breakfast cereal company in the country, and the top three US office furniture manufacturers – Haworth, Herman Miller, and Steelcase – all sit near one another in the Grand Rapids area.

But Michigan is a national leader in many other areas of manufacturing as well. It ranks near the top in production of a wide variety of goods, including automobile parts, sports equipment, steel springs, refrigerators, industrial products, tires, rubber goods, chemicals, and paper products. Facilities engaged in the production of these and other goods can be found throughout the Lower Peninsula, though southern Michigan remains the economic heart of the state. In recent years, its reliance on manufacturing has been eased somewhat by the rapid growth of a thriving high technology corridor in the state's southeastern corner.

Agriculture

Many Lower Peninsula communities also rely on agriculture for their economic well-being. About 80% of the country's red tart cherries are grown in Michigan, primarily in the Grand Traverse Bay region, and the state is among the US leaders in production of several other foods as well, including cranberries, navy beans, blueberries, cucumbers, sugar beets, and field beans. Corn, wheat, and hay crops account for the largest proportions of harvested land in the state.

Natural Resources

Up in the UP, folks have historically relied on the region's strong mineral and timber extraction industries to put food on the table. Some Upper Peninsula communities are still involved in copper and iron mining or timber harvesting, but over the last few decades tourism has emerged as a cornerstone of local economies.

People & Culture

The ethnic and cultural gulf between southern Michigan's major metropolitan areas and the state's northernmost towns and villages can hardly be overstated. Indeed, Michigan seems composed of three vastly disparate lands, each with its own unique atmosphere and sensibility. **Southern Lower Michigan** is the industrial, economic, and cultural heart of the state. Indeed, most of the state's major metropolitan areas, with the exception of Traverse City, can be found in this region. These areas – Detroit, Grand Rapids, Lansing, Flint, Saginaw, Kalamazoo, Ann Arbor – also are home to the state's largest universities, finest museums, most exciting nightlife, and most aggravating traffic jams.

Further north, however, the pace eases considerably. Sprawling suburbs and ubiquitous malls and shopping centers gradually give way to small towns and quiet two-lane byways. Those in search of nightlife are not without options in **northern Lower Michigan** – several cities (Traverse City, Cadillac, Alpena) offer a multitude of diversions, and a number of the state's finest resort towns can be found along the Lower Peninsula's northern coastline. But on the whole, life in the Lower Peninsula's North Country has a decidedly rustic, outdoorsy feel to it. This is true even at the height of summer, when cottage owners and vacationers flock to its woodlands, beaches, golf courses, and roads.

Further north, across the Mackinac Bridge, visitors are likely to remark that the **Upper Peninsula** seems to have only the most tenuous relationship to the rest of the state. Sometimes it seems like a lost island of Wisconsin (western UP gas stations are more likely to give away Packers paraphernalia than Lions gear), while at other times its attitude can be likened to that of a 51st state (UP residents call Lower Peninsula natives "trolls," since they live "under" the Mackinac Bridge, and grumblings about seceding from Michigan and forming a separate state called Superior have surfaced from time to time over the years). Hallmarks of the Upper Peninsula's small, scattered communities include independence, community spirit, and fierce pride in 1) the wild beauty that surrounds their homes, and 2) their ability to withstand the long, bone-chilling winters that characterize the region.

Travel Information

When to Go

Traveling in Michigan peaks during the summertime, as various communities stage popular festivals and other events and cottage owners and campers from Michigan's more populous southern realms make their Friday night pilgrimages northward, where many of the state's most popular resort communities, tourist attractions, and recreational opportunities lie. But while the state sees the majority of its visitors during the summer months, Michigan natives know that the state has a wonderful, chameleon-like ability to retain its charm with each passing season. Late autumn snow showers may signal the end of another season of backpacking and canoeing and bicycle touring, but they also remind folks to wax their skis and warm up their snowmobiles.

Costs

The cost of vacationing in Michigan varies considerably, depending on one's agenda and destination. The state's extensive park system – 96 state parks dot the woodlands and shores of Michigan's Upper and Lower Peninsulas, and state forest, national forest, and private campgrounds are present in abundance – provide families with ample opportunities for enjoyable, inexpensive excursions all around the state. Vacationers interested in having a roof over their heads can choose from quaint bed-and-breakfasts to inexpensive chain motels to plush accommodations such as Mackinac Island's celebrated Grand Hotel. Eating options run the gamut as well. Hundreds of inexpensive little restaurants thrive in Michigan's small towns and large cities, from Detroit's Coney Island joints to the ubiquitous pasty-oriented diners of the Upper Peninsula. Fast food chains are entrenched here, just as they are everywhere, but fine dining options are numerous as well, and not just in the state's major metropolitan areas. Indeed, Michigan's many harbor towns and resort communities offer some of the most delicious fare that you will find anywhere.

Not surprisingly, the price of vacationing is generally higher in the state's major cities – Detroit, Grand Rapids, Lansing, Kalamazoo, Traverse City – and in its more exclusive northern resort communities. On the other hand, the splendors of the UP generally are available at a reasonable price.

Transportation

The state's **highway system** can take travelers to any corner of the state, from Benton Harbor, tucked away in the Lower Peninsula's southwestern corner, to Copper Harbor, which lies at the tip of the UP's Keweenaw Peninsula. Major arteries include I-94, which straddles Michigan's southern reaches from Detroit to Kalamazoo and on to Chicago; I-75, which runs all the way from the UP's Sault St. Marie down to Florida; I-96, which connects Detroit, Lansing, Grand Rapids, and Muskegon; US-27 and US-131, both of which slice northward through the heart of the state; and US-2 and M-28, the major east-west passages across the Upper Peninsula. The state's Upper and Lower Peninsula road systems are connected by the incredible Mackinac Bridge, which spans the Straits of Mackinac.

For travelers in the state's southern region, **Amtrak** is another alternative. The passenger rail system makes stops in 20 Michigan cities – including Grand Rapids, Holland, St. Joseph/Benton Harbor, Port Huron, Lapeer, Flint, East Lansing, Battle Creek, Pontiac, Royal Oak, Detroit, Dearborn, Ann Arbor, Jackson, and Albion – and provides service to major cities outside Michigan's borders, most notably Toronto and Chicago. ☎ 800-USA-RAIL or 313-873-3442 for information on schedules and rates.

Michigan's busiest airport is **Wayne County's Detroit Metro Airport**. In 1996 this airport ranked as the world's fifth-busiest in terms of landings and takeoffs and 14th in passenger transportation (it served more than 30 million passengers that year). Northwest Airlines accounts for nearly three-quarters of all passenger traffic at the airport, but many other major airlines have regularly scheduled flights into and out of Detroit as well. Other Michigan airports of note include **Flint's Bishop International Airport**, **Lansing Capital City Airport**, the **Kalamazoo/Battle Creek International Airport**, and **Traverse City's Cherry Capital Airport**.

Special Concerns

The Great Lakes State contains a treasure trove of outdoor recreation attractions for adventurous travelers, but people who choose to explore Michigan's rivers and forests need to take appropriate precautions. A significant number of the state's most popular outdoor destinations are far from any medical facilities, and bad weather can dramatically change the complexion of backcountry excursions. Other factors, from *giardia* to Lyme disease to overly curious bears, can put a serious dent in a trip as well. The trick to avoiding such pitfalls? Proper prior research and planning.

Water

Always treat any water taken from lakes, rivers, or streams to avoid falling victim to giardia or other intestinal infestations. This can be accomplished through use of a good water purification filter or by bringing water to a sustained rolling boil of several minutes' duration.

Ticks

Check yourself for deer ticks, which can carry Lyme disease, a debilitating malady. Symptoms of this illness are often flu-like, and sometimes include an expanding bulls eye-shaped rash, fatigue, fever, achiness, and sore throat. See a doctor immediately if you develop these symptoms after spending time outdoors. If you find that one of these tiny fellows (maximum size about one-quarter of an inch) has made a home for itself on you or another member of your party, coat it with a drop of stove fuel, a bit of alcohol, or insect repellent. If the tick does not let go of its own volition, grasp it with tweezers as close to skin-level as possible and draw it out in a firm but gentle fashion, being careful not to crush it since bacteria could infect the area. After removal, wash the bite site with soap and water, iodine, or alcohol, and keep the tick in a sealable container for possible later identification if it seems likely that it has been attached for a few hours or more. Long pants and long-sleeved shirts can help minimize the risk of exposure to this nasty little bug.

Wildlife

Adventurers also need to practice common sense when encountering Michigan wildlife. Small animals can carry rabies and other diseases, no matter how adorable they might appear. **Moose** and **elk** can be dangerous, too – especially during rutting season or when cows feel their young are threatened – so keep your distance. But no Michigan wildlife encounter is likely to get your pulse racing like a run-in with a **black bear**. Such meetings are rare – and they almost always end in an anticlimactic fashion, for black bears are less aggressive than their grizzly cousins – but they do occur. To minimize the chances of a bear encounter, keep a clean camp. In the backcountry, prepare meals a good distance from your tent, and avoid leaving any food or scented items (such as toothpaste or deodorant) inside. Instead, hang food and scented items from campground bear poles (where available) or in trees (at least 20 feet above the ground and a good 100 feet from camp). Adventurers who do encounter a bear on the trail should keep calm and fight any impulse to flee, since running can trigger an aggressive response from the bear. Retreat slowly, making sure that you provide the bear with an avenue of escape. The most dangerous bears are sows with cubs, so immediately vacate any area where you find a cub. If the worst happens and you are attacked by a black bear, most bear experts contend that, whereas victims of grizzly attacks should play dead, victims of black bear attacks should fight back vigorously.

Know Your Limits

Finally, adventurers exploring Michigan's great outdoors should simply know their limits and recognize that the state's wild waters and woodlands are indifferent to human frailty. Casual weekend paddlers do not belong on the state's whitewater rivers, inexperienced divers have no business diving advanced sites, and folks unfamiliar with basic backcountry necessities (from clothes to first aid kits to survival gear) should think twice before tackling the rugged trails of the Porcupine Mountains or other wilderness areas. The state has plenty of great recreational options for people of all shapes, sizes, and fitness levels, so don't bite off more than you can chew. Assess your skills honestly and pick your destinations accordingly. Exploring the Wolverine State can be a delightful, exciting experience, as long as you plan for it in an intelligent and thoughtful fashion.

Important Phone Numbers

For general travel information on vacation opportunities throughout Michigan, call ☎ 800-5432-YES. To make reservations for accommodations at one of Michigan's state parks, call ☎ 800-44-PARKS.

How to Use This Book

We divide Michigan into three regions – the **southern Lower Peninsula**, the **northern Lower Peninsula**, and the **Upper Peninsula**. Each of these three chapters begins with an introduction to the region, then provides in-depth coverage of attractions – including such major parks as Isle Royale National Park, Sleeping Bear Dunes National Lakeshore, and Porcupine Mountains Wilderness State Park. Within each is transportation information, historical background, a discussion of flora and fauna, camping information, contact information, and full descriptions of outdoor recreation options (hiking, kayaking, canoeing, mountain biking, scuba diving, skiing, snowmobiling, dogsledding, fishing, etc.). Then each chapter moves on to discuss outdoor recreation options available elsewhere in the region, from major mountain biking destinations to prized shipwreck dive sites. Each chapter concludes with a brief rundown of notable restaurants, inns, and bed-and-breakfasts operating in the region.

In addition, this book includes several informative appendices: a guide to Michigan's state parks; a listing of major festivals and outdoor events around the state; contact information for outdoor and conservation organizations in the state; and a listing of notable Michigan guidebooks. Finally, the book features a comprehensive index to help readers find the specific travel information they need.

Southern Lower Michigan

Southern Michigan is the industrial, economic, and cultural heart of the state. Home to the state's major metropolitan areas – Detroit, Grand Rapids, Lansing, Kalamazoo, Ann Arbor – southern Michigan nourishes many of the finest museums, orchestras, and other cultural attractions; its largest universities (Michigan State University and the University of Michigan); its professional and semi-professional sports teams; and many of its most popular tourist destinations, from enormous shopping malls and busy parks and harbors to quaint antique shops and wineries.

Getting Around

The **highway network** in this region is an extensive one, although heavy use of area roadways necessitates a seemingly endless cycle of summertime repairs on major thoroughfares. Despite such inconveniences, however, southern Michigan's highways offer fairly direct routes between major metropolitan areas. Major east-west arteries include I-94, I-96, and I-69; primary north-south routes are US-31 and US-131 (on the west side), US-27 (central), and US-23, M-25, I-275, and I-75 (east).

Amtrak is another alternative for travelers. The passenger rail system has regularly scheduled service at most major southern Michigan cities, including Grand Rapids, Detroit, Flint, and Ann Arbor. The primary **airports** in this region of Michigan are also the two busiest in the state. Wayne County's Detroit Metro Airport is one of the busiest airports in the entire world, in part because it is the major US hub for Northwest Airlines. Other airports of note include Flint's Bishop International Airport and the Kalamazoo/Battle Creek International Airport. A wide range of car rental companies provide services at all three of these facilities.

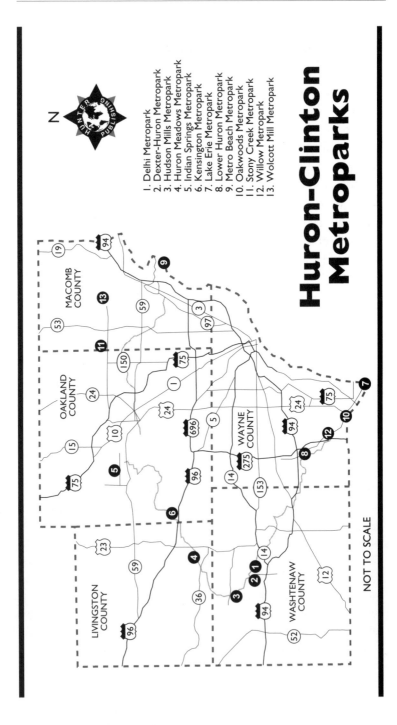

Huron-Clinton Metroparks

1. Delhi Metropark
2. Dexter-Huron Metropark
3. Hudson Mills Metropark
4. Huron Meadows Metropark
5. Indian Springs Metropark
6. Kensington Metropark
7. Lake Erie Metropark
8. Lower Huron Metropark
9. Metro Beach Metropark
10. Oakwoods Metropark
11. Stony Creek Metropark
12. Willow Metropark
13. Wolcott Mill Metropark

NOT TO SCALE

■ Huron-Clinton Metroparks

13000 High Ridge Drive
PO Box 2001
Brighton, MI 48116-8001
☎ 800-47-PARKS
http://www.metroparks.com

The Huron-Clinton Metroparks comprise an immensely popular system that attracts all kinds of folks from Detroit's metropolitan area. Metropark visitors won't encounter elk roaming in sepia autumn fields or black bears rooting around under vast canopies of green, but they will find an enormous array of scenic trails and waterways that are enjoyed by large numbers of users during all four seasons. None of these 13 parks will cut the mustard if you are in search of extended solitude or true wilderness experiences, but they are valuable nonetheless. Park officials estimate that the system serves 11 million visitors annually. Several of the parks feature swimming beaches, golf courses, and bodies of water large enough to accommodate motorboats; two of them – Metro Beach Metropark and Lake Erie Metropark – even have marinas. Indeed, most of the metroparks are more than 1,000 acres in size, and both Stony Creek Metropark and Kensington Metropark sprawl over more than 4,300 acres. All told, the Huron-Clinton Metropark system encompasses nearly 24,000 acres in southeastern Michigan.

This rolling acreage, coupled with the dearth of other outdoor options in the region, make the Huron-Clinton Metroparks a mecca for area residents. The various metroparks offer nice settings for picnics, birthday celebrations, and other occasions, as well as for jogging, in-line skating, bicycling, golf, swimming, fishing, softball, frisbee golf, and other activities. And for those men and women who impatiently watch the calendar, waiting for their next opportunity to escape into Michigan's northern realms, the system's ski trails and canoe-friendly waters can provide at least some relief for those "where did all my vacation time go?" blues.

Southern Lower Michigan

Getting There

The 13 parks that comprise the Huron-Clinton Metropark system form a wide half-circle around Detroit proper. The system begins at Macomb County's Metro Beach Metropark, which sits on the western shore of Lake St. Clair and ends at Lake Erie Metropark, on Erie's shoreline. In between, curving in a great arc across the entire metropolitan area, lie the other 11 parks, each of them a sanctuary of sorts.

Directions to each of the individual parks are as follows: **Metro Beach Metropark** (four miles east of Mt. Clemens, on Metropolitan Parkway); **Wolcott Mill Metropark** (in Ray Township southeast of Romeo, on Kunstman Road, just north of 29 Mile Road); **Stony Creek Metropark** (4300 Main Park Road, in Washington); **Indian Springs Metropark** (in Union Lake, on White Lake Road southwest of Clarkston); **Kensington Metropark** (near Milford/South Lyon off I-96); **Huron Meadows Metropark** (8765 Hammel Road, in Brighton); **Hudson Mills Metropark** (8801 North Territorial Road, in Dexter); **Dexter-Huron Metropark** (on Huron River Drive, seven miles northwest of Ann Arbor); **Delhi Metropark** (on Huron River Drive, five miles northwest of Ann Arbor); **Lower Huron Metropark** (17845 Savage Road, in Belleville); **Willow Metropark** (five miles northwest of Flat Rock, at I-275 and South Huron Road); **Oakwoods Metropark** (four miles northwest of Flat Rock, on Willow Road half a mile west of Huron River Drive); and **Lake Erie Metropark** (one mile south of Gibralter, on West Jefferson).

 Motor vehicle permits are required for entrance into all metroparks. Both daily and annual permits are available for purchase, and one permit is good for all parks in the network.

History

The Huron-Clinton Metropark system, which extends into Wayne, Oakland, Macomb, Washtenaw, and Livingston counties, was sanctioned by the Michigan state legislature as part of a piece of legislation known as the Public Acts of 1939. The parks were designed to take advantage of the presence of two major rivers in the region, the **Clinton** and the **Huron**. These two rivers offered both recreational opportunities and a pleasing appearance, and they became the cornerstones of the system. As the metropark concept took tangible form, its popularity with residents of southeast Michigan quickly became evident. And as the region continued to grow, both in population and development, the parks assumed even greater importance. The introduction of various outdoor programs, educational events, and nature centers further cemented the parks' place in the metro area, and use of the parks shows no signs of abating. Indeed, the major concerns confronting the metroparks today stem from overuse and their proximity to developed areas (Metro Beach, for example, has been forced to close its beach area to swimming on an embarrassing number of occasions over the last couple of years because of pollution). All in all, though, the metroparks remain clean and attractive.

Flora & Fauna

Several of the parks in the metropark system attract large numbers of birds, including such species as Canada geese, mergansers, mallards, herons, great horned owls, shrikes, woodpeckers, osprey, bald eagles, chickadees, egrets, and various other waterfowl and songbirds. Mammals making their home in one or more of the parks include white-tailed deer, raccoons, foxes, mink, muskrats, and squirrels.

Stands of hardwoods – oak, maple, beech, hickory, and aspen – dominate the landscape of most metroparks. Vegetation at most of the parks is fairly common for the region, but a couple of the parks do contain marshlands and bogs that nourish a wide variety of plant species, and the open meadows that can be found in several of the parks support an assortment of wildflowers.

Adventures

On Foot

Most of the parks in the metropark system feature hiking trails or paved bike-hike trails that wind through rolling woodlands or past glimmering ponds and streams. None of these trails are particularly demanding, which makes them ideal for family outings. Among the best of these footpaths are the nature trails at **Stony Creek, Indian Springs, Kensington, Metro Beach,** and **Oakwoods**. The Stony Creek offerings range from the half-mile **Reflection Trail** to the 2½-mile **Habitat Trail**, while Indian Springs is graced with the 3½-mile **Woodland Trail**. Kensington maintains five nature trails of varying lengths, and Metro Beach's South Marsh area attracts local birding enthusiasts. Oakwoods is home to three peaceful trails – **Long Bark Trail, Big Tree Trail,** and **Sky Come Down Trail** – that wind through woods and fields.

Several of the Metroparks also maintain longer paved trails that are used by bicyclists, walkers, joggers, and skaters alike. Of these, Kensington and Stony Creek have the longest pathways. The **Kensington Pathway** is more than eight miles long and swoops around Kent Lake, while the six-mile **Stony Creek bike-hike trail** takes users around the southern portion of Stony Creek Lake.

On Wheels

Most of the members of the Huron-Clinton Metropark system maintain fine biking trails that are ideal for a morning or afternoon of peddling. Paved pathways can be found at the **Metro Beach, Stony Creek, Indian Springs, Kensington, Hudson Mills, Lower Huron, Willow, Oakwoods**, and **Lake Erie** parks. The facilities at each of these parks require bicyclists to share the trail with skaters, joggers, and folks looking to give Fido some exercise (on a leash, of course), so many bicyclists choose to take mid-week or morning spins, when traffic is lighter.

The best of the metropark biking trails can be found at Kensington, in part because the sprawling park contains the longest (8¼ miles) pathway in the system. The **Kensington Pathway** loops around Kent Lake, a pretty, island-dotted lake in the center of the park. Unlike most bike trails at other metroparks, the Kensington Pathway throws an invigorating blend of terrain at peddlers, mixing reasonably strenuous up-and-down stretches with forays over wooden bridges and past shadowy woods. The pathway can be picked up at any number of places along the way.

On Water

Canoeing & Kayaking

Although the **Huron River** shared top billing with the Clinton River when the Huron-Clinton Metropark system was named, the Huron is the dominant of the two southeast Michigan rivers. Certainly it is of far greater importance to the metropark network than the Clinton. Whereas only one metropark sits astride any portion of the Clinton (the river's north branch runs through Wolcott Mill Metropark), nine of the parks make extensive use of the Huron. Indeed, the river winds through the southwestern metropolitan area in a vast liquid ribbon, attracting and discarding little pods of canoeists all along the way.

WHITEWATER CLASSIFICATION CHART		
CLASS	SKILL LEVEL	WATER CONDITION
I	Easy	Calm, moving water with occasional riffles.
II	Intermediate	Little bursts of bouncing rapids in clear, wide channels between long stretches of calm.
III	Difficult	Irregular waves through narrower channels where maneuvering around rocks is required.
IV	Very Difficult	Rapids are intense, loud, and long, with complex, rocky obstacles in the way.
V	Exceptionally Difficult	Rapids are long, loud, narrow, and violent, following one after the other without interruption.

Good paddling on the Huron starts in the **Proud Lake Recreation Area**, which lies just east of Kensington Metropark. Either area is a good one to launch from if planning an overnight trip (campgrounds can be found at several different spots on the river, including Lower Huron and Hudson Mills Metroparks; notify the offices of the parks in advance if you plan to camp there). From Kensington the river moves along at an easygoing pace, passing through the **Huron Meadows, Hudson Mills, Dexter-Huron, Delhi, Lower Huron, Willow**, and **Oakwoods Metroparks** before emptying out into Lake Erie. Canoeing is available in all of these parks. For more detailed information on canoeing or kayaking the Huron, see the Southern Michigan *On Water* section (page 46). To rent a canoe for a glide down the Huron, contact **Wolynski Canoe Rental** (☎ 248-685-1851), **Skip's Huron River Canoe Livery** (☎ 734-769-8686), or **Argo Canoe Livery** (☎ 734-668-7411).

A canoe livery is also maintained at **Stony Creek Metropark** for visitors interested in paddling around on the creek or the 600-acre Stony Creek Lake. Contact Stony Creek Metropark for more information on canoe rentals.

Fishing

Angling is available at most of the metroparks; in fact, the only parks that don't offer fishing are Indian Springs and Wolcott Mills. Of the parks that do, the best are **Kensington** and **Stony Creek**, which have good fishing on their inland lakes, and the **Metro Beach** and **Lake Erie** parks, each of which contains marinas that open out onto the Great Lakes network of waterways.

Sailing & Boating

Four of the Huron-Clinton Metroparks provide recreational options for operators of sailboats and motorboats. Each of these parks – **Kensington, Stony Creek, Metro Beach**, and **Lake Erie** – are on good-sized lakes or impoundments and have boat launching facilities. Both Metro Beach and Lake Erie provide boaters with easy access to Lake St. Clair, the Detroit River, Lake Erie, and points beyond, while Kensington and Stony Creek attract smaller vessels. Kensington especially sees a lot of boat traffic on warm summer weekends.

On Snow

The Huron-Clinton Metroparks are a true four-season haven. After winter snows chase the bicyclists and in-line skaters off the trails, cross-country skiers descend on the parks in large numbers, reveling in the rolling terrain and crisp, quiet air. Most of the trails are easy, making them ideal for beginners and children, yet they still offer the opportunity to replenish yourself in a scenic and peaceful winter setting. All the metroparks offer cross-country skiing with the exception of Wolcott Mill, and several (Kensington, Huron Meadows, Hudson Mills, Stony Creek, Willow, Lake Erie) even offer ski rentals. Top cross-country destinations in the park network include **Kensington, Stony Creek**, and Washtenaw County's Metropark chain **(Hudson Mills, Dexter-Huron**, and **Delhi)**.

In addition, ice skating and sledding facilities are available at several metroparks, including **Stony Creek, Willow, Lake Erie, Kensington, Metro Beach** (ice skating only), and **Indian Springs** (sledding only).

Camping

The parks at **Kensington, Hudson Mills**, and **Lower Huron** maintain camping facilities for canoeing parties and organized groups, and **Wolcott Mills** maintains a group campground for organized parties as well. Call ahead for reservations to use any of these camping areas.

To Find Out More

Call **Huron-Clinton Metroparks** at ☎ 800-47-PARKS for free *Metropark Guides* which include detailed maps of each park as well as a map of the larger metropolitan area. Contact information for individual parks is as follows: **Metro Beach Metropark** (31300 Metro Parkway, PO Box 46905, Mt. Clemens, MI 48046, ☎ 810-463-4581); **Wolcott Mills Metropark** (63841 Wolcott Rd., Ray Township, MI 48096, ☎ 810-749-5997); **Stony Creek Metropark** (4300 Main Park Rd., Shelby Township, MI

Southern Lower Michigan

48316, ☎ 810-781-4242); **Indian Springs Metropark**
(5200 Indian Trail, White Lake, MI 48386, ☎ 248-625-
7280); **Kensington Metropark** (2240 West Buno Rd.,
Milford, MI 48380, ☎ 248-685-1561); **Huron Meadows
Metropark** (8765 Hammel Rd., Brighton, MI 48116,
☎ 810-231-4084); **Hudson Mills Metropark, Delhi
Metropark**, and **Dexter-Huron Metropark** (8801 North
Territorial Rd., Dexter, MI 48130, ☎ 734-426-8211);
Lower Huron Metropark and **Willow Metropark**
(17845 Savage Rd., Belleville, MI 48111, ☎ 734-697-
9181); **Oakwoods Metropark** (PO Box 332, Flat Rock,
MI 48134, ☎ 734-782-3956); and **Lake Erie Metropark**
(32481 West Jefferson, PO Box 120, Brownstown, MI
48173, ☎ 734-379-5020).

■ Warren Dunes State Park

Red Arrow Highway
Sawyer, MI 49125
☎ 616-426-4013
Fax: 616-426-4829

A beautiful park that is among the most popular in the entire
Michigan system, Warren Dunes State Park is the southernmost
jewel in a vast necklace of white sand dunes that adorn the Lower
Peninsula's western shoreline. The towering dunes of the area,
which provide many scenic views of Lake Michigan's glimmering
expanse, are tremendously popular with Michigan natives and
out-of-staters alike. The mixture of sand and surf makes this an
ideal playground for sun-lovers. And for visitors who weary of the
park's often-crowded beaches, the park provides a refuge in the
form of the nearby Warren Woods Natural Area, a quiet 300-acre
unit known as a prime birdwatching area. This lovely preserve
augments Warren Dunes' already significant charms, making it
one of the most spectacular and enduring of Michigan's state
parks.

Getting There

Berrien County's Warren Dunes State Park can be reached by taking I-94 to Exit 16 (Bridgman). After exiting, turn south on Red Arrow Highway for two miles; the park entrance is on the right.

The Warren Woods Natural Area lies off I-94 as well, about 2½ miles east of Exit 6 on Elm Valley Road.

History

In the late 19th century local merchant Edward K. Warren purchased Warren Woods and the dunelands that would later become Warren Dunes State Park. The latter purchase was dismissed as folly at the time; the coastal land was considered worthless because no crops could be grown there. Warren knew better, though. An ardent conservationist, he recognized that with the region's rapid industrialization, "these lands would be of great value to thousands of people as a place of recreation." The dunelands remained private until 1930, when the Edward K. Warren Foundation gave the state the first 253 acres of what is now a 1,500-acre park.

Even back in its early years, the park was among the most popular in the state. Smitten by sandy beaches and hulking dunes, vacationers from nearby Indiana and Illinois drove through its gates in ever-growing numbers (natives of those two states continue to account for the majority of the park's one million annual visitors today). During the 1970s the park acquired a reputation as a mecca for hang gliders, and for several years the air above the dunes was thick with brightly colored gliders. Accidents and a general downturn in the sport eventually resulted in a decline in hang gliding activity. But many flyers from around the Midwest still return to its wind-swept dunes year after year (see *In The Air*, page 33 for more information).

Flora & Fauna

Warren Dunes State Park is best known for its massive dunes, but other natural features of the park deserve mention as well. Much of the park's acreage is actually a mix of oak and hickory wood-

Southern Lower Michigan

lands, and its coastal beach grasses give way to pockets of wild-flowers (white trillium, Dutchman's breeches, trout lily, jack-in-the-pulpit) further inland. This habitat supports an array of wildlife, including fox, deer, squirrel, opossum, and raccoon (the latter is a notorious nighttime campground visitor).

The Warren Woods Preserve contains one of the state's last remaining stands of virgin beech and maple forest. These venerable trees adds another dimension of tranquility to the preserve, one of the region's premier birdwatching sites. A wide range of birds, including a variety of warblers, barred owls, flycatchers, water-

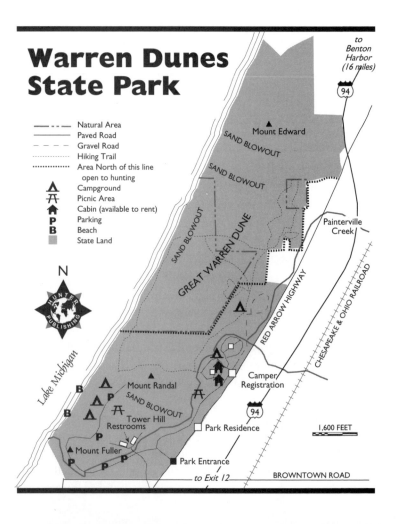

Warren Dunes State Park

to Benton Harbor (16 miles)

94 US

—··—··— Natural Area
———— Paved Road
— — — Gravel Road
··········· Hiking Trail
·············· Area North of this line
   open to hunting
▲ Campground
⅄ Picnic Area
♠ Cabin (available to rent)
P Parking
B Beach
▮ State Land

N

HUNTER PUBLISHING

Mount Edward
SAND BLOWOUT
SAND BLOWOUT
SAND BLOWOUT
GREAT WARREN DUNE

Painterville Creek

RED ARROW HIGHWAY
CHESAPEAKE & OHIO RAILROAD

Lake Michigan

B ▲
P ▲
B ▲ Mount Randal
SAND BLOWOUT
⅄
Tower Hill
Restrooms
P
▲ Mount Fuller
P P P

Camper/ Registration

94

Park Residence

1,600 FEET

Park Entrance
to Exit 12
BROWNTOWN ROAD

thrushes, and woodpeckers, can be found fluttering around in the preserve's lofty upper reaches.

Adventures

In The Air

 Warren Dunes State Park is a hang-gliding paradise. The park's giant dune formations provide gliders with fabulous aerial views of Lake Michigan's coastline, and the winds here are ideal for soaring. In addition, the area's relatively forgiving sand makes it attractive for beginning gliders. Hang gliders can chase thermals from any number of dunes in the park, but the most popular launch point is **Tower Hill**. Looming 240 feet above Lake Michigan's surface, Tower Hill is the highest dune in the park.

Hang-gliding at Warren Dunes State Park (Vito Palmisano).

Warren Dunes is the only Michigan state park that allows hang gliding, but they do impose some restrictions on the practice. A hang-gliding permit is required, and these can be obtained only by visitors who have an accompanying instructor or their own gliding license. Check with the park office for a listing of area instructors. In addition, the park has established launch zones that gliders must use when visiting Warren Dunes. Students and Hang I-rated flyers launch from the zone marked with red posts on the northwest face of Tower Hill, while Hang II-rated flyers are permitted to launch from the zone marked with blue posts further up the hill. Hang

III- and IV-rated flyers may launch from the zone marked with black posts along the top of the ridge.

On Foot

Many visitors to Warren Dunes forsake the park's trails to spend hours exploring the park's sprawling sand dunes, happily tromping around them at random. But the park does feature six miles of hiking trails. The best is the one-mile **Warren Dunes Nature Trail**, which provides great snapshot examples of the varied habitats within the park. Over in the Warren Woods area, a pleasant 3½-mile trail is maintained for birders and nature lovers. It winds through thick hardwood forest for its entire length, making it a favored afternoon destination in the fall after the colors turn.

On Snow

Six miles of cross-country ski trails draw folks to Warren Dunes during the winter. They are not groomed, but are on relatively flat inland terrain and are easily accessible. The park maintains three small cabins for winter sports enthusiasts. These have electricity and sleep four on bunk beds. Snowmobiling is not permitted in the park, another factor that makes it appealing to Nordic skiers.

Camping & Accommodations

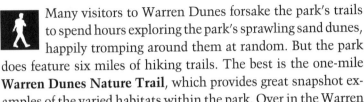

Recognizing the popularity of the park, the state has made efforts to accommodate as many overnight visitors as possible. Warren Dunes' largest campground holds 180 decently spaced sites with all the modern amenities, including electricity and access to showers. Another campground, more rustic in character, is also maintained from Memorial Day to Labor Day. It offers 122 beach campsites down along the park's southern reaches. Finally, Warren Dunes State Park has three "mini-cabins" available year-round. They are in the same area as the modern campground, have electricity and comfortably sleep four. To make overnight camping reservations at Warren Dunes, ☎ 800-44-PARKS.

To Find Out More
Contact Warren Dunes State Park, Red Arrow Highway, Sawyer, MI 49125, ☎ 616-426-4013.

■ Waterloo-Pinckney Recreation Areas

WATERLOO RECREATION AREA
16345 McClure Road, Route 1
Chelsea, MI 48118
☎ 734-475-8307

PINCKNEY RECREATION AREA
8555 Silver Hill
Pinckney, MI 48169
☎ 734-426-4913

Southcentral Michigan's Pinckney and Waterloo state parks offer a wide range of outdoor recreation activities. Combined, the two parks encompass more than 30,000 acres of glacier-carved ridges, hardwood forest, lakes, and ponds that serve as an attractive playground for Lower Michigan anglers, backpackers, canoeists, mountain bikers, hunters, and equestrians.

Getting There

The Pinckney and Waterloo recreation areas are actually two separate entities, but their proximity to one another, similar geography, and closely linked activities contribute to a sense that the parks are really two halves of a single, sprawling whole.

Washtenaw County's **Waterloo Recreation Area** lies between Jackson and Ann Arbor and can be approached from several directions. Six different I-94 exits between Ann Arbor and Jackson provide access to various portions of the park from the south: Race Road (Exit 147) will deliver you to Big Portage Lake, as will Mt.

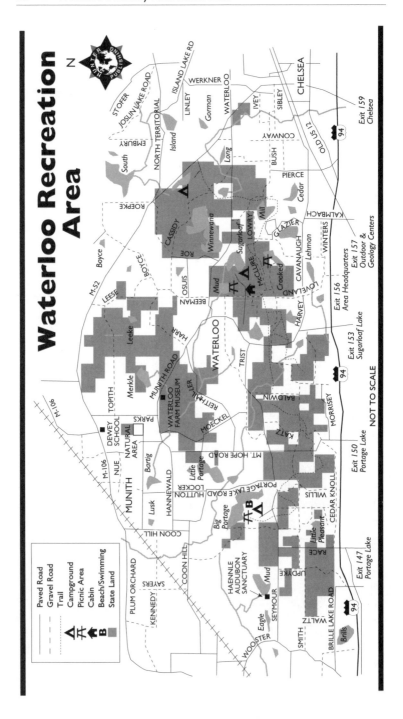

Hope Road (Exit 150); Clear Lake Road (Exit 153) leads to Sugar-loaf Lake; Kalmbach Road (Exit 156) winds northward to park headquarters; Pierce Road (Exit 157) directs you to the park's out-door centers and geology center; and M-52 (Exit 159) provides ac-cess to Green Lake Campground.

The **Pinckney Recreation Area** lies southwest of the town of Pinckney in Livingston County. To reach the park, take M-52 to North Territorial Road. Turn east on North Territorial, then turn north on Dexter-Townhall Road and follow the signs. Travelers from the east can pick up Dexter-Townhall Road by taking North Territorial Road west from US-23.

History

Both Waterloo Recreation Area (which currently holds more than 20,000 acres of lakes, streams, and woodlands) and Pinckney Recreation Area (11,000 acres) were created in the early 1940s, as part of a series of such areas in the Lower Peninsula. These areas were added to the state park system in 1943 and 1944, dramati-cally expanding the size and quality of the state's outdoor recrea-tion offerings. In subsequent years, both parks experienced modest increases in size as private and state property was added to their boundaries (the Waterloo Recreation Area is the Lower Peninsula's largest state park). These additions served to consoli-date their standing among Michigan sportsmen and outdoor lov-ers, though both Waterloo and Pinckney continue to be honeycombed with pockets of private property. The value of the Waterloo Recreation Area as an educational destination was dra-matically heightened with the 1989 unveiling of the **Gerald E. Eddy Geology Center**, dedicated to documenting the geologic history of Michigan and the Great Lakes region.

Today, the two parks attract more than one million visitors annu-ally, the vast majority of them from Ann Arbor, Lansing, Jackson, metro Detroit, and other southern Michigan population centers. These run the gamut, ranging from families looking to enjoy a day at the beach to hardy folks in search of quiet woodlands.

Southern Lower Michigan

Pinckney Recreation Area

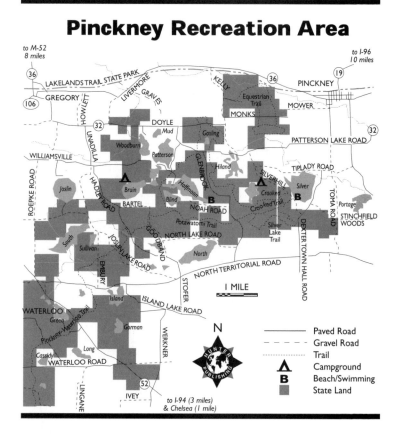

Flora & Fauna

Hardwood forests dominate the landscape at both parks. Thick stands of maple, oak, beech, and hickory bristle throughout the rolling terrain of the two parks. Elsewhere, the wetland regions feature such endangered plant species as pitcher plants and pink lady slippers, and open meadow areas support a variety of wildflowers.

Waterloo and Pinckney are home to numerous white-tailed deer within their boundaries, but the parks are perhaps better known for the variety of birds and waterfowl that can be spotted in their trees and on their waterways. The many lakes and streams in Waterloo are primarily responsible for this region's reputation as a birdwatching mecca. Birds that have been spotted include sedge and marsh wrens, sandhill cranes, Acadian flycatchers, Virginia rails, Louisiana waterthrushes, and cerulean and hooded warblers.

Adventures

On Foot

Southern Lower Michigan's primary backpacking trail threads its way through both areas. Bobbing and weaving through a menagerie of lakes, ponds, and rustling woodlands for a good deal of its 35-mile length, the **Waterloo-Pinckney Trail** is a nice option for hikers looking to hit the trail for three or four days (the hike can be lengthened by another dozen miles or so if you tack on a portion of the Potawatomi Trail). Reminders of civilization are never too far away on this trail; the well-marked path crosses several roads, borders on private property at a couple different junctures, and most of the designated campgrounds along the trail are popular with a variety of park users. Nonetheless, the trail does wind through some indisputably pretty forests and wetlands, and its location makes it an attractive alternative to southeast Michigan hikers.

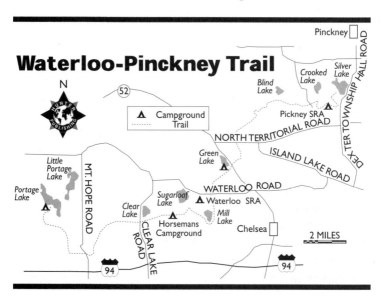

The western trailhead is at Portage Lake in Waterloo; its eastern trailhead is in Pinckney's Silver Lake day-use area. Backpackers can camp at any of the campgrounds in the recreation area, but be forewarned that several of these are not ideal if you are hoping for a backcountry experience. Both Big Portage Lake and Sugarloaf Lake, for instance, are large campgrounds that feature all the modern amenities. Solitude is in short supply at those camps. On the other hand, those amenities make them popular for back-packers determined to grab one last shower before hitting the trail. In addition, rustic cabins can be reserved at Burns, Mill Lake, and Cedar Lake Outdoor Centers.

The parks also feature several day-hiking trails for less adventur-ous souls. In Waterloo, hikers can choose from seven different na-ture trails of varying lengths, including the **Hickory Hills Trail**, a 5.3-mile loop that traverses a very hilly stretch of hardwood for-est; the **Bog Trail**, a popular 1½-mile round-trip jaunt to a bog that is home to an array of interesting plant species; and the 1.3-mile **Oak Woods Trail**, with scenic views of Mill Lake and a nearby pond. Other Waterloo nature trails include the **Old Field Trail** (less than a mile), the **Lowland Trail** (1.1 miles), the **Spring Pond Trail** (one mile), and the **Lakeview Trail** (3.6 miles). The Pinckney Recreation Area also has a couple of nice trails for day-hiking, but the recreation area draws large numbers of mountain bikers on these pathways as well. The only one of these trails that is open exclusively to foot traffic is the **Losee Lake Trail** (a three-mile loop); on the others – the **Potawatomi** (17 miles), **Crooked Lake** (five miles), and **Silver Lake** (two miles) trails – hikers and bikers are required to follow markers that keep them going in opposite directions.

On Wheels

Mountain Biking

The Pinckney Recreation Area is home to the legendary **Potawatomi Trail**. The 17-mile "Poto" Trail, which straddles Livingston and Washtenaw counties, offers some of the most physically demanding fat tire biking in the Lower Peninsula. The single-track pathway winds through a

Potawatomi Trail

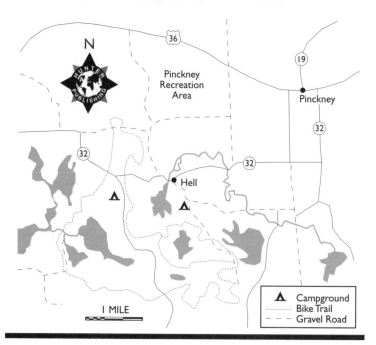

pretty mix of hardwood forest, quiet lakes, and marshy wetlands, but bikers are far more likely to remember Poto's other characteristics. Pocked with long uphill climbs, mach-speed downhill runs, heavily rutted sections, and pockets of treacherous loose debris, the trail is a paradise for diehard members of the knobby-wheeled set. Less experienced bikers would do well to turn instead to the **Crooked Lake Loop**, an enjoyable but less demanding five-mile trail that connects to the Potawatomi, or the two-mile **Silver Lake Trail**.

On Water

Canoeing

Pinckney's so-called "**Chain of Lakes**" is a pleasant option for Lower Michigan canoeists who feel like taking a break from the usual downstream treks. The Chain of

Lakes is a cluster of seven lakes tenuously joined to one another by small channels or streams. Blessed with pretty shorelines and good protection from wind for much of their lengths, these small lakes can provide a placid afternoon of paddling. However, the seven – **Halfmoon Lake, Blind Lake, Bruin Lake, Watson Lake, Patterson Lake, Woodburn Lake**, and **Hiland Lake** – are also immensely popular with anglers, who can set out from boat launches at Bruin, Halfmoon, or Hiland Lakes. Bass, panfish, northern pike, and crappie are all present in good numbers on the Chain of Lakes. Other lakes in the Pinckney Recreation Area that draw boaters include **Joslin Lake, South Lake, North Lake, Pickerel Lake, Crooked Lake**, and **Gosling Lake**.

The Waterloo Recreation Area is a popular destination for boaters and anglers. The park provides access to 16 different lakes that hold a variety of gamefish. The most popular of these are **Crooked Lake** (bluegill, sunfish, bass), **Sugarloaf Lake** (northern pike, rainbow trout), and **Big Portage Lake** (walleye, bass, bluegill, northern pike). Other Waterloo lakes suitable for fishing include **Cassidy, Crooked, Cedar, Clear, Doyle, Hankard, Little Portage, Merkle, Mill, Walsh**, and the **Wimmewana Impoundment**.

On Horseback

Both recreation areas maintain facilities for equestrians. Indeed, Waterloo and Pinckney hold some of the most popular bridle trails in the entire Lower Peninsula. Approximately 26 miles of riding trails can be found in the Waterloo Recreation Area, as well as the **Horsemen's Campground** and staging area. This rustic campground includes 25 roomy sites, and although backpackers and other non-equestrians are permitted to camp there, it often takes on a decidedly horsey atmosphere during the fall, when horse lovers rush to the park to immerse themselves in the autumn colors. The family-oriented nature of many of these trips – and the easy camaraderie that passes between most riding parties – can make the Horseman's Campground a particularly congenial place to while away an October evening.

The Pinckney Recreation Area has eight miles of bridle trails. The trails here are not as extensive as those at Waterloo, but you can take guided horseback tours through the area via nearby Hell Creek Ranch. Call the ranch at ☎ 734-878-3632 for more information.

On Snow

 Both Pinckney and Waterloo are popular during the winter. Hundreds of acres are set aside for snowmobiling enthusiasts, and several cross-country trails are available to skiers. The two trails in Pinckney are the **Alpha Ski Trail** (a two-mile loop) and the **Bravo Ski Trail** (a four-mile circuit), both of which traverse hilly, wooded terrain. Both trails are marked, but neither is groomed. Waterloo has a number of loops starting out from the park's **Cedar Lake Outdoor Center**, which lies off Pierce Road. About eight miles of marked ski trails are here, but, as with Pinckney, they are not groomed.

Camping & Accommodations

Waterloo offers four camping areas. The two main ones are lakeshore facilities with all the modern amenities. The **Sugarloaf Lake Campground** has 180 open sites, a boat launch, and a small beach area; it can be reached by taking Kalmbach Road north from I-94, then turning west on Cavanaugh Lake Road. The **Big Portage Lake Campground** is accessed by taking Mt. Hope Road north from I-94, then turning west on Seymour Road. It has 194 sites and beach access, and is open year-around (Sugarloaf is open only during the summer). Two rustic campgrounds can also be found within Waterloo. The 25-site **Horseman's Campground**, which is open to both equestrian and foot traffic, lies in the park's southeastern section, and the **Green Lake Campground** (25 wooded sites) lies just off M-52 in the park's northern region.

Another option is Waterloo's network of rustic cabins that are nestled in the park's rolling woodlands. Some of these cabins are small, comfortably housing four-six people, while others are cavernous buildings that can hold a group of 20. All of the cabins are accessible by car, and the majority feature electric stoves and

Southern Lower Michigan

lights. A total of 13 cabins are scattered around the recreation area; for reservations, call park headquarters.

Pinckney Recreation Area maintains two campgrounds. The first of these – **Bruin Lake** – is a modern, 200-site facility that is equipped with a boat launch, fishing pier, swimming beach, and playground. **Crooked Lake Campground** offers camping in a decidedly more rustic setting, with 25 sites spread out on a hillside overlooking the lake. The campground features vault toilets and a hand pump for water.

To Find Out More
Waterloo Recreation Area, 16345 McClure Rd., Rte. 1, Chelsea, MI 48118, ☎ 734-475-8307. **Pinckney Recreation Area**, 8555 Silver Hill, Pinkney, MI 48169, ☎ 734-426-4913.

■ Adventures Region-Wide

On Horseback

Horseback riding thrives in Michigan's southern regions, supported by an abundance of riding facilities. Equestrian facilities and bridle trails are relatively sparse in the UP and the northern Lower Peninsula, although horseback riding is permitted on most roads and two-tracks in state and national forests. Down in southern Lower Michigan, however, thick clusters of horsemen's facilities are maintained in state parks and recreation areas. These range from riding trails of modest size to parks equipped with extensive trails, equestrian campgrounds, and well-maintained staging areas. Of the 17 parks and recreation areas that maintain such facilities, here are a few of the best:

Brighton Recreation Area

A favorite of area equestrians, this Livingston County area features 18 miles of bridle trails, a concession-operated riding stable within the park, and a nice staging area. The park lies three miles southwest of Brighton off Chilson Road. ☎ 810-229-6566.

Highland Recreation Area

Located in Oakland County, the park maintains more than 13 miles of marked bridle trails and a horsemen's campground with two dozen sites. The park sits 15 miles west of Pontiac on M-59. ☎ 248-685-2433.

Ionia Recreation Area

Facilities at this park include a horsemen's campground, 20 miles of marked bridle trails, and a large day-use staging area. The park lies a few miles north of I-96, on Jordan Lake Road (Exit 64). ☎ 616-527-3750.

Pontiac Lake Recreation Area

This Oakland County facility includes 17 miles of marked horse trails, a horsemen's campground with 25 sites, and rental horses. To reach the park, take M-59 west to Williams Lake Road. Turn north onto Williams Lake Road and west onto Gale Road.

Proud Lake Recreation Area

More than eight miles of bridle trails wind across the rolling terrain of this western Oakland County park, which also features a staging area. To reach the park, take the Wixom Rd. Exit off of I-96 and go north for six miles.

Yankee Springs Recreation Area

Five miles of marked bridle trails that provide access to an additional 10 miles of trails in the Barry State Game Area. This park also maintains a horsemen's campground. To reach Yankee Springs, take M-37 west to Gun Lake Road and continue west for 14 miles or so, or take Exit 61 off US-131 and head east for eight miles on CR-A42.

Other state parks maintaining equestrian facilities include the **Ortonville Recreation Area,** the **Holly Recreation Area, Maybury State Park, P.J. Hoffmaster State Park, Hart-Montague State Park, Kal-Haven State Park**, and **Lakelands Trail State Park**. In addition, the Waterloo and Pinckney Recreation Areas maintain good equestrian facilities; see above. For more information on equestrian opportunities elsewhere in the state, contact the Michigan **DNR's Recreation and Trails Section** at PO Box 30452, Lansing, MI 48909-7952, ☎ 517-373-4175.

On Water

Canoeing & Kayaking

 See the whitewater chart on page 27. Some major outdoor recreation activities in Michigan – backpacking, for instance, or snowmobiling – are primarily based in the state's more northern reaches, where population density plunges and public land is plentiful. But canoeing is one outdoor activity that thrives in Michigan's southern environs as well. In fact, rivers of markedly varying sizes and temperaments thread all through the southern part of the state, providing paddlers with an abundance of water options. These range from the west side's Grand River, the state's longest stream at more than 300 miles, to the Huron River, an easygoing, heavily trafficked ribbon of water that cuts through Michigan's eastern ramparts. Southern Michigan's rivers may not offer the thrills and spills of their cousins to the north, but they still provide paddlers with ample opportunity to leave traffic jams and deadlines far behind. Following are brief

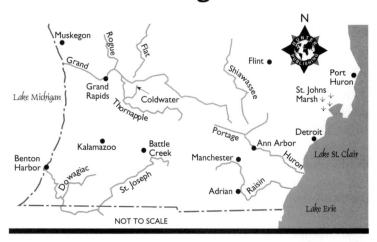

South Michigan Rivers

descriptions of some of southern Michigan's best canoeing and kayaking destinations.

Dowagiac River (Class I)

This is a 14-mile tributary of the St. Joseph River in the state's southwestern corner. The upper part of the river – from the M-62 bridge to Niles Dam – is mellow. Less than 50 feet wide, it winds through woodlands and fields at a leisurely pace, making it attractive for beginners. Some canoeists disembark at Kinzie Road Bridge, off M-51. Paddlers who choose to continue on past the Niles Dam (which requires a portage) will find more challenging water, especially in the spring. The current quickens and maneuvering skills take on added importance as sharp turns and sweepers become more prevalent. Canoeists and kayakers floating below the dam can take out at the US-31 bridge outside of Niles or wait until after the Dowagiac joins up with the St. Joseph. Canoe rentals for the Dowagiac are available through **Niles Canoe Rental** (☎ 616-683-5110).

Flat River (Class I)

This placid mid-Michigan stream runs through a mix of woodlands and residential areas for most of its length. The upper portions of the 60-mile river are shallow and choked with fallen trees, making it unsuitable for canoeing, but from Greenville Dam down, the Flat attracts lots of folks looking for a peaceful afternoon float. In addition, good camping options are available (with permits) at three different state game areas along the way (Langston State Game Area, Flat River State Game Area, and Lowell State Game Area). Rentals are available from **Double R Ranch Resort** (☎ 616-794-0520).

Grand River (Class I)

Michigan's longest river is an ideal testing ground for beginners. Wide and tranquil for much of its length, the Grand is lined with dozens of access points at parks, bridges, and dams. The river offers lots of pleasing scenery and opportunities for wildlife viewing. Its current is sluggish above Lansing, but quickens and widens (to more than 1,000 feet in some areas) with the appearance of a steady diet of major tributaries, including the Red Cedar, Looking Glass, Flat, Thornapple, and Rogue Rivers. Beginning canoeists

Canoeing the Huron River (Thomas A. Schneider).

and kayakers should note that dams along the way create both portages and impoundments that can get tricky in windy conditions. Paddlers looking to rent a canoe for use on the Grand can call **Grand Rogue Campgrounds and Canoe (☎ 616-361-1053)**.

Huron River (Class I-II)

This pleasant river starts in Oakland County and winds its way through Livingston, Washtenaw, and Wayne Counties before emptying into Lake Huron 100 miles later. It sees a tremendous amount of traffic from metro Detroit-area residents. Some sections still offer a measure of privacy and quiet; others do not, especially on weekends. The river features numerous campgrounds and canoe liveries and nearly a dozen portages around dams (most of them easy and on the river's lower reaches).

Good paddling on the Huron starts at Proud Lake, southeast of Milford off Wixom Road. The upper third of the river is characterized by narrow spans and a moderate current. It passes through Kent Lake (which can produce some decent waves on windy days), the hugely popular Kensington Metropark, and a string of other small lakes in these first 30 miles. The river then passes through four other Huron-Clinton Metroparks – Huron Meadows, Hudson Mills, Dexter-Huron, and Delhi – before visiting Ann Arbor and Ypsilanti. The Huron widens out through here, becoming up

Huron River

Origins to Commerce Lake

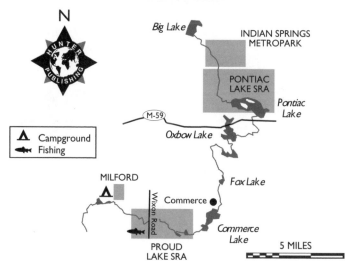

Commerce Lake to Baseline Dam

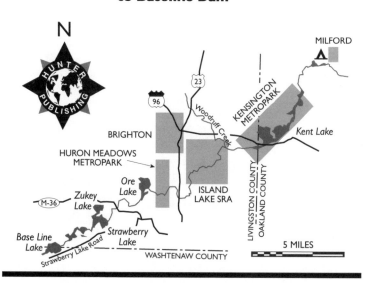

Huron River
Base Line Dam
to Barton Impoundment

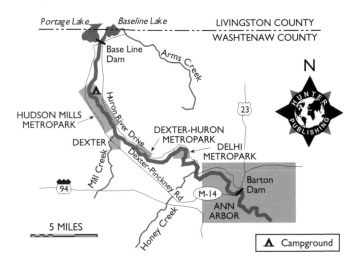

Barton Impoundment
to French Landing Dam

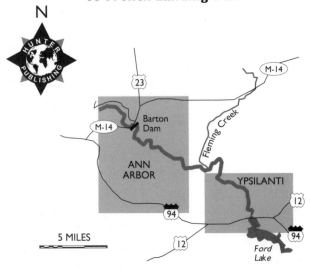

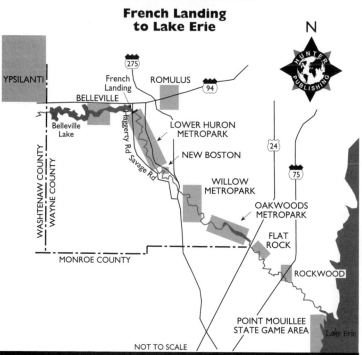

Huron River
French Landing to Lake Erie

N

to 90 feet wide in places, and attracts a good deal of day traffic. This area also features the river's lone stretch of whitewater, just above Delhi Road Bridge west of Ann Arbor. The Delhi Rapids churn up waves of two to three feet in the springtime. These rapids, which attract area kayaking enthusiasts, are fully capable of dumping uncertain canoeists (portages are present on both sides of the river). After the river passes through Ypsilanti and Belleville Lake, the current dawdles through a mix of forest and development, swinging through three more metroparks (Lower Huron, Willow, and Oakwoods) on its way. Leading canoe liveries on the Huron include **Argo Canoe Livery**, 1055 Longshore Drive, Ann Arbor MI 48105 (☎ 734-668-7411), **Skip's Huron River Canoe Livery** (☎ 734-769-8686) and **Wolynski Canoe Rental** (☎ 248-685-1851), but there are many others as well; contact individual metroparks for canoe livery information.

Raisin River (Class I)

The Raisin wanders through southeastern Michigan in a lackadaisical fashion, spurning straight lines in favor of a seemingly endless series of twists and turns. Indeed, the Raisin has been cited in *Ripley's Believe It or Not* as "the world's most crooked river." This can be especially problematic in its upper reaches, which are narrow and infested with downed trees. But in time the river broadens out, making it a good choice for family outings (though not a passive one; the river's geography, coupled with the presence of sweepers, call for nearly constant steering). Paddlers planning an extended trip on the Raisin often put in at Swain Park in Brooklyn, while daytrippers can put in at several access sites along the river's 149-mile length. These are primarily in small towns along the river's shoreline (Manchester, Tecumseh, Adrian, Blissfield, etc.). Rentals for the Raisin are available through **Sharon Hollow Acres Canoe** (☎ 734-428-0100) and **River Raisin Canoe Livery** (☎ 734-529-9029).

Rogue River (Class I)

Forty-two miles in length from its beginnings in Newaygo County to its union with the Grand River, the Rogue picks up speed gradually, transforming itself from a molasses-slow stream into one of southern Michigan's faster-paced rivers. This is due to both a good gradient and the high number of tributaries that feed into it. Indeed, paddlers are discouraged from putting in until Sparta, when the river hits its stride. The river's last 10 miles or so – from Rockford to the Grand River – are top-notch for afternoon excursions, although there is a portage at Childsdale Dam. Rent kayaks or canoes from **AAA Rogue River Canoe Rental** (☎ 616-866-9264).

Shiawassee River (Class I)

Located at the base of Michigan's thumb, the Shiawassee is ideal for family outings or showing the ropes to novice paddlers. The only exception to this is in the spring, when higher water levels can give the river a somewhat more surly temperament. The Shiawassee runs through sections of farmland, forest, and residential areas. The headwaters and upper portions cannot be easily navigated, but from Byron on down, the Shiawassee widens to

50 feet or more, and numerous bridges and shoreline parks provide users with access spots. Some of the river's prettiest stretches are between Corunna and Chesaning; here the river widens to 65-80 feet and runs two-six feet deep. But as with the rest of the river, the absence of shoreline camping spots precludes overnighters, at least on the river itself. Most paddlers take out before hitting the marshland of Shiawassee River State Game Area. Prime take-out spots include the West Gary Bridge and Fergus Road. Contact **Walnut Hills Campground and Canoe** (☎ 517-634-9782) about rentals.

St. Joseph River (Class I)

Southwestern Michigan's St. Joseph River, which winds through six Michigan counties (and a small portion of northern Indiana) before emptying out into Lake Michigan, is one of the state's most robust. Nourished by a wide assortment of good-sized tributaries, the St. Joseph is both wide and deep, and canoeing is good below Tekonsha. But the river is saddled with a large number of dams and impoundments that detract from its appeal, and access sites are generally limited to bridge crossings. Canoes and kayaks are available for rent from **Niles Canoe Rental** (☎ 616-683-5110).

Thornapple River (Class I)

Although the Thornapple flows across about 100 miles of Michigan countryside, relatively little of it is suitable for paddling. Its upper reaches are narrow and draped in a canoeist's nightmare of brush, logs, and fallen trees, and its last third is pocked with dams and impoundments and a rash of heavy development. The Thornapple's midsection, though, offers undemanding floats through attractive woodlands. The Thornapple Lake area has multiple access options, including Nashville Dam, Thornapple Road, Barger Road, and Charlton County Park. Although cottages and other signs of civilization are ubiquitous in this area, views of field and forest become more frequent as the miles float on by. For the next 20 miles or so the stream's width reaches 45-65 feet and the current moves along at a steady clip. Paddlers should take out at Irving Dam to avoid the river's dam-riddled lower stretches. Rentals are available at **Indian Valley** (☎ 616-891-8579) and **Whispering Waters Campground Canoe** (☎ 616-945-5166).

Other canoeable rivers in southern Michigan include the **Cass, Coldwater, Flint, Kalamazoo, Looking Glass, Portage**, and **Red Cedar** rivers.

Southeast Michigan is home to several larger bodies of water that attract area kayaking enthusiasts. The **Detroit River, Anchor Bay**, and the **St. Clair River** all receive attention from intrepid sea kayakers. These waters may not offer wilderness experiences, but they do provide paddlers with interesting perspectives on Belle Isle and various fixtures of the Detroit skyline (on the Detroit River) or the imposing petrochemical plants and oil refineries of Canada's shoreline (on the St. Clair River).

Perhaps the best destination for kayaking enthusiasts in southeastern Michigan, however, is the **St. Clair Flats State Wildlife Area**. This wildlife sanctuary is one of the state's largest remaining wetlands, and it is home to a stunning array of mammals, waterfowl and other birds. The highlight of the Flats area, which formed as a result of the messy way in which the St. Clair River goes about emptying itself into Lake St. Clair, is **St. John's Marsh**, a particularly rich haven for wildlife. A lush maze of placid water and towering vegetation, this 3,000-acre region is home to more than 150 kinds of birds (including rare king rails, bald eagles, and crowned night herons) and nearly two dozen mammals, including mink and red fox. The most visible of the marshland's inhabitants, however, are the swans, which glide about in great abundance on the water's glass-like surface. To reach St. John's Marsh – which also attracts large numbers of canoeists (and blissfully few watercraft of any other type) – take Exit 243 off I-94 and head east on M-29 through New Baltimore. After about 15 miles, travelers will see Anchor Bay on the right and St. John's Marsh on the left; keep your eye out for the state-maintained public access launch site a few miles down on the left. Both kayaks and canoes are available for rent at nearby **Great Lakes Docks and Decks** (☎ 810-725-0009), or from **Anchor Bay and St. John's Marsh Canoe and Boat Rental** (☎ 800-292-3625).

Fishing

Many of Michigan's best trout streams are found in the UP or the northern Lower Peninsula, but the state's southern reaches compensate by offering some of the best walleye and bass (both large-mouth and smallmouth) fishing in the entire Midwest. Moreover, the waters off Michigan's southern coastlines offer superb Great Lakes fishing in southern Lake Michigan (on the west coast) and western Lake Erie and southern Lake Huron (on the east coast).

Rivers

Southwestern Michigan holds several top fishing rivers, including the **Cass** (panfish, northern pike, catfish, white and smallmouth bass), **Coldwater** (brown trout), **Detroit** (walleye, bass, Great Lakes muskie, northern pike), **Dowagiac** (steelhead and brown trout), **Flint** (northern pike, walleye, smallmouth bass, catfish), **Grand** (catfish, walleye, pike, salmon, smallmouth bass), **Kalamazoo** (smallmouth bass, rock bass, walleye, brown trout, northern pike, bluegill, catfish), **Maple** (catfish, northern pike), **Paw Paw** (bass, brown trout, bluegill, walleye, northern pike), **Raisin** (smallmouth bass, rock bass, and northern pike), **Rogue** (brown and steelhead trout, chinook salmon), **St. Clair** (walleye, yellow perch, bass, bluegill, catfish, black crappies, northern pike), **St. Joseph** (smallmouth bass, walleye, steelhead, and catfish), **Shiawassee** (smallmouth bass, rock bass, northern pike, walleye), and **Thornapple** (smallmouth bass, rock bass, and pike).

In addition, the **Muskegon River** – which rises from the Lower Peninsula's northern midsection but empties into Lake Michigan way down by Muskegon – is perhaps the state's premier trout stream.

Inland Lakes

Southern Michigan is also replete with fetching inland lakes. The finest in this region is undoubtedly **Muskegon Lake**. This outstanding fishing lake supports large numbers of walleye, catfish, smallmouth bass, yellow perch, northern pike, and bluegills, among others. Other top lakes in the region include **Big Fish Lake** (largemouth bass, brown trout, bluegill, black crappies), **Coldwater Lake** (bass, bluegill, northern pike), **Duck Lake** (bluegill, walleye, black crappies, bass), **Fremont Lake** (bluegill, crappies, largemouth bass, northern pike), **Gull Lake** (largemouth and smallmouth bass, bluegill, yellow perch, northern pike), **Gun**

Lake (walleye, bluegill, yellow perch, smallmouth and large-mouth bass), **Ousterhout Lake** (bluegill, yellow perch, large-mouth bass), **School Section Lake** (bluegill, largemouth bass, northern pike, crappies), and **Thornapple Lake** (northern muskie, walleye, bluegill, big and smallmouth bass). Other good fishing lakes on Michigan's southwest side include **Big Whitefish Lake, Fish Lake, Long Lake, Marble Lake, Miner Lake, Nevins Lake, Pickerel Lake, Proud Lake, Reeds Lake, Sessions Lake, Tamarack Lake**, and **Union Lake**, but there are literally dozens of other decent lakes to choose from as well.

Michigan's southeastern side houses many good inland lakes as well, although powerboating and waterskiing is even more en-demic here than it is over on the state's west side. Top-notch fish-ing lakes in Southeast Michigan include **Belleville Lake** (channel catfish, largemouth bass, smallmouth bass, bluegill, northern pike, walleye, and others), Jackson County's **Big Portage Lake** (sunfish, black crappies, bluegill, largemouth bass), **Big Wolf Lake** (largemouth bass, bluegill, walleye), **Cass Lake** (large and smallmouth bass, walleye, northern pike, bluegill), **Deer Lake** (smallmouth and largemouth bass, rock bass, bluegill, walleye, crappies, northern pike, rainbow trout), **Holloway Reservoir** (walleye, channel catfish, black crappies, largemouth bass), **Pon-tiac Lake** (northern pike, largemouth bass, channel catfish, bluegill), **Orchard Lake** (smallmouth bass, largemouth bass, northern pike, yellow perch), **Sand Lake** (smallmouth bass and bluegill), **Stony Creek Impoundment** (walleye, crappies, channel catfish, largemouth bass, northern pike), and **Wamplers Lake** (yellow perch, bluegill, small and largemouth bass). Other lakes worth checking out include **Devils Lake, Kent Lake, Lake Che-mung, Lake Nepessing, Lake Orion, Maceday Lake, Sylvan Lake, Vineyard Lake, White Lake**, and **Whitmore Lake**.

Great Lakes

Michigan's southern harbors serve as primary gateways to splen-did Great Lakes fishing in **Lake Erie, Lake Huron**, and **Lake Michigan**. Anglers flock to western Lake Erie primarily for its un-paralleled trophy walleye fishing, but the lake also boasts tremen-dous smallmouth bass fishing. Southern Lake Huron offers a great variety of gamefish, including trout, salmon, and walleye.

And over on the other side of the state, lower Lake Michigan's silvery surface is dappled every summer with boaters gleefully pulling in coho and king salmon, steelhead, brown trout, lake trout, walleye, and other popular fish. With the exception of perch stocks, which have plummeted dramatically in all three lakes, fisheries in lakes Erie, Huron, and Michigan are expected to maintain their strength for the next several years.

Adjacent to the Great Lakes is **Lake St. Clair**. Often overshadowed by its much larger cousins, Lake St. Clair is nonetheless an essential link in the Great Lakes chain, for it connects Lake Huron to Lake Erie. It is also a notable fishing destination in its own right. About 540 square miles in size, Lake St. Clair's shallow and weedy bottom supports good quantities of smallmouth bass, muskie, and walleye. Unlike the Great Lakes, it has been able to maintain its sizable yellow perch population.

Scuba Diving

Sport diving enthusiasts have a variety of scuba destinations, from the shipwrecks of the Sanilac Shores and Thumb Area Underwater Preserves to the wrecks of the St. Clair River. All three of these areas are in relatively close proximity to metropolitan Detroit, making them among the state's most heavily used dive areas. As with other Michigan bottomland preserves, removal of

Exploring a Great Lakes shipwreck (Travel Michigan).

Southern Lower Michigan

artifacts and other materials from wreck sites is strictly forbidden, and transgressors are subject to penalties ranging from fines to boat confiscation to jail time.

Sanilac Shores Underwater Preserve

Lake Huron's Sanilac Shores Preserve covers 163 square miles and includes several great wrecks. The single greatest attraction here is probably the *Regina*, a 250-foot steel-hulled freighter that was lost at sea during an infamous 1913 storm (the storm sank 12 ships). The bodies of some of the *Regina*'s crew washed ashore in the days following the storm, but the vessel itself was not found until 1986. Upon its discovery, it immediately became one of the most popular dive sites in all the Great Lakes. The massive ship rests in about 80 feet of water (55 feet at its highest point) and can be penetrated. Cargo from the ship is scattered all around the wreck site. A haven for experienced divers, the *Regina* sits about 7½ miles southeast of Port Sanilac. Another recent discovery, the *Mary Alice B.*, sits a few miles north of the *Regina* at about 95 feet. Sitting upright and mostly intact, the *Mary Alice B.* has quickly become a favorite of top divers.

Another immensely popular Sanilac dive site is the *Sport*, a 57-foot tug that was abandoned in heavy seas in 1920 after its boilers went out. It can be found about three miles east of the coastal town of Lexington. Although the tug sits upright in about 50 feet of water, its upper portions are only 25 feet below the surface, making exploration easy. In 1992 the *Sport* became the first wreck in the state's preserve system to receive an underwater historical marker.

Two other well-known wreck sites here should be explored only by experienced divers. Both the *Checotah* (a scow schooner) and the *New York* (a steamer) lie in the far northeastern corner of the preserve, within a few hundred yards of one another. The depth at which they lie – 120 feet – prevents most divers from investigating either site, but advanced sport divers who make the descent will find many fascinating artifacts down in the darkness.

Other dive sites in the Sanilac Shores Preserve include the *North Star*, the *Colonel A. B. Williams*, the *Charles S. Price*, the *Eliza H. Strong*, and the *Charles A. Street*. These sites require different levels of expertise, so inform yourself about each wreck before hitting the water.

DIVE SHOPS. Many southeast Michigan dive shops provide services to Sanilac Shores divers. Perhaps the best known of these is Four Fathoms Diving, in part because its owner discovered the *Regina* and was instrumental in establishing the preserve. **Four Fathoms Diving** can be contacted at 7230 Main St., PO Box 219, Port Sanilac, MI 48469, ☎ 810-622-DIVE. Other dive shops in the area include **All Seasons Diving Company** (3910 Lake George Road, Dryden, MI 48428-9709, ☎ 810-796-2357), **Great Lakes Odyssey** (355 Connecticut, Marysville, MI 48040, ☎ 810-364-4974), **Bruno's Dive Shop** (34740 Gratiot, Clinton Township, MI 48035, ☎ 810-792-2040), **Dive Inn** (3858 24th Ave., Port Huron, MI 48060, ☎ 810-987-6263), **Lakeshore Charters & Marine Exploration** (4658 S. Lakeshore, Lexington, MI 48450, ☎ 810-359-8660), and **Macomb Scuba Center** (13465 W. 12 Mile, Warren, MI 48093, ☎ 248-558-9922).

Thumb Area Underwater Preserve

This region's reputation as a fishing paradise sometimes overshadows its other qualities, but knowledgeable sport divers recognize that possession of a fishing rod is not a prerequisite for enjoying its waters. In fact, the preserve, which lies off the shoreline of eastern Lower Michigan's "Thumb," attracts large numbers of sport divers and has many boat launch and marina facilities.

As with the Sanilac Preserve, the importance of the Thumb Area Preserve has become more evident in recent years with the discovery of new wrecks. But the Thumb's most popular dive sites continue to be the *Philadelphia*, the *Albany*, and the *Chickamauga*, vessels whose whereabouts have long been known. The stories of the *Philadelphia* and the *Albany* are closely intertwined. Back in 1893, the two steamers collided about a dozen miles off Pointe Aux Barques. The crash left the *Albany* in particularly bad shape, and so the crew of the *Philadelphia* took the vessel in tow and set out for the nearest port. The 267-foot *Albany* was unable to make it, however, and sank about eight miles northeast of the Pointe Aux Barques Lighthouse. The *Philadelphia* limped along, but it too proved fatally crippled by the collision, and it sank a few miles later. It currently rests 5½ miles northeast of the lighthouse. Today, both vessels lie in 120 to 140 feet of water, a depth that limits the number of visitors they receive. The *Philadelphia* is generally regarded as the better destination of the two; it lies intact and upright and includes opportunities for penetration diving.

The *Chickamauga* is a great wreck for divers who are not quite ready for the challenges of the *Philadelphia* or *Albany*. It is a 322-foot double deck schooner that was lost in 1919. It can be found

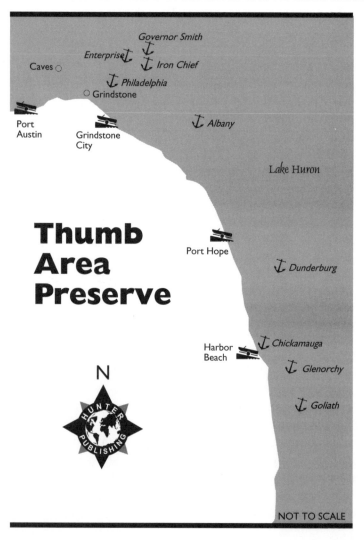

approximately half a mile east of Harbor Beach in 35 feet of water. The dive site enjoys greater protection from heavy seas than many other areas of the preserve, and visibility is fairly good.

Other noteworthy dive sites in the Thumb Area Underwater Preserve include the *Glenorchy*, a 365-foot steamer that lies 10 miles south-southeast of Harbor Beach in 120 feet of water (penetration diving is possible); the *Iron Chief*, a 212-foot wooden steamer located three miles northeast of Grindstone City in 130-140 feet of water; and the *Governor Smith*, a steamer four miles northeast of Grindstone City in 190 feet of water.

 All of these sites are inappropriate for inexperienced divers. They should only be undertaken by advanced divers with proper gear.

Other shipwrecks known to be within the preserve include the *Hunter Savidge, Dunderburg*, and *Enterprise*.

DIVE SHOPS. Diver services for the Thumb Area Preserve are available from **All Seasons Diving Company** (3910 Lake George Rd., Dryden, MI 48428-9709, ☎ 810-796-2357), and **Macomb Scuba Center** (13465 W. 12 Mile, Warren, MI 48093, ☎ 248-558-9922).

For more information on the preserve itself, contact the **Lighthouse County Park** at 7400 Lakeshore, Port Hope, MI 48468, ☎ 517-428-4749.

St. Clair River

The St. Clair River, which links Lake St. Clair to Lake Huron, provides diving experiences that are fundamentally different from those in the Great Lakes in several essential respects.

 The St. Clair is a busy shipping channel, a factor that accentuates the importance of topside attentiveness. In addition, two primary characteristics of the river are strong current and limited visibility, both of which can get divers in trouble. In addition, large – and potentially deadly – snarls of fishing line

have sprouted in certain areas, a development that has made the dive knife an obligatory piece of equipment on underwater excursions.

Despite some risks, the St. Clair River is a big attraction for area sport divers. The river holds several major wreck sites. One of the most popular is the *John B. Martin*, a 220-foot schooner that can be found 100 yards north of the Blue Water Bridge, where the river meets Lake Huron. Many divers approach the wreck by entering from a beach at the end of Riverview Street, in Port Huron. After visiting the wreck, which lies in 60 feet of water, divers get out on the US side of the Blue Water Bridge.

Visits to the Martin should be undertaken only by advanced divers familiar with the river; divers visiting this site have told harrowing tales about the strength of the river's current.

A short distance south of the Blue Water Bridge lies the *Monarch*, a tug boat that sank in 50 feet of water more than 60 years ago. Whereas current is a major concern just a few hundred yards up the river, here it is usually a negligible factor. A steel cable guides divers from the Canadian shoreline to the wreck.

Other wreck sites in the river include the *M.E. Tremble, Ben Hur*, and *A. R. Colburn*. In addition, a few stretches of shoreline are commonly used to introduce new divers to the river. These include the Pine Grove Park area and the "Backwash," a stretch of river that allows divers to be gently pulled up and back to their starting point by a quirk in the current (the backwash disappears below 40 feet, though, so divers are advised to keep track of their whereabouts). For more information on the St. Clair River, contact the **St. Clair County Convention and Visitors Bureau** at 520 Thomas Edison Parkway, Port Huron, MI 48060, ☎ 800-852-4242.

Southwest Michigan

The underwater preserves along Lake Huron receive the bulk of attention from southern Michigan's sport diving community, but the western side of the state is by no means barren of attractions for underwater explorers. In fact, proposals have been made to add a southern section of Lake Michigan to Michigan's bottomland preserve system. The boundaries of this proposed preserve would stretch from the Michigan-Indiana border up to a point two miles north of Holland and extend out from shore to create a 370-square-mile preserve. If approved, the preserve would become the largest in the entire bottomland system.

The two major shipwrecks in this area are the *Rockaway* and *Ironsides.* The **Rockaway** is a 106-foot schooner that sank in a fierce November storm in 1891. Its remains lie in three pieces in about 70 feet of water, and although penetration diving is not possible, the site's many artifacts make it a popular destination.

The steamer **Ironsides** was lost in 1873. Located four miles west of Grand Haven, the 233-foot vessel lies at a depth of about 115 feet. As with the *Rockaway,* the boat's interior cannot be explored, but its condition and design make it a favorite of experienced divers.

Other area wrecks include the **Havana** and the **Verano**. For more information on the proposed preserve, contact the **Michigan Maritime Museum** at PO Box 612, South Haven, MI 49090, ☎ 616-637-8078.

Boating & Sailing

Thanks to its 3,000 miles of Great Lakes shoreline and 11,000 inland lakes, Michigan can claim more boats than any other state. On summer weekends, it often seems as though all of them are being used at once on Lake St. Clair and its connecting waterways in the southeastern Lower Peninsula. Still, the southernmost part of the state has much to offer boaters, including quaint resort towns and endless beaches along Lake Michigan; excellent fishing in Saginaw Bay and the St. Clair Flats; quiet harbors and a friendly, small-town atmosphere along the Thumb in Lake Huron; and a mixture of parks, cottages, stately homes, city skylines, and industrial complexes along the Detroit and St. Clair Rivers.

*Sailing on the Great Lakes
(Randall McCune).*

Lake Michigan

Southwestern Michigan features the longest stretch of freshwater beach in the world. The sands are deposited along shorelines and piled into dunes by Lake Michigan, which is 307 miles long and 118 miles wide, and averages 400 feet in depth. In addition to the nearly endless expanses of sand, the coast between the Indiana border and Pentwater features eight recreational harbors, a number of quaint resort towns, and many city and state parks. Beginning at the state line in the southern end of the lake, boaters will encounter harbors at New Buffalo, St. Joseph, South Haven, and Saugatuck. The latter is a haven for artists and features a pleasant downtown shopping area with unique galleries and appealing restaurants. Seven miles later is another harbor on Lake Macatawa near the aptly named city of Holland, which celebrates its Dutch heritage with windmills, wooden shoe factories, and an annual tulip festival. The next harbor comes 20 miles later in Grand Haven, with its popular beaches and a 2½-mile boardwalk along the lake. Additional harbors can be found in Muskegon – the area's largest city – and Whitehall. The coastline becomes more wooded and wild as boaters continue into the north end of the lake.

Lake Huron

At 223 miles long, 183 miles wide, and an average of 195 feet deep, Lake Huron is the second largest of the Great Lakes (after Superior). In fact, early explorers arriving on the eastern shore were convinced that China must lie on the opposite side. The southern portion of the lake wraps around the thumb of Michigan's mitten – a friendly, laid-back, agricultural area. It has largely escaped the throngs of summer tourists that descend on the state's northern regions. The 150 miles of coastline encircling Saginaw Bay features six recreational harbors – in Au Gres, Bay City, Saginaw, Sebewaing, Bayport, and Caseville – and three sizeable state parks with beaches and campgrounds – Port Crescent, Albert E. Sleeper, and Bay City. Boaters stopping in Port Austin, at the tip of the thumb, can watch the sunrise over Lake Huron and the sunset over the bay. Continuing south, boaters will find recreational harbors in Harbor Beach, Port Sanilac, and Lexington before reaching Port Huron at the mouth of the St. Clair River.

St. Clair River

The sights along the shores of the 39-mile St. Clair River – which connects Lake Huron to Lake St. Clair – range from wild, marshy wetlands to pleasant residential communities to giant factories and power plants. The busy waterway also provides plentiful opportunities for viewing the big freighters as they pass close to shore. Beginning at the north end of the river, boaters will find ample docking space along the Black River in Port Huron, with access to restaurants, shops, and parks. There are recreational harbors in St. Clair and Marine City before the river divides into several branches near its mouth, creating the island-strewn St. Clair Flats. Harsens Island, the largest on the American side, was once a resort for wealthy vacationers who arrived on steamers from Detroit.

Lake St. Clair

At 26 miles long, 24 miles wide, and an average of only 10 feet deep, Lake St. Clair may seem small compared to the others in the Great Lakes watershed. But it is actually among the largest lakes in the country, excluding the Great Lakes. Its close proximity to Detroit's northern suburbs means that it sees more than its share of boat traffic during the summer months. In fact, the Michigan shoreline is lined with marinas, yacht clubs, and private docks from Grosse Pointe to Anchor Bay. Sailing regattas take place nearly every night of the week in the southern end of the lake, while the northern reaches are extremely popular with fishermen, cruisers seeking protected anchorages, and boaters who like to hang out and party in shallow, sandy areas. Recreational harbors on Lake St. Clair include Metro Beach – a metropark with a large public beach that is usually crawling with boats – and the Clinton River in Mt. Clemens.

Detroit River

Heading south from Lake St. Clair, boaters enter the 32-mile Detroit River. Forming the border between Michigan and Ontario, Canada, it is one of the busiest waterways in the world. Near the headwaters of the river is Belle Isle, a wooded park that has been providing urban Detroiters with relief from the confines of the city for generations. Home to two venerable yacht clubs, Belle Isle is also the site of annual hydroplane boat races and the Detroit Grand Prix. Continuing southward, boaters encounter imposing industrial complexes, the towering Detroit skyline, and the more subdued city of Windsor before reaching the Ambassador Bridge. There are two recreational harbors along the river – at the Erma Henderson marina and at St. Aubin Park. Continuing toward Lake Erie, boaters pass Boblo (Bois Blanc) Island – once the site of an amusement park – and several industrial downriver communities offset by the stately homes on Grosse Isle.

Lake Erie

The southeastern corner of Michigan borders Lake Erie, which is 241 miles long, 57 miles wide, and the shallowest of the Great Lakes at an average of 62 feet. It was once by far the most polluted of the Great Lakes, but has made a nice recovery in recent years. Recreational harbors along the short Michigan shoreline include Lake Erie Metropark, Monroe, and Bolles Harbor.

Inland Lakes and Rivers

Inland lakes of all shapes and sizes liberally dot the landscape in the southern half of Michigan's Lower Peninsula. Nearly 600 public access sites allow boaters to use these waters, as well as connecting rivers, for cruising, fishing, swimming, waterskiing, or simply relaxing in the sun.

On Wheels

Mountain Biking

 Thanks in large part to the presence of several good-sized state recreation areas, southern Michigan mountain bikers can enjoy a variety of scenic trails in their own backyards. Trails here satisfy every knobby's appetite, from relatively mellow dirt road forays to white-knuckle scab-makers that will test even technically advanced riders. In fact, several of the state's most notorious mountain biking destinations are in this region. Here are a few of southern Michigan's better known trails:

Addison Oaks Trails

The five-mile system in this Oakland County park is a big favorite with locals. The loop is moderately difficult, with numerous wooded sections. To reach Addison Oaks County Park, take Rochester Road north to Romeo Road west; the park entrance lies about two miles down. For more information, ☎ 248-693-2432.

Fort Custer Trails

The Fort Custer Trail system offers a great mix of easy trails for beginners and technically daunting loops for more advanced bikers. In fact, challenging segments such as the Amusement Park, the Trenches, Sand Trap, and Granny's Garden are among the best-known in the entire Lower Peninsula. The network offers varied scenery as well, with both single-tracks and double-tracks winding through meadows, hardwood forest, and clusters of streams and ponds. Grab a map from park headquarters before heading out, though; the system, which has many unmarked portions, includes numerous trails that can lead riders astray. Fort Custer Recreation Area can be reached by taking M-96 (Dickman Road) east out of Kalamazoo for about 10 miles. For more information, contact park headquarters at ☎ 616-731-4200.

Highland Trails

This 14½-mile system in Oakland County's Highland Recreation Area is probably the most technically challenging circuit in the entire state. The network consists of four loops of varying lengths, but the most notorious is Loop D, a four-mile trail that will destroy all but the hardiest of bikers. The Highland Recreation Area lies on the south side of M-59, between Milford Road and Bogie Lake Road. For more information, contact park headquarters at ☎ 248-685-2433.

Holdridge Lakes Trail

This modest system, which is in the Holly Recreation Area, is expected to become considerably more popular when 10 miles of new mountain biking trails are completed. The new section should be open by the time you read this. For more information, ☎ 248-634-8811.

Island Lake Trails

A relatively mellow biking experience awaits in the Island Lake Recreation Area. The park lies near Brighton, making it a favorite destination for casual Detroit-area riders. The system's main track is particularly popular. A 10-mile single track, it takes riders through quiet meadows and tall clusters of oak and other hardwoods, with views of the Huron River thrown in along the way. The system does require a basic level of fitness and ability, but its gently rolling terrain is pretty forgiving, and the layout makes it easy for bikers to attack the course at their own pace. The trailhead is at park headquarters, which is just south of I-96, at the intersection of Kensington Road and Old Grand River Road.

Lawless Park Trails

Less than 10 miles from the Indiana border, Lawless County Park is one of Michigan's newest mountain biking destinations. It became an immediate favorite of northern Indiana mountain bikers after it opened in the mid-1990s and is now getting popular with Michigan bikers as well. Dedicated exclusively to mountain biking, the narrow single-track trail winds through a 200-acre section of the park for 10 miles. The trail is tough, but fun. Lawless County Park lies 12 miles west of Three Rivers and US-131. To reach the entrance, take M-60 west through Jones to Lewis Lake Road and follow the signs. For more information, ☎ 616-445-8611.

Pontiac Lake Trails

Bikers will feel every inch of this system, which lies within the Pontiac Lake Recreation Area. The single-track trail is marked by grinding climbs, steep downhill runs, and a variety of technical challenges, and is fully capable of wreaking havoc on even experienced mountain bikers. The tough layout, though, makes the course a favorite training ground for competitive riders. To reach the trailhead, take Williams Lake Road north from M-59 to Gale Road; turn west and park in the Pontiac Lake beach lot on the south side of the road. For more information about the trail, call park headquarters at ☎ 248-666-1020.

Yankee Springs Trails

Yankee Springs is perhaps the most heavily visited of this region's mountain biking options. Nestled deep in Barry County's Yankee Springs Recreation Area, this single-track system is good for bikers of varying abilities. Its southeastern segments are fairly flat (though some small ravines spice things up), providing less experienced bikers with a good workout. The northern stretches of Yankee Springs take bikers up and down over rugged – and often steep – terrain. These exhilarating and challenging trails are some of the very best that the state has to offer. To reach the park, take US-131 to Exit 61 and go east on CR-A42 for about eight miles. Turn south on Gun Lake Road (CR-430); the headquarters lie less than a mile down the road. For a trail map or other information, ☎ 616-795-9081.

In addition, southern Michigan's Pinckney Recreation Area is home to the **Potawatomi Trail**, one of the state's true biking meccas. See page 40 for more information.

Bicycling

Bicyclists can choose from literally hundreds of rewarding routes in southern Michigan. The region may hold most of the state's largest metropolitan areas, but it also boasts a multitude of placid lakes, shady rivers, quiet roadways, and bustling mid-sized towns that can be enjoyed from a bicycle seat. In fact, the southern reaches of the Lower Peninsula are home to many of the state's most enthusiastic cyclists (and to its largest and most active bicycling clubs). The Lower Peninsula's southwest corner, in particu-

Bicyclists enjoying one of Michigan's many quiet roadways
(Crystal Mountain Photo).

lar, is a hotbed of bicycling activity. This is due in large measure to the energy and enthusiasm of a local bicycle club known as the **Three Oaks Spokes**, which developed a menu of cruises collectively known as the **Backroads Bikeway**. These 10 tours, all of which have been posted with color-coded signs, ramble all across southeast Michigan. State parks, wineries, quaint villages, and cider mills figure prominently on these routes.

So although southern Michigan cyclists will concede that the North Country features some pretty spectacular rambling options, they have some pretty fine close-to-home options as well. So here's a sampling of some – but by no means all – of the best bicycling routes in Lower Michigan.

Frankenmuth Fahrrad Ramble

One of the most popular annual bicycling events in Lower Michigan is the Frankenmuth Fahrrad Bicycle Tour, held each May in Frankenmuth. This tour includes loops of 25, 50, and 100 kilometers on gently rolling terrain through picturesque woodlands and farm country. The 50-kilometer (31-mile) loop is a particularly pleasant ride. The circuit, which begins and ends in Frankenmuth's Heritage Park, extends eastward to the pretty little town of Vassar. For more information, contact the **Frankenmuth Convention and Visitors Bureau** at ☎ 517-652-6106.

Grand Mere Trail

Every year, on the last weekend of September, bicyclists from all around the Midwest descend on Three Oaks, Michigan, a small town in the state's southwestern corner, to take part in the **Apple Cider Century**. This bicycle tour, which includes loops of 25, 50, 75, and 100 miles, has been nurtured by the Three Oaks Spokes bicycle club into one of the Midwest's best and most popular tours. The Grand Mere Trail follows the route of the 50-mile loop and is part of its Backroads Bikeway selection. The cruise, which bicyclists often launch from the Three Oaks Bicycle Museum, takes peddlers through several small villages (New Troy, Glendora, Baroda, Stevensville, Sawyer), sprawling orchards, and a couple of the state's prettiest parks, Warren Dunes State Park and Grand Mere State Park. For more information on the annual cruise, contact **Apple Cider Century** at PO Box 7000, Three Oaks, MI 49128, ☎ 616-756-3361.

Kal-Haven Trail

This western Michigan rail-trail gets a variety of traffic near its east and west hubs, including strolling couples, in-line skaters, and other bicyclists, but it remains a worthwhile cycling destination nonetheless. The Kal-Haven is 34 miles long, but many bicyclists take it round-trip, making for a full day of peddling. Their reluctance to leave the trail is understandable, though, because it's a beauty. It passes through a wonderful hybrid of town and country, mixing scenic woodlands and meadows of wildflowers with attractive little towns that are ideal for lunch or ice cream stops. The rail-trail's eastern trailhead can be found on 10th Street in Oshtemo Township (near Kalamazoo, two miles north of M-43 and just west of US-131). Its western trailhead is in South Haven. To reach it, take US-131 to Exit 22 (North Shore Drive). Head west on North Shore for about a quarter-mile to CR-A2 and turn left; a gravel parking lot is less than a mile down the road on the left, just after a bridge. For more information on the trail, contact **Kal-Haven State Park** at ☎ 616-637-2788. For more information on the **Rails-to-Trails Conservancy**, contact

Kal-Haven Trail Sesquicentennial Park

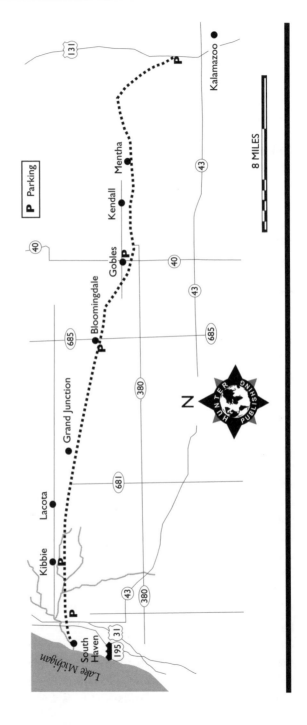

the organization's Michigan chapter at PO Box 23032, Lansing, MI 48909, ☎ 517-393-6022.

Lake Shore Avenue Trail

This 20-mile Ottawa County bike path parallels Lake Shore Avenue all the way from Grand Haven to Holland. The pathway is an exceptionally scenic one, for it takes bicyclists through miles of pretty woodlands and dunes, skirting the vast blue waters of Lake Michigan the entire time. Even the launching points for this trek – Holland's Tunnel Park or Grand Haven State Park – are pleasant, though the latter gets ridiculously crowded during the summer. Given that reality, bicyclists who wish to place a car at both ends of the pathway and avoid a 40-mile round-trip cruise would do well to grab their Grand Haven parking spot at an early hour.

Muskegon Cruise

This 25-mile circuit takes full advantage of the western Michigan coastline, cobbling together stops at Muskegon State Park and Duck Lake State Park with lightly traveled country roads further inland to create a scenic and invigorating ride. Most cyclists begin at the huge (1165 acres, 300+ campsites) Muskegon State Park. From there they head west on Scenic Drive, which lives up to its name with spectacular views of Lake Michigan and Muskegon Lake. Nine miles later, in the Duck Lake State Park area, the circuit begins its inland stretch. Turn east on Michillinda Drive, which meets Orshal Road after a couple of miles. Take a right on Orshal and follow all the way down to River Road. Turn right on River Road until you reach Buys Road. Turn left on Buys and follow for two miles until you take a right on Fenner. The latter road leads back into Muskegon State Park.

Thumbs Up Bicycle Cruise

Located in the upper crescent of Michigan's thumb, this enjoyable cruise follows one of the routes of the annual Thumbs Up Bicycle Tour, which launches from Port Austin every June. The tour includes five different circuits of varying lengths; the one described here is the 62-mile cruise, the second longest of the five. It is marked by superb and varied scenery – the route passes by two state parks and a state game area and follows the Lake Huron coastline for about half of its length – and a fair amount of traffic (plan a weekday trip if possible). The loop starts in Port Austin's Gallop Park and heads west on Port Austin Road (M-25) all the way down to Caseville. Take Kinde Road east out of Caseville to Lewisville (you'll go through the villages of Pinnebog and Kinde). Take Huron City Road out of Lewisville to Stoddard Rd.; turn right on Stoddard, left on Minden Road, and left again on Lighthouse Road. After four miles on Lighthouse, turn right on M-25 (Grind Stone Road), then right on Pearson Road into Grind Stone City. From there, take a right on Point aux Barques Road, which eventually merges with Port Austin Road.

These are just a few of the many great bicycling routes in southern Michigan. The areas surrounding Lansing, Ann Arbor, Kalamazoo, Grand Rapids, Saginaw, and Port Huron, among others, offer plenty of options, and metro Detroiters have ready access to the Huron-Clinton Metropark system, a 24,000-acre network that includes 13 different parks (see page 23 for a detailed description of the metroparks). In addition, organized rides of all shapes and sizes have proliferated throughout the Lower Peninsula over the last few years. Contact local chambers of commerce or regional bicycling clubs for additional information. Finally, bicycles are permitted on trails in many of Lower Michigan's state park and recreation areas. For further information on these options, contact the **Michigan Department of Natural Resources' Parks Division** at ☎ 517-373-1270.

On Snow

Cross-Country Skiing

Numerous Nordic skiing trails can be found in the southern half of the Lower Peninsula. These trails – which range from novice-friendly circuits over flat terrain to hilly loops suitable for more advanced skiers – are primarily in state parks and recreation areas. Here are some of the region's best:

Bald Mountain Trails

The Bald Mountain Recreation Area grooms eight miles of trails for cross-country in its northernmost section (Bald Mountain has three distinct units). The trails are clear of the snowmobile traffic that can be found in its other sections. Bald Mountain Nordic skiing is challenging and scenic, with lots of rolling hills punctuated by the odd lake or stream. The recreation area lies seven miles north of Pontiac; to reach park headquarters, go north on M-24 to Greenshield Road and turn east. Call the park at ☎ 248-693-6767.

Highland Recreation Area Pathway

Cross-country skiing is a popular activity in this Oakland County recreation area. Skiers can choose from among three loops of varying length, all of which run through heavily wooded and rolling terrain. This no-frills (ungroomed, no shelter) system runs through the park's attractive Haven Hill Natural Area, which is off-limits to snowmobilers. Highland Recreation Area lies near the intersection of M-59 and Milford Road. For more information, ☎ 248-685-2433.

Ionia Recreation Area Trails

This mid-Michigan site grooms nine miles of trails for cross-country skiing. A couple of small loops are suitable for less-experienced skiers, but the park's main attraction is a six-mile loop that will challenge advanced skiers with its very hilly route. This is a handsome area, with lots of woods, lakes, and streams, but it also gets a lot of attention from snowmobilers. Ionia Recreation Area lies 3½ miles north of I-96 on Jordan Lake Road. ☎ 616-527-3750.

Maybury State Park Trails

Ten miles of groomed trails lie within this popular Wayne County park. Most of the system will likely frustrate beginners, but Maybury is a nice getaway for more experienced skiers. Equipment rental is available. Maybury lies on Eight Mile Road, about five miles west of I-275. For more info, ☎ 810-348-1190.

Muskegon State Park Trails

This picturesque park offers two lighted trails (2½ kilometers and five kilometers) for Nordic skiing. Both loops are ideal for intermediate skiers, with varied terrain that ranges from mild rolls to more heart-pumping fare. The cross-country ski trails are part of

Bountiful lake-effect snow provides southwestern Michigan Nordic skiers with plenty of trails (Travel Michigan).

the park's immensely popular winter sports complex, which also provides ice skating and luge opportunities (see the "Luge" section, below). The park can be accessed from both the north and south. From the north, take Scenic Drive southbound out of Whitehall; from the south, take M-120 southwest to Memorial Drive and follow the signs. ☎ 616-744-9629.

Proud Lake Trails

Proud Lake Recreation Area holds one of the most popular cross-country skiing networks in southeastern Michigan. Officially, the park has eight miles of forest-rimmed trails – including one lighted loop – but more experienced skiers often light out for more challenging terrain elsewhere in the recreation area. To reach Proud Lake, take Wixom Road north from I-96 or Duck Lake Road south from M-59. ☎ 248-685-2433.

Saugatuck Dunes State Park Trails

Nordic skiers flock to Saugatuck State Park's tough but handsome trails. Constantly replenished by lake-effect snow, the Saugatuck system maintains a fresh feel to it all through the season. Saugatuck Dunes' 13 miles of groomed trails are among the most demanding in southern Michigan, but the park's scenic offerings –

views of Lake Michigan, hulking dunes – keep folks coming back. The park also includes a 2½-mile loop that can be easily negotiated by beginners. To reach the park, take Blue Star Memorial Highway west from I-96, turn north on 64th Street, and turn west on 138th Avenue; the park entrance lies a mile up the road. ☎ 616-399-9390.

Sleepy Hollow State Park Trails

More than seven miles of groomed and tracked trails await in mid-Michigan's Sleepy Hollow State Park. The trails pass through a number of open areas, making for sometimes windy conditions, but the system does offer nice views of Lake Ovid. To reach the park, take US-27 to Price Road and head east for seven miles. ☎ 517-651-6217.

Yankee Springs Trails

This Barry County park is a haven for cross-country skiers. Blessed with scenic countryside and an interesting blend of terrain, the Yankee Springs Recreation Area maintains half a dozen loops for skiers of varying abilities. The longest of these is a five-mile chug through challenging but pretty woodlands. Park trails are periodically groomed, and a warming shelter is available. To reach the park, take US-131 to Exit 61 and go east on CR-A42 for about eight miles. Turn south on Gun Lake Road (CR-430); the park's headquarters is less than a mile down the road. ☎ 616-795-9081.

South Michigan offers a variety of other Nordic skiing options in addition to the ones mentioned above. A number of county parks offer nice cross-country skiing, and the Huron-Clinton Metropark system attracts thousands of Detroit-area skiers each year (see the section on Huron-Clinton Metroparks, page 29). Finally, several other state parks (Van Buren, P.J. Hoffmaster, Warren Dunes) feature small cross-country systems.

Downhill Skiing & Snowboarding

No one argues that the ski areas in the southern half of Michigan's Lower Peninsula can compare to those in the northern half or in the Upper Peninsula. In most cases, the vertical drop is less than half as high, the longest run is a third as long, and the snow

Southern Lower Michigan

tends to be of the granular, artificial variety. Another striking difference is a conspicuous lack of trees on most southern Michigan ski hills. Still, these ski areas are extremely popular with locals who only have an afternoon or evening to spend, rather than the entire weekend it takes to make the trip up north. They all offer instruction and equipment rentals and allow snowboarding. Most feature snow-making on all slopes and are fully lighted for night skiing. Overall, these slightly less glamorous ski areas are excellent places for beginners to practice before venturing up north. And each one offers a few challenges that can keep more experienced skiers in condition until they find the time and money to take their next ski vacation.

Alpine Valley

Located on Highland Road in White Lake Township, Alpine Valley wins hands down for the Detroit-area ski hill with the most trees. It features 25 runs, with a 300-foot vertical drop and a longest run of 2,000 feet, served by 10 chairlifts. ☎ 248-887-4183.

Bittersweet

Located on River Road in Otsego, north of Kalamazoo, Bittersweet receives a good amount of lake-effect snow off nearby Lake Michigan. It features 15 runs served by five lifts, a 300-foot vertical drop, and the longest run in southern Lower Michigan at 2,300 feet. ☎ 616-694-2820.

Cannonsburg

Just northeast of Grand Rapids, Cannonsburg offers 17 runs served by three lifts, with a 250-foot vertical drop and 1,800-foot longest run. ☎ 616-874-6711.

Mt. Brighton

Though rather sparse and windswept, Mt. Brighton – just off I-96 in Brighton – is quite popular with the college crowds from nearby Ann Arbor and East Lansing. It features 25 runs and a terrain park served by seven chairlifts. The longest run is 1,800 feet, and the vertical drop is 250 feet. Particularly entertaining is the "midnight skiing" offered on weekends. ☎ 810-229-9581 for conditions and information.

Mt. Holly

On Dixie Highway in Holly, about an hour north of Detroit, Mt. Holly features the highest vertical drop in the area at 350 feet, and a longest run of 2,100 feet. Some of its 16 runs and eight chairlifts – including a brand-new, high-speed quad – pass through semi-wooded areas. It also has decent moguls (sometimes), a snowboard park with jumps, and a nice view of the surrounding countryside from the top of the hill. ☎ 248-634-8260 for information or 800-582-7256 for a snow report.

Pine Knob

Off Sashabaw Road in Clarkston, the Pine Knob ski area is part of the concert venue/entertainment complex of the same name. It offers 16 runs served by five lifts, a 300-foot vertical drop, and a longest run of 1,600 feet. ☎ 248-625-0800 for more information, or reach the snowline at ☎ 800-642-7669.

Swiss Valley

Swiss Valley is just north of the Indiana border in Jones, off Mann Road. Its 11 runs – with a vertical drop of 225 feet and a longest run of 1,800 feet – are served by three lifts. ☎ 616-244-5635.

Timber Ridge

Another prime spot for lake-effect snow, Timber Ridge is in Gobles, just west of Kalamazoo. It has 15 runs served by four lifts, a 250-foot vertical drop, and a 2,000-foot longest run. ☎ 616-694-9449.

Luge

Western Michigan's **Muskegon State Park** maintains one of only three luge tracks in the entire country (the other two are at Lake Placid, New York, and at Northern Michigan University's Lucy Hill Naturbahn Luge Track in the UP). Muskegon's luge run is open to the public. Beginners receive tutoring on basic concepts like steering and braking on a 150-meter training run. The layout of this section of the track is pretty relaxed, with speeds rarely exceeding 15 miles per hour or so. But another, more adrenaline-inducing section is also available to lugers itching to pick up the pace. The advanced option lets lugers take on the bottom 300 meters of the complex's icy, 450-meter competition track. Because of

Southern Lower Michigan

the dramatically increased speed, the latter run is a considerably wilder ride.

Basic tutorials, equipment, and runs on the training track are available for $15; an additional $10 is necessary to try the 300-meter run. Weekday nights are reserved for luge leagues, and large groups (12 or more) can reserve the track on selected weekday afternoons. For more information, ☎ 616-774-9269.

Snowmobiling

The forested ridges and valleys of Michigan's North Country are universally recognized as terrific terrain for snowmobiling, but the state's southwestern counties also boast several trails of considerable size. Situated to the west of Lake Michigan's sprawling seas, the region regularly gets sizable quantities of lake-effect snow. This is bad news during rush hour, but it does enable snowmobiling enthusiasts to disappear into the woods for hours at a time without having to slog their way north.

Southwestern Michigan's primary trails include the **Niles-Sister Lakes Trail** (58 miles in Berrien County), the **Berrien County Trails** (more than 50 miles), the massive **West Michigan Trail** network (well over 200 miles stretched across several counties), the **Newaygo County Trail** network (60 miles), the **Northwest Shore Trails** (150 miles), and the **Southwest Shore Trails** (112 miles). These pathways run through a blend of private and public land in Berrien, Cass, Van Buren, Allegan, Ottawa, Kent, Muskegon, Oceana, and Newaygo counties; contact the appropriate visitor's bureau or chamber of commerce for information on snowmobiling in particular counties.

Snowmobilers across the entire southern half of the Lower Peninsula also migrate to many of the region's state parks and recreation areas. Indeed, a number of southern Michigan's parks – from southeast Michigan's Pontiac Lake Recreation Area and central Michigan's Fort Custer Recreation Area to the Kal-Haven and Hart-Montague rail-trails of the state's west side – allow snowmobiling, though some impose restrictions.

For detailed maps and information about Michigan's snowmobile trail system, contact the **Michigan Snowmobiling Association** at ☎ 616-361-2285 or the **DNR's Forest Management Division** at ☎ 517-373-1275.

■ Where To Sleep

 Southern Michigan communities provide ample accommodations for all tastes and budgets. In addition to dozens of quaint bed-and-breakfasts (many of them on or near scenic Great Lakes shorelines), there are literally hundreds of hotels of all shapes and sizes – from modest independently owned and operated ranch-style facilities and fully equipped chain hotels (Holiday Inn, Best Western, Red Roof Inn, etc.) to beautiful country inns and plush resorts. Following is just a sampling of some of the finest.

Price Guide	
$	up to $50 per night
$$	$50-$100
$$$	$100-$175
$$$$	more than $175

Southwest Michigan

Amway Grand Plaza Hotel (187 Monroe NW, Grand Rapids, MI 49503, ☎ 616-774-2000, $$-$$$). This huge (30 stories, 682 rooms) spectacular hotel is in the heart of downtown Grand Rapids, making it an ideal base from which to explore the city. Nicely decorated rooms, elegant public areas, a gracious staff, and a huge array of accoutrements – including six restaurants, lighted tennis courts, heated indoor pool, exercise room, etc.

Boyden House Inn Bed and Breakfast (301 S. Fifth St., Grand Haven, MI 49417, ☎ 616-846-3538, $$-$$$). Built in 1874, this cozy seven-room home features fireplaces, whirlpool baths, homemade breakfasts, and easy access to the beach.

Inn at Union Pier (9708 Berrien, Union Pier, MI 49129, ☎ 616-469-4700, $$$). Nestled in the state's far southwestern corner,

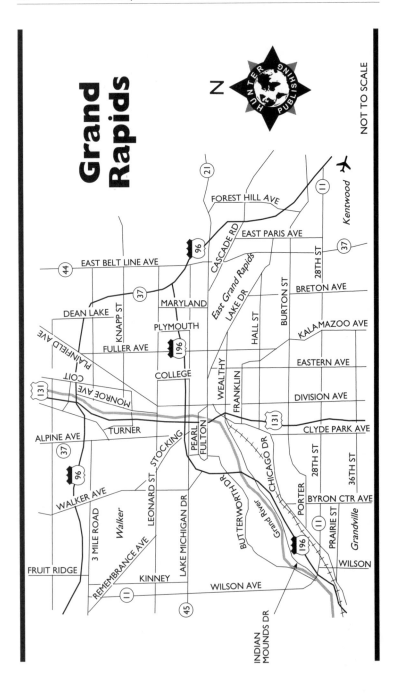

the Inn is immensely popular with Chicago natives and other visitors of Lake Michigan's eastern shores. It features 15 tastefully decorated rooms, each with private baths, and beautiful common areas (including an eight-person hot tub cradled out on a long deck area). Full breakfast is included with the stay, and an array of restaurants lie a few miles' drive away.

Nickerson Inn (262 W. Lowell, Pentwater, MI 49449, ☎ 616-869-6731, $$-$$$$). A 1914 historic B&B, this fine 12-room facility features a wide veranda that looks out on scenic woodlands.

Snow Flake Motel (3822 Red Arrow Highway, St. Joseph, MI 49085, ☎ 616-429-3261, $$). This unusual inn, which is shaped in an ornate snowflake pattern, was designed by the Frank Lloyd Wright Foundation. The motel's 57 rooms open out onto a courtyard and feature plenty of amenities.

Stuart Avenue Inn Bed and Breakfast (229 Stuart Ave., Kalamazoo, MI 49007, ☎ 616-342-0230, $$-$$$). This historic B&B offers 18 beautiful rooms and suites (14 of which include fireplaces) in two elegant Victorian homes and a small carriage house. A major draw is the inn's spectacular English garden, renowned throughout the area.

Wickwood Country Inn (510 Butler St., Saugatuck, MI 49453, ☎ 616-857-1465, $$$-$$$$). Luxurious accommodations in one of Southwest Michigan's most popular and picturesque villages. Each of the 11 rooms (all with private baths) is tastefully furnished, and the first floor of the two-story building features a dark mahogany library/bar, garden room, screened deck, and formal living room.

Southcentral Michigan

National House Inn (102 S. Parkview, Marshall, MI 49068, ☎ 616-781-7374, $$-$$$). This 16-room facility is Michigan's oldest operating inn. Originally used as a stagecoach stop in 1835, the building now features a pleasing blend of Victorian and country-style furnishings. The inn looks out on Marshall's picturesque town square and is within walking distance of antique shops.

Lansing

N

NOT TO SCALE

Radisson Hotel Lansing (111 N. Grand Ave., Lansing, MI 48933, ☎ 517-482-0180, $$-$$$). Only two blocks east of the state Capitol Building, this 259-room hotel has nicely decorated rooms, a handsome lobby, and many perks for guests, including heated indoor pool, sauna, whirlpool, and exercise facility.

Victorian Villa Guesthouse (601 North Broadway, Union City, MI 49094, ☎ 517-741-7383, $$$). This gorgeous Victorian inn has eight rooms, two suites, and succulent English-themed dining options, with massive breakfasts (included with the room) and dinners. The Guesthouse also hosts a dazzling array of special events, from Sherlock Holmes mystery weekends in the spring and fall to elaborate nine-course roast goose Christmas dinners with a decidedly Dickensian flair.

Southeast Michigan

The Atheneum (1000 Brush Ave., Detroit, MI 48226, ☎ 313-962-2323, $$$-$$$$). This luxury 10-story hotel in the heart of Greektown has many amenities, including a complete exercise room. A great – if expensive – base from which to explore the Motor City.

Dearborn Inn (20301 Oakwood Blvd., Dearborn, MI 48124, ☎ 313-271-2700, $$$). This 222-room hotel, which operates under the Marriott banner, provides elegant and tasteful accommodations. Behind the main hotel are five bed-and-breakfast homes – all of which are replicas of homes of famous Americans. Excellent meals are offered.

Garfield Inn (8544 Lake St., Port Austin, MI 48467, ☎ 517-738-5254, $$). This refurbished Victorian mansion – once a favorite stay of President Garfield – includes six tastefully decorated rooms and a highly regarded restaurant. Only a short stroll away from Lake Huron.

Montague Inn (1581 South Washington Ave., Saginaw, MI 48601, ☎ 517-752-3939, $$-$$$). Nestled on sprawling, beautifully landscaped grounds, this elegantly restored Georgian mansion overlooks Lake Linton and Ojibway Island. The Inn maintains 15 nicely decorated rooms, a suite, and an excellent dining room.

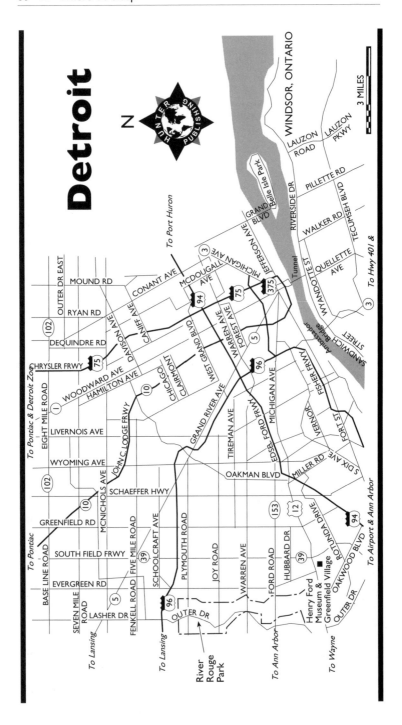

Detroit

St. Clair Inn (500 N. Riverside Ave., St. Clair, MI 48079, ☎ 810-329-2222, $$-$$$). Located on the St. Clair River, this English country-flavored hotel includes 78 rooms, an indoor pool, a scenic boardwalk, and boat docking facilities.

■ Where To Eat

 The vast majority of Michigan residents make their home in the southern half of the Lower Peninsula (about half of the state's population lives in Metro Detroit alone). Consequently, the cities of this region support a dizzying array of restaurants, from ubiquitous fast food joints to four-star restaurants that are among the finest in the Midwest. Dining options run the gamut in terms of ethnicity as well, ranging from localized caches (the Polish fare served in Hamtramck's family restaurants, for example) to the thick carpeting of Mexican, Chinese, German, and Italian restaurants that can be found across the entire region.

Price Guide
$ . . . . Inexpensive
$$ . . . . moderately priced
$$$ . . . . expensive

Ann Arbor

Angelo's (1100 E. Catherine, Ann Arbor, MI, ☎ 734-761-8996, $). Few restaurants enjoy the devoted following that this breakfast eatery does. Great chow and lots of it, but bring a newspaper; you'll stand in line for awhile on most mornings.

Casey's Tavern (304 Depot at 5th, Ann Arbor, MI, ☎ 734-665-6775, $). Casey's bills itself as Ann Arbor's favorite neighborhood bar, for good reason. A popular destination of U of M football boosters and local softball teams, the restaurant offers quality pub food inside walls festooned with Michigan sports paraphernalia.

Cottage Inn Pizza (512 E. Williams, Ann Arbor, MI, ☎ 734-663-3379, $$). Perennially popular with students and professionals alike, Cottage Inn serves a variety of Italian dishes, though pizza remains its staple.

Grizzly Peak Brewing Company (120 W. Washington, Ann Arbor, MI, ☎ 734-741-7325, $$). This popular microbrewery offers a variety of quality suds and tasty pasta and pizza options.

Moveable Feast (326 W. Liberty, Ann Arbor, MI, ☎ 734-663-3278, $$$). This highly regarded restaurant serves French-American cuisine under the roof of a restored Victorian home.

Real Seafood Company (341 S. Main, Ann Arbor, MI, ☎ 734-769-5960, $$). A warm, roomy restaurant that specializes in tasty seafood and shellfish dishes.

Zingerman's Deli (422 Detroit, Ann Arbor, MI, ☎ 734-663-3354, $). One of the most famous delicatessens in the eastern US, Zingerman's cultivates a fanatical, and large, customer base with its amazing array of deli and gourmet foods.

Detroit

Atwater Block Brewery (237 Joseph Campau, Detroit, MI, ☎ 734-393-2337, $$). A bright, cavernous gathering spot for downtown professionals, this trailblazing Motown microbrewery offers a great variety of pub food and a separate lounge area (complete with big humidor) for cigar aficionados.

Camp Ticonderoga (5725 Rochester, Troy, MI, ☎810-828-2825, $$$). The menu in this big, rustic watering hole is weighted toward game, though less exotic fare is also available. The restaurant's patio looks out on the Sylvan Glen public golf course.

Fishbone's Rhythm & Blues Café (400 Monroe, Detroit, MI, ☎ 734-965-4600, $$). This cajun-flavored eatery made a big splash at its Motown debut, and its still making waves. Great Louisiana-style fare in a big, lively dining room decorated with a blues/jazz theme. A sister restaurant is also in operation on Northwestern Highway in Southfield.

Ja-Da (546 E. Larned, Detroit, MI, ☎ 734-965-1700, $$). BBQ dishes and a hip urban sensibility are the hallmarks of this popular eatery, which lies on the fringes of the Motor City's Greektown area. Live jazz is a regular feature. Friendly but less-than-speedy service.

The Lark (6430 Farmington, West Bloomfield, MI, ☎ 248-661-4466, $$$). A visit to The Lark is an evening in itself. This French country inn, which is known for both its exquisite food and attentive service, was voted best restaurant in the entire country by *Condé Naste Traveler* in 1995.

C.J.'s Café (21 Flint St., Lake Orion, MI, ☎ 248-693-8291, $). A casual breakfast restaurant featuring a small-town atmosphere and good food (highlighted by great homemade cinnamon-raisin bread). A big favorite of local bicyclists.

Memphis Smoke (100 S. Main, Royal Oak, MI, ☎ 248-543-4300, $$). This rollicking joint sets itself apart from the rest of Royal Oak's crowded restaurant scene with scrumptious Southern-style pulled pork and beef brisket dishes served against a backdrop of live blues and a motif of prancing pigs.

Moose Preserve (2395 Woodward Ave., Bloomfield Hills, MI, ☎ 248-858-7688, $$). This wild and wooly restaurant bristles with North Country atmosphere and tasty entrées that run heavily toward fish and game. Reward yourself with a plate of piping hot chocolate chip cookies if you're fortunate enough to get one of the Preserve's popular pool tables.

Thai House (25223 Gratiot, Roseville, MI, ☎ 810-776-3660, $$). Remains a standout destination for Thai fans despite ever-growing metro area competition.

Xochimilco (3409 Bagley, Detroit, MI, ☎ 734-843-0179, $). A longtime staple of Detroit's Mexicantown area, this sprawling Mexican restaurant draws big lunch and dinner crowds with sizable portions and cheap pitchers.

Whistle Stop (501 S. Eton, Birmingham, MI, ☎ 248-647-5588, $). Breakfasts are the main draw at this cozy diner.

The Whitney (4421 Woodward, Detroit, MI, ☎ 734-832-5700, $$$). Great food and drink in an opulent setting.

Southern Lower Michigan

Flint

Churchill's Food & Spirits (340 S. Saginaw, Flint, MI, ☎ 810-238-6777, $). This raucous pub and grub joint is a favorite hang-out for U of M-Flint students.

The Speakeasy (Pearson Road, Flushing, MI, ☎ 810-659-7630, $$). Nice and casual, with an emphasis on pasta, ribs, and seafood.

Whitey's (State Road, Davison, MI, ☎ 810-653-6666, $$). This popular suburban restaurant offers a variety of seafood, including a yummy fish-and-chips dish.

Grand Rapids

Cygnus (187 Pearl St., Grand Rapids, MI, ☎ 616-774-2000, $$$). Located on the 27th floor of the Amway Grand Plaza Hotel, Cygnus provides elegant dining and dancing under the stars.

Great Lakes Shipping Company (Corner of Breton Ave. and Burton St., Grand Rapids, MI, ☎ 616-949-9440, $$). This restaurant serves up delicious steak and seafood in a handsome, fireplace-studded setting.

1913 Room (187 Pearl St., Grand Rapids, MI, ☎ 616-774-2000, $$$). Another option in the Amway Grand Plaza Hotel, this main-floor restaurant serves top-notch food in a comfortable setting.

Schnitzelbank (342 Jefferson Ave SE, Grand Rapids, MI, ☎ 616-459-9527, $$). German-American cuisine served up in a warm Old World atmosphere.

Holland

The Hatch (1870 Ottawa Beach Rd., Holland, MI, ☎ 616-399-9120, $$). Fine dining just minutes from Lake Michigan. The Hatch menu offers a range of dishes, from monster steaks to seafood and pasta.

Pietros Trattoria (175 E. 8th St., Holland, MI, ☎ 616-396-1000, $$). This downtown eatery is the place to go for Italian and Mediterranean cuisine.

Sandpiper (2225 S. Shore, Macatawa, MI, ☎ 616-335-5866, $$$). Gorgeous harbor views and classy entrées are hallmarks of this Holland-area restaurant, which is a favorite haunt of area boaters.

Wooden Shoe Restaurant (US-31 N. & 16th St., Holland, MI, ☎ 616-392-8521, $). Family-oriented restaurant packs 'em in for breakfast.

Kalamazoo

Black Swan (3501 Greenleaf Blvd., Kalamazoo, MI, ☎ 616-375-2105, $$). This lakeside establishment maintains a terrific menu and warm ambiance.

Cosmo's Cucina (804 W. Vine, Kalamazoo, MI, ☎ 616-344-5666, $$). Diverse contemporary cuisine in a modern setting.

Olde Peninsula Brewpub and Restaurant (200 E. Michigan, Kalamazoo, MI, ☎ 616-343-2739, $$). Located in the downtown area, the Olde Peninsula offers tasty sandwiches, burgers, and dinner entrées.

Webster's (100 W. Michigan Ave., Kalamazoo, MI, ☎ 616-343-4444, $$$). Nestled in the heart of downtown, Webster's offers fine dining in a refined atmosphere.

Lansing

Blue Coyote (113 Pere Marquette, Lansing, MI, ☎ 517-485-2583, $$). Popular brewpub attracts an electic crowd.

Chesapeake Crab House (300 M A C, Lansing, MI, ☎ 517-337-4440, $$$). Delicious steak, seafood, and pasta dishes served in a peaceful atmosphere.

Clara's (637 E. Michigan Ave., Lansing, MI, ☎ 517-372-7120, $$). Ideal for family outings, Clara's offers a diverse menu of American-style entrées and a sinful smorgasbord of desserts.

El Azteco (106 W. Saginaw, East Lansing, MI, ☎ 517-485-4589, $). This casual restaurant, which specializes in Mexican fare, is a big favorite of the college crowd.

Southern Lower Michigan

The Landshark (101 E. Grand River, East Lansing, MI, ☎ 517-351-8973, $). Classic college bar, which means loud and crowded. But if you're in the mood to dive headfirst into Spartanland, this is the place.

The Peanut Barrel (521 E. Grand River, East Lansing, MI, ☎ 517-351-0608, $). The floor of the always popular Barrel gets lost under a blizzard of discarded peanut shells on big game days. Cozy and relaxed atmosphere.

Rum Runners (601 E. Michigan Ave., Lansing, MI, ☎ 517-482-4949, $$). Across from Oldsmobile Park, where the city's single A Lugnuts play ball, Rum Runners attracts customers of all shapes and sizes with its beer selection, tasty food, and dueling piano players.

Port Huron

River Crab (1337 N. River Road, St. Clair, MI, ☎ 810-329-2261, $$$). Renowned for its great seafood, Sunday brunch, and view of the St. Clair River.

Thomas Edison Inn (500 Thomas Edison Parkway, Port Huron, MI, ☎ 810-984-8000, $$$). In a striking setting, the dining room provides great views of the Blue Water Bridge to Canada. The Inn specializes in delicious fresh fish.

Victorian Inn (1229 Seventh St., Port Huron, MI, ☎ 810-984-1437, $$$). Fine dining in an elegant Victorian setting. One of the best restaurants in the entire Thumb area.

Saginaw/Bay City

Chesaning Heritage House (605 W. Broad, Chesaning, MI, ☎ 517-845-7700, $$$). This gorgeously maintained building is one of mid-Michigan's most popular dining destinations. Once inside, customers will find exceptional food served in a congenial atmosphere.

Montague Inn (581 Washington Ave., Saginaw, MI, ☎ 517-752-3939, $$$). The Montague provides fine dining in a handsome historical setting.

Yesterdays (607 E. Midland, Bay City, MI, ☎ 517-894-2809, $$$). Elegantly appointed, this restaurant features a delightful array of choices and two bars (Little Bourbon Street and The Lumberjack).

Zehnders (730 S. Main, Frankenmuth, MI, ☎ 517-652-9925, $$). This legendary restaurant draws people from miles around with its all-you-can-eat chicken buffet. Great home cooking on a massive scale.

Southern Lower Michigan

Northern Lower Michigan

This is a handsome region of cool woodlands, rolling hills, valleys, and winding rivers. The Lower Peninsula's northern regions attract large numbers of hunters, anglers, snowmobilers, and other outdoor lovers from all over the state, to say nothing of the thousands of families who spend sizable chunks of their summers at cottages or campgrounds here. Any area that can quench the thirst of both solitude-seeking canoeists and shoppers with an appetite for fine food is bound to be popular, and northern Michigan is no exception.

Getting Around

The region's major roadways see a great deal of traffic on weekends and during the summer from residents of metropolitan Detroit, Grand Rapids, Lansing, and other areas further south. The primary north-south arteries leading into Michigan's North Country are US-31 and US-131 (on the west side), US-27 (right up the middle of the state), and I-75 and US-23 (on the east side). The only large airport in the area is Traverse City's Cherry Capital Airport, where a number of car rental companies maintain services.

■ Huron National Forest

Huron-Manistee National Forest
1755 S. Mitchell Street
Cadillac, MI 49601
☎ 800-821-6263 or 616-775-2421

Recreation opportunities abound throughout this forest, which is administered jointly with Manistee National Forest (the latter is over on the northwestern side of the Lower Peninsula). Popular with everyone from backpackers to anglers to cross-country skiers, Huron attracts visitors from all over the state and the greater

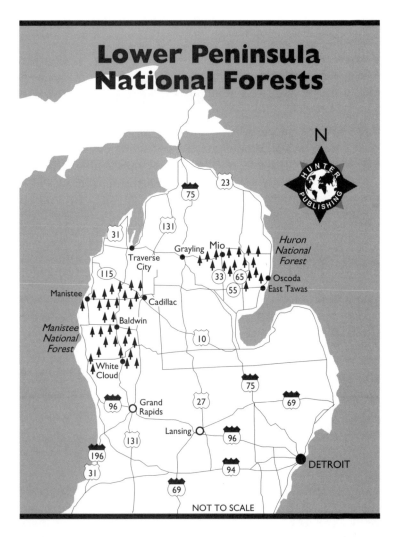

Midwest. Indeed, its lakes, deep jack pine forests, and rolling terrain make it a natural haven for all kinds of outdoor enthusiasts. It also attracts birders and wildlife lovers, for Huron and its surrounding environs are home to the Kirtland warbler, one of the continent's rarest birds, and a wide assortment of other creatures. Its single biggest attraction, however, is the mighty Au Sable River, which runs through much of the forest's length. The Au Sable, which enjoys Wild and Scenic River status, is a mecca for fishermen and canoeists alike, and ranks as one of the state's most beloved natural resources.

Getting There

Travelers from the south can take Interstate 75 north to Grayling, where it hits M-72; travelers turning east on M-72 will enter Huron through its western boundary. Some, however, choose to forsake further motorized transportation in Grayling, preferring the Au Sable River, which winds through the center of town as it rushes eastward to Lake Huron. If you care to bring or rent a canoe, you can ease into Huron National Forest via paddle power.

You can also take M-33 or M-65, both of which run north-south through the forest, into Huron. From the north, both M-33 and M-65 can be picked up on M-72; from the south, both roads can be picked up via M-55, an east-west road that meets I-75 in the small town of West Branch. Finally, the forest can also be reached via US-23, which parallels Michigan's Lake Huron coastline. Roads lead into Huron from two towns along US-23 – Oscoda and Tawas City. From Oscoda you will take River Road west. If you are entering from Tawas City, look for Monument Road. Both of these roads will eventually take you to Lumbermen's Monument, a visitor center that features a 14-foot bronze statue dedicated to past generations of Michigan loggers.

History

Back in the late 19th century, the land now known as Huron National Forest had been reduced to a near wasteland, laid low by feverish and indiscriminate logging. Many of Michigan's woodlands were staggering under the weight of similar short-sighted practices, but few felt the blows as acutely as northeastern Michigan. Wildlife habitats and watersheds were obliterated with stunning speed, and by the turn of the century the future good health of the region was in serious doubt.

In the early 1900s, however, the fledgling American conservation movement found a powerful friend in the White House – Theodore Roosevelt. The bespectacled former Rough Rider, a long-time outdoorsman, was determined to preserve America's wild places, and he formulated policy accordingly. During his presidency, five new national parks and 51 national wildlife refuges were established around the nation, and forests were given new

Northern Lower Michigan

protections. In 1909 Roosevelt's push to acquire public land for use by all Americans resulted in the establishment of the Michigan Forest. This region, later renamed the Huron National Forest, was cobbled together from already decimated woodlands and abandoned farms. At its inception, Huron was a decidedly unimpressive area, but concerted efforts to reforest the area gradually paid off, thanks in large part to the Civilian Conservation Corps programs in the 1930s. By the time of the CCC's departure from the area in the early 1940s, they had planted an estimated 485 million trees and completed an ambitious restocking of fish in the region's wounded waterways. Now, more than 50 years later, Huron National Forest stands as one of Michigan's crown jewels.

Flora & Fauna

Huron National Forest is home to a wide variety of creatures. **Tuttle Marsh**, a wetlands area within the forest, is known for its wildlife, including waterfowl, beaver, and various reptiles. You also are apt to run into a number of other beasts in the forest. Wild turkeys, deer, red foxes, raccoons, porcupines, coyotes, and black bears all roam across Huron's hills and valleys, while its skies contain bald eagles, ospreys, loons, and the Kirtland's warbler, a rare songbird found nowhere else in the world during the summer months. Kirtland's warblers are drawn to the forest because of its unique combination of sandy soil, young jack pines, and grassy openings. Automotive tours designed to provide glimpses of the Kirtland's warbler are available, but don't bet the farm on seeing one; there are only about 3,000 of the songbirds left, and they tend to favor the deep woods.

Huron offers an interesting range of trees and plants as well. In addition to the large stands of jack pine clustered throughout the forest, Huron supports northern red oak, aspen, red pine, black spruce, tamarack, red maple, balsam fir, and other species. Notable flora growing within Huron include the rare Allegheny plum and Hill's thistle, as well as a variety of edible mushrooms. The most popular of these are morel mushrooms, a tasty treat that grows in the forest's Maltby Hills area.

! TAKE CARE *Be careful what you pick here. Some of the mushrooms sprouting amid the shadows of Huron's woodlands are poisonous, so if you don't know what you're doing, leave it be.*

Adventures

On Foot

 Huron National Forest offers more than 330 miles of trails for backpackers and hikers. Most of these paths are short interpretive trails or modest ones suitable for day-hiking, but there are a few that cannot be undertaken without an overnight stay. Huron's best backpacking trails are the Hoist Lake Trail and the national forest segment of the Shore-to-Shore Trail that winds across the length of the state's northern Lower Peninsula, from the coast of Lake Huron to that of Lake Michigan.

Hoist Lake Trail

The Hoist Lake Hiking Area, in the forest's northern section, is a 10,000-acre region with more than 20 miles of trails. The area features several loops that can add or subtract miles from your hike, depending on your wind and/or the weather. In terms of scenery, this trail is a rewarding one. The gently rolling terrain offers marshes, small lakes, and a nice variety of trees, including pine and aspen. Wildlife is abundant, too, so pack and care for your food and toiletries accordingly. Backcountry camping is allowed at a number of spots along the trail, including rustic sites at South Hoist Lake (on the southeastern side of the trail network) and Byron Lake (on the southwestern side). The campsites on Byron Lake's northern shore – it also has backcountry sites on the south side of the lake – are probably the best of the lot. All sites have fire rings. If you can manage it, plan a mid-week trip; the South Hoist Lake area can get a little congested during weekends and holidays. The South Hoist Lake Trail can be accessed from both its western and eastern ends. If you're coming in from the west, take M-72 eastbound to F-32 (Aspen Road). Follow Aspen Road southbound to a parking lot on the west side of the road; the

Northern Lower Michigan

trail enters the forest on the other side of the road from the lot. If you're looking to begin from the east, the trail starts off M-65, just south of M-72.

Michigan Shore-to-Shore Trail

This 219-mile trail (excluding spurs) extends from the town of Empire, on Lake Michigan's shores, all the way to Oscoda, which looks out on Lake Huron. (Hikers also have the option of beginning or ending the eastern part of their tromp in Tawas City via a small trail spur.) The Huron National Forest section of the trail is among its most picturesque. Backpackers (and equestrians, who also use the trail) follow a mix of trails and two-tracks through much of the length of the forest, paralleling the course of the beautiful Au Sable for significant stretches. Backcountry travelers are permitted to camp along the trail, provided they adhere to the various rules (camp at least 200 feet from designated trails and bodies of water, etc.). There are also a number of campgrounds spaced at intervals along the trail. These include – marching eastward – 4 Mile Camp, Luzerne, McKinley, South Branch, Gordon Creek, Monument, and Old Orchard Park. Since the trail crisscrosses several roads in the area, backpackers who don't have the time or inclination to haul their loads across the entire state can begin their journey within a few miles of nearly all of these sites.

On Wheels

 Northeastern Michigan does not have the same quality mountain biking trails as some other sections of the state, but Huron National Forest does provide a couple of trails. The best of these is the **Midland-to-Mackinac Pathway**, a 12-mile segment that runs all the way up to the straits of Mackinac. Another option is the **Eagle Run Trail**, a seven-mile trail on the forest's eastern boundary.

Bicycling enthusiasts can follow the Au Sable for a good deal of its length by taking **River Road** out of Oscoda. The road is a busy one, but its wide, paved shoulders give cyclists some breathing space, providing them with the opportunity to enjoy both the river and Huron's rolling forestlands. Riders taking this route who don't want to backtrack have the option of taking River Road all the way inland to M-65 north. After a few miles, M-65 hits Bissonette Road, which can be taken most of the way back to Oscoda (take a right on Rea to rejoin River Road for the last few miles).

On Water

Canoeing & Kayaking

See the whitewater chart on page 27. The **Au Sable River**, home to the famous Au Sable River Canoe Marathon, is one of the best rivers in the entire state for canoeing. As Jerry Dennis mused in *A Place on the Water,* a lovely book about growing up in Michigan's North Country, "early in the morning, on certain stretches of the Au Sable River, you can imagine northern Michigan has changed very little over the centuries. The river is alive and clean, and flows over the same sand bottom French fur traders noticed two hundred years ago, when they first began calling it 'River of Sand.'" Blessed with clear water, a steady current, and beautiful and varied shoreline for much of its length, the 114-mile Au Sable (Class I) is ideal for canoeists looking for a mellow, visually rewarding journey. Indeed, its beauty, plentiful shoreline campground options, and easygoing character has historically made the Au Sable a natural destination for families. But as with other beloved natural attractions across the country, the Au Sable has, at least to some degree, become a victim of its own beauty. Thick clots of boorish canoeists and rowdy tubing enthusiasts crowd its waters on some summer weekends. Those who truly love the river and forest focus on mid-week or off-season trips.

The Au Sable is commonly understood to begin in **Grayling**, even though its genesis is actually more than 10 miles further north, west of I-75. But whereas the river north of Grayling is less than ideal for canoeing because of its modest size and brushy quality, from Grayling on it is ideal for paddlers. Many canoeists begin their journey in Grayling proper, but if you decide to do so, make sure you launch downstream from the M-72 bridge; a water-control dam is under the bridge. Several canoe liveries are east of the bridge, making rentals easy. Most outfits will allow you to launch non-rental canoes from their property as well, but secure

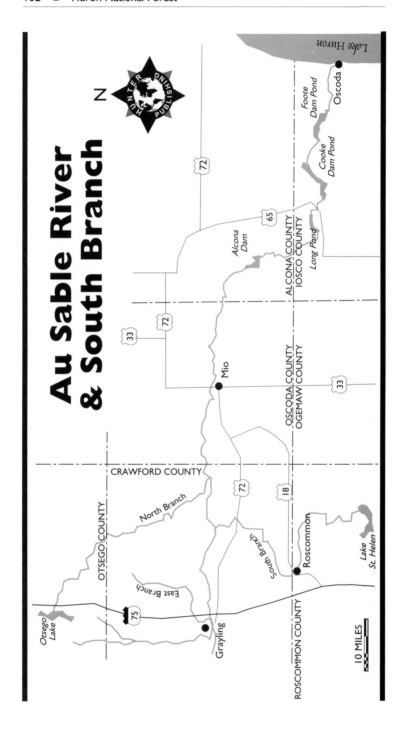

Au Sable River & South Branch

permission first. You can also put in a little further down-stream at one of the numerous access sites that dot the Au Sable's shoreline.

The river quickly grows in strength and size a short distance downstream, when it meets the East Branch of the Au Sable. For the next 60-70 miles the river's depth is generally two to three feet (somewhat deeper in springtime), while it spans 30-40 feet from shore to shore. From McKinley Bridge on, however, some stretches of the Au Sable – such as the Foote Dam area – are quite wide (80 to 100 feet) and deep. Major markers/ac-

The awesome Au Sable is perhaps the most famous river in Michigan (Huron-Manistee National Forests).

cess points along the Au Sable include **Wakeley Bridge** (14 miles from Grayling, five-seven hours from Grayling, **Parmalee Bridge** (16½ miles from Wakeley, four-six hours), **Mio Dam** (12½ miles from Parmalee, three-five hours), **McKinley Bridge** (15 miles from Mio Dam, four-five hours), **Alcona Dam** (12 miles from McKinley, three hours), **Five Channels Dam** (17½ miles from Alcona Dam, four-seven hours), and **Foote Dam** (15½ miles from Five Channels Dam, five-eight hours). Portages are required at the various dams.

The Au Sable flows directly through Huron National Forest for much of its length, and 23 miles of that stretch have been given National Scenic River status. The forest boasts 15 different access points for canoeists and kayakers, and contains dozens of nice camping spots along its shores. The last exit point within the Huron is at Five Channels Pond. Numerous canoe liveries provide services for would-be explorers of the Au Sable. Operators in Grayling include **Au Sable Canoes**, ☎ 517-348-5851; **Borcher's Canoe Livery**, ☎ 517-348-4921; **Carlisle Canoes**, ☎ 517-348-

2301; **Hutt's Canoeing**, ☎ 517-348-8405; **Jim's Canoe Livery**, ☎ 517-348-3203; **Penrod's Au Sable Canoe Rental**, ☎ 517-348-2910; **Ray's Au Sable and Manistee Canoeing**, ☎ 517-348-5844; and **Wyandotte Lodge**, ☎ 517-348-8354. For a complete list of canoe liveries operating along the Au Sable, contact the offices of Huron-Manistee National Forest.

The other major option for canoeists in the Huron area is the **Au Sable River's South Branch**, which is notable in its own right. A little over 37 miles in length, the South Branch is less predictable than the main stream. Water levels can vary by several feet from spring to summer, and its waters can get cloudy after heavy rainfall. The river from Chase Bridge (take Chase south from M-72) down can be run in one full day, however, and although the South Branch – like the Au Sable – can get too crowded on summer weekends, it offers a variety of pleasing scenery. In fact, much of it flows through the **Mason Tract**, a large nature sanctuary that was bequeathed to the state back in the 1950s. Despite recent tornado damage, it remains a jewel of the forest. The South Branch meets up with the main stream of the Au Sable a couple of miles downstream from Wakeley Bridge.

Fishing

Huron National Forest is an angler's dream (though the grayling, which first attracted Michigan sportsmen to the area, is long gone). Largemouth and smallmouth bass, northern pike, walleye, chinook and coho salmon, and trout (brookies, brownies, and rainbow) all lurk or leap in one area or another, and many can be found in several different spots. Huron is dotted with more than a dozen small "walk-in" lakes that can be quite rewarding for sports fishermen, including **Bliss Lake** (largemouth bass and bluegills), **Reid Lake** (rainbow trout), **South Hoist Lake** (rainbow trout), and **Jewell Lake** (northern pike, bluegill, and largemouth bass). Nearby **Wakeley Lake** is a hot spot for bluegill and bass. Wakeley Lake is just off M-7, east of Grayling, near Five Corners.

It is the Au Sable and its dam-created ponds, however, that bring anglers from far and wide. The river is a legendary destination for fishermen on the prowl for brook, brown, and rainbow trout to fry. But the river is also home to healthy populations of salmon below Foote Dam. **Cooke Pond** holds fat walleye and both large-mouth and smallmouth bass, while **Alcona Pond** boasts northern pike, walleye, and smallmouth bass.

*In 1993 Huron National Forest established a floating fishing pier for anglers with disabilities (though it is open to everyone). The pier is at **O'Brien Lake**, a remote, trout-stocked lake surrounded by woodlands a few miles east of the small town of McKinley. It can be found east of F-32, at the end of Forest Road 4838.*

On Snow

Cross-Country Skiing

Huron offers several fine cross-country skiing trails, from Hoist Lake to Eagle Run, Corsair to Highbanks, as detailed below.

Hoist Lake Trail

This 20-mile trail is probably the best of the bunch, at least for experienced skiers. It provides a great combination of challenging terrain and remote backcountry camping sites. For additional information on this trail, see the *On Foot* coverage of Huron. But the forest contains a number of other notable cross-country ski trails as well:

Reid Lake Trail

This six-mile route covers gently rolling hills and passes by a number of abandoned fields and orchards. Equipped with backcountry sites for winter campers, the Reid Lake Trail can be picked up on M-72 west of Harrisville.

Corsair Trail

The 27-mile Corsair Trail network, while primarily utilized by cross-country skiers, is also sometimes explored by hikers. It is regarded as one of the best cross-country trails in eastern Michigan, and offers a pleasant variety of scenery, including plentiful woods, open meadows, and several small creeks and lakes. Its trails are groomed, and the loops range from basic to advanced. The Corsair Trail is in the southeastern section of the forest; it can be reached by taking Monument Road north from Tawas City.

Eagle Run Trail

Ideal for beginning skiers, the Eagle Run Trail is level for much of its seven-mile length. The trailhead is at the forest's Eastgate Welcome Center outside of Oscoda, on River Road.

Mason Tract Pathway

This mellow route wanders beside nearly 10 miles of the magnificent Au Sable River, meandering along the river bank and periodically darting into and out of the forest. It is almost a straight north-south shot, unless you decide to return via a loop midway down the pathway, but parties of two or more skiers can easily leave cars at both ends. The northern trailhead to the pathway is about 15 miles east of Grayling off M-72; the southern trailhead lies at Chase Bridge, on CR-519.

Highbanks Trail

This scenic backcountry trail winds from the high bluffs of the Au Sable River Valley to the stream's southern shores. This linear trail is seven miles and is a favorite of summer dayhikers. Terminals are at Iargo Springs and Sid Town Village, but the trail can also be accessed from Lumbermen's Monument and Canoer's Memorial.

Other notable cross-country ski trails in the area include a 54-mile network of groomed trails in nearby **Au Sable State Forest** and 24 miles of trails at **Hinchman Acres**.

Snowmobiling

Several popular snowmobile trails pass through parts of Huron National Forest and the surrounding region. These include the 64-mile **Oscoda County Trail** network, which begins just outside of Mio on the northern border of the forest and extends to the edge of Alcona County; and the **Roscommon-St. Helen Trail**, a 25-mile route southwest of the forest near Roscommon.

Camping

Huron National Forest maintains 10 campgrounds within its boundaries, many of them on lakes that are attractive to those equipped with rod and reel. In addition to the established campgrounds, numerous campsites can be found along the Au Sable River shoreline. Huron campgrounds in the western half of the forest include **Island Lake**, a 17-site campground equipped with a beach for swimming and access to fishing at Loon Lake; **Kneff Lake**, a 26-site facility on a lake known for rainbow trout; **Mack Lake**, a campground with 42 sites; and **Wagner Lake**, a secluded area with 12 sites.

On the eastern side of the forest are another half-dozen campgrounds. Perhaps the most popular of these is at **Jewell Lake,** which attracts anglers because of its plentiful stores of perch, bass, bluegill, and pike. The campground has 32 sites spread over more than 190 acres, and includes a boat launch. Other campgrounds in the area include the **Monument Campground**, a 20-site area that is a favorite with families; the 19-site **Rollways Campground**; **Round Lake**, which features 33 sites and a boat launch; **Horseshoe Lake**, a modestly sized facility (nine sites); and **Pine River**, which has 11 campsites and good fishing.

To Find Out More

There are two ranger stations in Huron, each responsible for a section of the forest. The **Mio Ranger Station**, which oversees the western portion of Huron, can be reached at ☎ 517-826-3252. The **Huron Shores Ranger Station** looks over Huron's eastern sections. ☎ 517-739-0728.

■ Manistee National Forest

Huron-Manistee National Forest
1755 S. Mitchell Street
Cadillac, MI 49601
☎ 800-821-6263 or 616-775-2421

Northern Lower Michigan

The Manistee National Forest contains so many adventures, one hardly knows where to begin. Located in the western Lower Peninsula, Manistee spreads over most of three large and beautiful counties – Wexford, Lake, and Newaygo – and portions of several others. Heavily quilted with burly forests of pine, oak, hickory, aspen, and other varieties of trees, Manistee's rolling terrain explodes with color in the fall. These magnificent woodlands, coupled with the stunning array of lakes, streams, and rivers, make Manistee a favorite destination for outdoor adventurers, from trout fishermen and Nordic skiers to backpackers and canoeists.

Getting There

Primary north-south routes to Manistee National Forest include US-31, which passes along the western boundary of the forest; US-131, a major artery east of Manistee; and M-37, which slices through the heart of the forest. East-west roads that intersect with these highways include M-20, the southernmost of the roads; M-10, which parallels the beautiful Pere Marquette River for some of its length; and M-55, which provides access to the majority of the national forest's campgrounds.

History

Like many other regions of Michigan, the area now known as Manistee National Forest was exploited by generations of lumbermen and developers. Indeed, in the latter part of the 19th century, Michigan was the leading producer of timber in the entire nation. This timber contributed greatly to America's expansion, but logging practices were short-sighted. The feverish pace of extraction took its toll, and by the early 1900s the lumber mill owners were drifting away, leaving decimated woodlands and dying mill towns in their wake. In the 1920s, however, the state began to deed great swaths of tax-delinquent lands to its department of conservation, and Civilian Conservation Corps programs set about revitalizing the area. Obstacles inevitably arose (in 1936, for instance, CCC workers fought a desperate battle against a massive invasion of grasshoppers), but over time a vibrant new forest of largely second-growth trees was prospering along Lake Michigan's shores. Manistee was established as a national forest in 1938. It is currently administered jointly with Huron National Forest, which is in Michigan's northeastern Lower Peninsula.

Flora & Fauna

The forest lands of Manistee include a wide variety of trees – spruce, oak, aspen, birch, cedar, maple, beech, hemlock, elm, hickory, and many kinds of pine. Many different types of plants make their home on the sun-dappled forest floor as well; the **Loda Lake Wildflower Sanctuary**, just west of M-37 about seven miles north of White Cloud, displays these ferns, flowers, and berries. To reach the sanctuary, turn west off M-37 onto 5-Mile Road, then turn north on Felch Ave., a gravel road that leads to the entrance. Manistee also includes the **Newaygo Prairies**, remnants of the tall grass prairies that used to carpet much of America's midsection. More than 100 different plant species thrive in these patches, including Indian grass, June grass, heath aster, prairie cinquefoil, prairie smoke, and blazing stars. On the forest floor, morel mushrooms can be found from late April to June.

Manistee supports many different types of animals as well, including deer, coyote, porcupine, fox, racoon, beaver, and an assortment of songbirds and waterfowl such as sandhill cranes, great blue herons, loons, and northern harriers. Game birds like spruce grouse and turkeys also roam underneath Manistee's vast canopy.

Adventures

On Foot

Backpackers can choose from several trails, each featuring a unique blend of terrain and vegetation. Backcountry trails range from the Manistee River Trail, which takes hikers through the Manistee River valley, to the Nordhouse Dunes trails, which provide access to a magnificent stretch of windblown dunes opening out onto chilly Lake Michigan.

Manistee River Trail

This pathway, nestled in the national forest's northernmost reaches, offers a great opportunity to explore the outdoors in the company of one of Michigan's prettiest rivers, the Manistee. The 12-mile trail, which also connects to the North Country Trail via a 1½-mile spur, offers up a nice blend of pines and hardwoods as it darts back and forth across the valley, opening up to great views of the river and forest at a number of junctures. There is no established campground on the trail, but backcountry camping is permitted (as it is everywhere in the forest).

The trail can be reached via several trailheads. One northern trailhead is at Seaton Creek Campground, a few miles west of Yuma. To reach this trailhead, take M-37 south or M-55 north to 26 Mile Road. Take 26 Mile Road west for 1.7 miles, then take a right on O'Rourke Drive. After following O'Rourke for 1.3 miles, take a right on F-5993 for half a mile. Some backpackers simply canoe to the campground via Hodenpyle Dam Pond. Another trailhead at the north end of the valley is off Beers Road, five miles west of Mesick. The primary trailhead at the southern end is at Red Bridge, on Coates Highway. To reach Red Bridge, take M-37 to 30 Mile Road west. Follow it until you take a left curve onto Warfield Road. After 1½ miles take a right on Coates Highway to Red Bridge, which overlooks the Manistee itself. The parking lot is on the west side of the river.

Nordhouse Dunes Trail System

This 3,450-acre area, composed of massive sand dunes, hardwood forests, and extensive interdunal wetlands, extends a mile inland from Lake Michigan's shore and abuts Ludington State Park. Hikers thus have miles of unspoiled shoreline to explore.

Privacy can be easily obtained by setting up camp behind any of the hulking dunes that look out on the lake, or deeper in the forest (Campsites and campfires, though, must be more than 400 feet away from Lake Michigan and 200 feet away from Nordhouse Lake).

Further inland, more than 14 miles of trails provide hikers with multiple beach access points. Bicycles, motorized vehicles, and horses are not permitted in the area.

Boaters can reach Nordhouse Dunes simply by dropping anchor offshore and wading in, while those traveling by more ho-hum modes of transportation can reach the trailhead via US-31 southbound out of Manistee; turn right on Nurnberg Road.

North Country Trail

This trail, which will be a 3,200-mile thread through seven northern states when it is completed, slices directly through Manistee's midsection. It presents a diverse range of woodlands, streams, lakes, and wildlife along its length. The trail can be reached at several different points. Working southward, major trailheads that take you through Manistee National Forest are at **Marilla** (take Beers Road two miles east out of Marilla); **Udell** (take M-55 six miles west out of Wellston); **FreeSoil** (take FreeSoil Road 9½ miles east out of FreeSoil); **Timber Creek** (take M-37 north out of Baldwin to US-10 and then go west on US-10 for 7½ miles to Timber Creek Campground); **Bowman Lake** (take 56th Street west out of Baldwin for five miles to Bowman Bridge Campground Spur; trailhead is another 1½ miles west); **76th Street** (take M-37 south three miles out of Baldwin to Big Star Lake Road, also known as 76th Street; the trailhead lies 2½ miles down the road); **Nichols Lake** (at Nichols Lake Recreation Area); **M-20** (take M-37 one mile north out of White Cloud to M-20, then west on M-20 for almost three miles); **40th Street** (take M-37 five miles south out of White Cloud to 40th Street, then turn west for three-quarters of a mile to trailhead); and **Croton Dam** (east of Newaygo at the dam site).

On Wheels

Mountain Biking

Manistee National Forest contains three major trails that are of interest to both mountain bikers and Nordic skiers, depending on the season. Perhaps the most exciting development for mountain bikers here has been the recent emer-

Northern Lower Michigan

gence of the Big M cross-country ski area as a destination for the fat-tired set. The original **Big M Trail system** provides 15 miles of trails for bikers, and plans have been hatched to put together an additional 32 miles of trails for mountain biking use. Volunteers from local and state mountain biking organizations are expected to shoulder most of the burden for this ambitious initiative. The new trails will include loops of varying size through a mix of terrains and challenging elevation changes. For information on the progress of this effort, contact the Manistee ranger station at ☎ 616-723-2211. Big M is off M-55, midway between Manistee and Wellston.

Forest officials decided to expand the Big M area for mountain bikers in part because of clashes on the North Country Trail between hikers and mountain bikers. But while the opening of Big M to bikers should do much to relieve that situation, the **North Country Trail** still boasts stretches that will tantalize mountain bikers. Foremost among these is a 10-mile single track that winds through the Manistee District of the forest from Hodenpyle Dam, midway between Marilla and Mesick off Beers Road, to Red Bridge, on Coates Highway.

Other recommended mountain biking trails within the forest include the **Mackenzie Trail** and the **Hungerford Lake Trail**. For more information on these routes, see the *On Snow* section below.

On Water

Canoeing & Kayaking

See the whitewater chart on page 27. Canoeing and kayaking opportunities are plentiful in Manistee National Forest, with stretches of eight major Michigan rivers.

Pere Marquette River (Class I)

The Pere Marquette, which originates a few miles west of Reed City and joins Lake Michigan just south of Ludington, is the largest of the group. A good portion of the river rushes through the forest's interior, hurrying along through thick forest at a pace that is swift but manageable for canoeists with limited experience. Many

Pere Marquette River

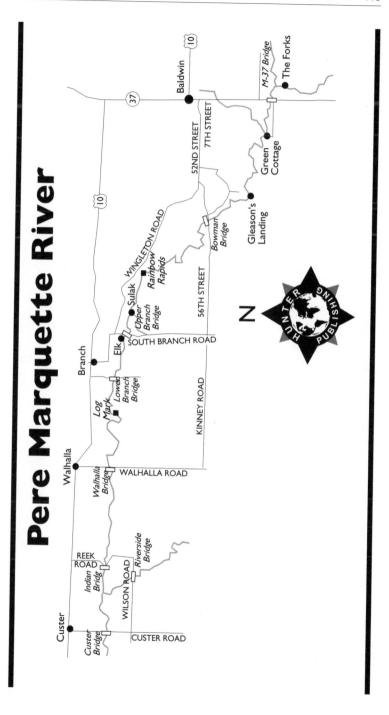

paddlers embark on the river at the M-37 Bridge south of Baldwin; those who choose to ride the stream all the way from there to the US-31 Bridge east of Ludington (the usual take-out point) will enjoy 56 miles of good canoeing. The scenery along the Pere Marquette – which was designated the state's first National Scenic River back in 1978 – is lovely at many points, and its length makes it suitable for longer trips.

Be forewarned; the river gets mighty congested during the summer with canoeists, anglers, and other folks. In fact, a permit system for watercraft has been implemented; (☎ 616-745-3100 to reserve). This has relieved the situation somewhat, but if crowds aren't your scene, you should still look elsewhere for your canoeing pleasure.

Luckily, the national forest offers several alternatives. The best of these are the Pine, Manistee, and Little Manistee, although the placid temperament of the White River makes it an attractive option for some canoeists as well.

Pine River (Class I-II)

One of the state's swiftest rivers, thanks to its relatively sharp gradient, the Pine offers handsome scenery for much of its 57 miles. Most of the shoreline is state or federal land, so it remains in good condition. The river passes through hills festooned with hardwoods, pines, and cedars in its early stretches. Its depth rarely exceeds four feet during the first 20 miles, but it's 25 to 40 feet across for much of this stretch. After passing under Dobson Bridge, a popular launching point midway up the river, the speed of the river increases and obstacles – rocks, submerged logs, the odd sweeper – become more numerous, especially below M-37's Peterson Bridge (the river is Class II in some parts). Moderately capable paddlers should not find any of this to be insurmountable (experienced paddlers can bag the fast-moving river in a day), but novices could come out on the other end looking a little (or a lot) bedraggled. The last 10 miles of the river are marked by high bluffs, tight bends, and the usual pleasant array of pines and hardwoods. The Pine can be accessed at several bridges and other sites along its route, but its extreme popularity made it necessary for the Forest Service to establish a permit system and limitations on shoreline camping; call ☎ 616-745-3100 for reservations and additional information.

Manistee River (Class I)

The Manistee measures more than 230 miles long from its headwaters in Antrim and Otsego Counties to its mouth on Lake Michigan. The mighty Manistee has been a long-time favorite of Michigan canoeists. The river's length eases congestion – although raucous parties descend here on summer weekends – while its largely undeveloped shoreline makes for an aesthetically pleasing journey. For paddlers, the Manistee begins in Crawford County's northwestern corner. At this point the stream's depth ranges from one to four feet (with some deeper holes), and gradually expands to widths of 50 to 90 feet. Below Lower Sharon Bridge the current lessens somewhat and it becomes deeper, though depths of three-four feet still prevail. From the M-66 Bridge on, the river passes tall banks bristling with pine, birch, and maple, as well as occasional meadows. The water through this segment is often slow, though some stretches pick up the pace. The final 30 miles are quite pretty, and sightings of wildlife are common, but during the spring and fall areas such as Tippy Dam attract many anglers.

Little Manistee River (Class I-II)

The obstacle-infested upper reaches of the river are virtually impassable by canoe, and the river feels the effects of dry periods to a greater degree than do some others, but the last 25 miles of the Little Manistee's 67-mile length generally provide one of the Lower Peninsula's underrated canoeing experiences. The best up-river site to put in at is **Fox Bridge** (Bass Lake Road), although **Dewitts Bridge**, less than a mile further upstream, also provides access. A short way downstream from Fox Bridge is **Driftwood Valley Campground**, on the left; from there the river moves toward Lake Michigan at a moderately fast pace, throwing in challenging bends here and there to keep everyone awake. Some choose to leave the river at **Nine Mile Bridge**, mindful of the more demanding stretch of water that looms ahead. Indeed, the four-mile stretch immediately below Nine Mile is characterized by a fast current, horseshoe bends, logjams, and sweepers. Experienced canoeists and kayakers will love it; beginners, however, are likely to have a far different reaction. This challenging stretch ends around **Six Mile Bridge**, and the last few miles are mild.

White River (Class I)

Blessed with a steady current and few obstacles, the 80-mile long White River is a favorite for inexperienced paddlers and families (tubing is a favorite pastime as well). Upstream from Hesperia, though, the river is narrow and shallow, pocked with logs and other obstacles, and canoeists avoid that stretch. Instead, they begin their journeys at **Hesperia** or other points downstream, taking advantage of the river as it widens and deepens. Good shoreline campsites are scarce – the river banks are steep in some areas and swampy in others – but a scattering of public and private campgrounds make overnighters possible. Access points are relatively few, too (the best are at **Pine Point Campground** and **County Line Bridge**), but this also helps to keep the crowds down.

Canoe Liveries

Canoe liveries operating in the Manistee area include: **Baldwin Canoe Rental** (☎ 616-745-4669) on the Pere Marquette, Pine, and Little Manistee; **Pine Creek Lodge** (☎ 616-848-4431) and **Wilderness Canoe Trips** (☎ 800-873-6379) on the Manistee; **Enchanted Acres Camp** (☎ 616-266-5102) on the Little Manistee; **Happy Mohawk Livery** (☎ 616-894-4209) and **Kellogg's Canoes** (☎ 616-854-1415) on the White; and **Horina's Canoe Rental** (☎ 616-862-3470), **Famous Jarolim Canoe** (☎ 616-862-3470), and **Carl's Canoe Livery** (☎ 616-797-5156), all on the Pine.

Fishing

Manistee features major rivers and streams, hundreds of ponds and lakes, and close proximity to Lake Michigan (Great Lakes angling opportunities are available at Manistee). It offers some of the best fishing in the entire Midwest.

The dazzling array of options in the region can be strangely paralyzing; after all, Newaygo County alone contains 234 lakes, and the overwhelming majority of Lake County's 156 lakes are within the national forest. Wherever your eventual destination, chances are good that you will be rewarded. Some of the larger lakes in the region (such as **Mitchell Lake, Big Star Lake, Hamlin Lake, Cadillac Lake**, and the **Tippy Dam Impoundment**) offer tremendous walleye and pike fishing, while their smaller cousins (including **Bass Lake, Loon Lake, Robinson Lake, Wolf Lake**) are havens for bass and bluegill. Other lakes popular for panfishing include **Bluegill, Twinwood, Indian, Brush**, and **Shelley**.

While the area's inland lakes are popular destinations for fishermen, the rivers remain the premier attraction for many anglers. The **Pere Marquette** is one of the country's best free-flowing trout streams, and flyfishermen and spincasters roam all through its waters. Steelhead, brown trout, and chinook salmon are all abundant, but northern pike, brookies, and coho salmon also ply its waters. The **Manistee, Little Manistee, White, Sable, Muskegon**, and **Pine** are favorites for trout and salmon, and smaller streams throughout the area are favorites for the locals.

On Snow

Downhill Skiing & Snowboarding

 Caberfae Peaks Resort, in the northeastern corner of Manistee National Forest, provides downhill skiers and snowboarders with 23 runs, four chair lifts, and two T-bars, as well as cross-country trails for Nordic skiers. Caberfae has one of the largest vertical drops (490 feet) in the Lower Peninsula, and it is both less expensive and less crowded than **Boyne**, the region's largest ski resort. The resort's lodge is modest but clean. Caberfae is 15 miles west of Cadillac on M-55. ☎ 616-779-0685.

Cross-Country Skiing

Manistee National Forest is a mecca for Nordic skiers. Even the distant whine of snowmobiles cannot disrupt the sense of calm and tranquility that marks many of the forest's cross-country trails. The **Mackenzie Ski Trail system** is no exception, despite its proximity to Caberfae (in fact, after a day out on the trails, the lodge at Caberfae can be a welcome sight). Comprised of four groomed trails that run a total of 14 miles, the Mackenzie system takes skiers through a pleasing blend of forest types and terrain. The system is suitable for skiers of all skill levels, though expert skiers might stifle a yawn by the end of the day. It can be accessed via Caberfae Road, west of Cadillac.

Another favorite destination for cross-country skiers is the **Big M Trail system**, which is nestled in the Udell Hills area. In fact, this groomed trail is touted by experienced skiers as one of Michigan's most diverse and imaginative. And while the network features some relatively flat terrain, especially at its northern end, a number of the trails will give the old cardiovascular system a vigorous workout. The **Catamount** run, for example, includes old downhill slopes in its circuit, as do a couple of others, and some loops climb to ridges that provide pleasing scenic vistas (some of these can be bypassed, but of course you lose the views, too). The Big M ski trails are west of Wellston on Udell Hills Road, 3½ miles south of its juncture with M-55.

The **Hungerford Ski Trail** is a groomed, 13-mile loop that takes skiers through a mix of pine, aspen, oak, and other hardwoods. It provides a number of nice views of winter-varnished creeks and lakes. Located on the eastern outskirts of the national forest, Hungerford can be accessed by taking M-20 west from Big Rapids to Cypress Avenue north, to Forest Road 5134. The trail features several short, steep hills, but for the most part it is an easy one for both Nordic skiers and mountain bikers.

Other Nordic skiing trails in the Manistee National Forest include the **North Country Trail**, described on page 111, the **Nordhouse Dunes** area, **Caberfae's** cross-country offerings (nine miles of groomed trails), and the **White River Trail**, a relatively easy 12-mile trail that begins at the Pines Point Campground.

Snowmobiling

Bountiful lake-effect snow makes much of Michigan's western coastline particularly appealing to snowmobilers, who can choose from countless trails that thread through Manistee National Forest. The most established of the trails in Manistee and surrounding environs include:

Honeymoon Lake Snowmobile Trail

This 50-mile trail, a mix of two-track, Forest Service, and county roads, is southwest of Baldwin in the Big Star Lake area.

Caberfae Way Snowmobile Trail

Accessible from the Caberfae Resort area, this fine – albeit heavily used – trail heads through more than 30 miles of rolling woodlands.

Ward Hills Snowmobile Trail

Accessible from Timber Creek Campground, this 10-mile route goes through Manistee's midsection and connects to 40 miles of trails in the Wellston area.

Lincoln Hills Trail

A 24-mile trail 15 miles north of Baldwin on M-37.

Blood Creek Trail

Twenty-three miles in length, the Blood Creek Trail is a few miles southeast of Baldwin off M-37.

Udell Hills Snowmobile Trail

This relatively short 18-mile loop system is east of Stronach, a little town at the southern end of Manistee Lake, on Stronach Road. It consists primarily of unplowed county and Forest Service roads.

Several towns in the area are surrounded by extensive systems as well, including **Wellston** (40 miles of trails), **Newaygo** (75 miles of trails), and **Manistee** (a whopping 200 miles of trails – both marked and unmarked – extending to Cadillac; the Udell Hills Trail is a part of this network).

Camping

The Forest Service maintains 18 campgrounds within Manistee National Forest. Campgrounds within the Manistee-Cadillac District are: **Hemlock**, a 15-site campground five miles west of Cadillac on Lake Mitchell, which is known for its northern pike and walleye; **Peterson Bridge**, a 20-site campground along the Pine River; **Seaton Creek**, a 17-site area near Hodenpyle Dam Pond; **Bear Track**, which boasts 20 sites and close proximity to both the North Country Trail and the Little Manistee River; **Dorner Lake**, with only eight sites; **Driftwood Valley**, a 21-site campground accessible from the North Country Trail; **Pine Lake**, which offers 12 sites and good fishing; **Sand Lake**, a campground that includes barrier-free facilities and 45 sites; and **Udell Rollways**, a 23-site campground overlooking the Manistee. The largest of the campgrounds in the Manistee District, however, is the **Lake Michigan Recreation Area**. Located 13 miles south of Manistee on the shores of Lake Michigan, this campground includes 99 sites and access to Nordhouse Dunes. For more information on these campgrounds, call the **Manistee District Station** at ☎ 616-723-2211.

Campgrounds within the more southern Baldwin-White Cloud District include **Bowman Bridge**, which features 20 family sites and four group sites; **Diamond Point**, an isolated, rustic campground popular with White River canoeists; **Gleason's Landing**, with six walk-in sites and a boat launch; **Highbank Lake**, which offers nine well-spaced campsites; **Old Grade**, a 20-site campground on the Little Manistee that is a favorite of anglers; **Timber Creek**, a nine-site area; **Nichols Lake**, a barrier-free 28-site campground; **Benton Lake**, a campground of 24 sites near the Loda Lake Wildflower Sanctuary and the Mena Creek Waterfowl Area; and **Pines Point**, a barrier-free campground with 33 sites. Backpackers can access the North Country Trail from many of these campgrounds. Trailheads are at Nichols Lake, Timber Creek, and Bowman Bridge. Highbank Lake and Benton Lake are both in close proximity to the trail. For additional information, call the **Baldwin-White Cloud District Station** at ☎ 616-745-4631.

▪ Pigeon River Country State Forest

9966 Twin Lakes Road
Vanderbilt, MI 49795
☎ 517-983-4101

The Pigeon River Country State Forest is, at 98,000 acres, the Lower Peninsula's largest wilderness preserve. It is part of Michigan's Mackinaw State Forest, one of three state forests in the Lower Peninsula. This handsome land of rolling hills and valleys, winding rivers, and verdant woodlands is home to the largest elk herd in America east of the Mississippi River, and it is the allure of these majestic beasts that draws many visitors, especially during the fall rutting season. But "Pigeon River Country," as it is commonly called, holds myriad other charms for outdoor adventurers.

Getting There

The Pigeon River Country State Forest area sprawls across southern Cheboygan and northern Otsego counties. It can be reached by taking I-75 to Exit 290 and heading on into Vanderbilt. Once in town, turn east on Main Street. Take the road, which changes into Sturgeon Valley Road, for 13 miles. The Pigeon River Country headquarters is just off Sturgeon Valley Road, on Twin Lakes Road. Elk tour maps, campground maps, and other information on the forest is available at the headquarters.

History

The Pigeon River Country was one of Lower Michigan's most beloved regions in the first years of this century, regardless of its many blemishes. Indeed, significant expanses had been reduced to near wasteland by a devastating one-two punch of forest fires and logging, and its incredible flocks of passenger pigeons were wiped out by hunters. But some men and women recognized that those remaining pockets of forest and wildlife provided tantaliz-

Northern Lower Michigan

ing indications of what could be, and champions such as P.S. Lovejoy emerged to fight on behalf of that vision.

P.S. Lovejoy

Lovejoy, who headed the state's Department of Conservation for two decades, was guided by an abiding passion for preserving the wilderness character of the region: "I'd like to see the Pigeon opened up to insure really good fire protection and damn little more," he wrote. "So that it isn't too damn easy for the beer-belly gents and the nice old grandmaws to get to, set on and leave their tin cans at." Shortly after his arrival in Michigan, Lovejoy launched a campaign to establish a preserve in the area, scrambling to add various state and private lands as they became available. He also led efforts to resuscitate the region's many scarred hillsides and meadows, instituting state reforestation programs that breathed new life into the wilderness. In addition, the character of the Pigeon River area was fundamentally transformed with the introduction of two dozen Rocky Mountain elk to the region in 1918 (elk herds native to the state had been hunted to extinction many years earlier). Today's thriving herd is the result of that transplant effort.

By the 1990s Pigeon River Country was firmly entrenched as one of Michigan's wilderness prizes. In recent years, however, the region has been dogged by disputes between developers and conservationists. Oil and gas companies that have already made inroads into the forest's southern reaches continue to clamor for increased access, and a variety of private groups, developers, and others have been lobbying to open up the forest to other uses. On the other side of the fence are a coalition of area residents, conservationists, sportsmen, and state officials battling to preserve the work that Lovejoy and his allies undertook years before. But while the spectre of condominiums and other emblems of civilization chill those who hope to preserve the wilderness character of the Pigeon River Country, its defenders are increasingly concerned that an even bigger threat may come from people who enjoy and appreciate the region. Overuse is a significant problem in a number of areas, particularly from equestrian traffic, and eroding trails and riverbanks have led the DNR to consider closing or limiting use on some trails.

Flora & Fauna

The Pigeon River Country State Forest includes a wide range of hardwoods (including beech, oak, and hemlock), cedar, and white and red pine, and its swampy lowlands support a broad array of vegetation, including a variety of berries and flowering plants. The forest's wildlife is abundant and varied as well. The elk herd gets the headlines, but white-tailed deer, black bears, bobcats, wild turkeys, and pine martens also roam within its boundaries. In addition, bald eagles, loons, ospreys, and many other bird species glide across its skies.

Adventures

On Foot

A good portion of the 50-mile **High Country Pathway** winds through the heart of Pigeon River Country State Forest. This trail, while not as extensive as the Shore-to-Shore Trail or the still-coalescing North Country National Scenic Trail, continues to stand as the best one in the Lower Peninsula for extended wilderness backpacking. The High Country Pathway is in essence a giant loop situated in the center of northern Michigan. The trail snakes through wonderfully remote woodlands for much of the circuit, and it can be accessed from any number of points along the way. Access points include the state forest campgrounds at **Pigeon Bridge, Round Lake, Pigeon River, Tomahawk Lake**, and **Shoepac Lake**. The most popular spot from which to launch High Country backpacking trips, though, is probably **Clear Lake State Park campground** (10 miles north of Atlanta on M-33) because of its size (200 sites) and modern facilities.

High Country Pathway

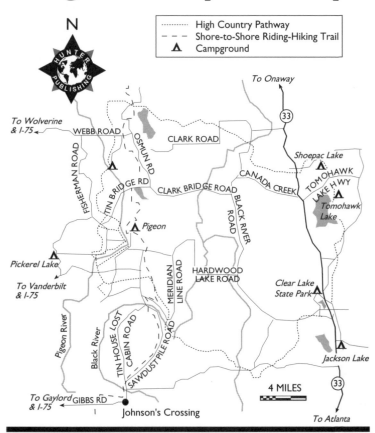

The High Country Pathway also features two offshoots that can be tackled over the course of a weekend. The **Shingle Mill Pathway** (10 miles) is a pleasant trail through rolling woodlands, running alongside the Pigeon River on the eastern end of its loop.

> *Shingle Mill hikers should note that the trail is also popular with mountain bikers.*

The **Clear Lake-Jackson Lake Pathway** (eight miles) is another option, but it pales next to the forest's other backpacking alternatives.

Finally, those without the time or inclination to throw on a backpack can take any of the many foot trails that thread through the state forest; even an afternoon stroll can give a tantalizing taste of Pigeon River Country wilderness.

On Wheels

Mountain Biking

Mountain biking enthusiasts have a couple different trails to choose from in Pigeon River Country. The first of these lies in the forest's Green Timbers area. This 6,300-acre parcel, which sits on the Pigeon's far western border, was adopted as part of the forest in 1982. Unlike the rest of the forest, it is closed to all motor vehicles, including snowmobiles. The **Green Timber Trail**, which also sees use from day hikers, includes several loops of two-track of varying size that wind through a mix of northern Michigan hardwoods and open meadows.

The forest's other main mountain biking trail is the **Shingle Mill Pathway**, a 10-mile single-track trail that offers great scenery and a rugged workout. The trailhead to the pathway is near Pigeon River Forest headquarters.

On Water

Canoeing & Kayaking

Pigeon River (Class I-II)

Two picturesque rivers flow through the boundaries of Pigeon River Country State Forest. The first of these is the Pigeon, the river for which the region is named. The Pigeon is one of the most challenging rivers in the Lower Peninsula. It features a swift current, numerous hairpin turns, vigorous rapids (especially below the M-68 Bridge), and a wide array of sweepers and other obstacles. In addition, portages are apt to be numerous and difficult in the river's upper reaches. All of these factors combine to make the river a poor choice for inexperienced paddlers. Still, it will delight veteran kayakers and canoeists. The Pigeon runs through beautiful country, and its surly qualities help

Mullet Lake

CLEMENT ROAD

BOWERSOCK ROAD

ONAWAY ROAD

N

HUNTER PUBLISHING

To Indian River & I-75 (9 miles)

Afton

M-68

M-68 Bridge

AFTON ROAD

MONTGOMERY ROAD

PIGEON RIVER ROAD

△ Campground

MUNGER ROAD

McIntosh Landing

Little Pigeon River

WEBB ROAD

Red Bridge

OSMUN ROAD

Pigeon River

TIN BRIDGE ROAD

STURGEON RIVER VALLEY ROAD

To Vanderbilt & I-75 (10 miles)

4 MILES

keep river traffic light, providing those paddlers who do travel its length with a number of quality campsites from which to choose. Good launch points can be found at the Pigeon Bridge and Pigeon River campgrounds within the forest. Canoeists and kayakers who decide to brave the rapids below M-68 can take out at the Clement Road Bridge on the south side of Mullett Lake; others can take out at the M-68 Bridge or at the bridge on Pigeon River Road. Area liveries providing services on the Pigeon include **Tomahawk Trails Canoe Livery** (☎ 616-238-8703) and **Sturgeon & Pigeon River Outfitters** (☎ 616-238-8181).

Black River (Class I)

Further to the east lies the Black River, the Pigeon's mild-mannered cousin. Whereas the Pigeon pushes and shoves its way northward, the Black takes its time, wandering through the forest at a generally leisurely pace. Significant stretches of the Black run through private land, so contact forest headquarters for guidance on access points and campsites. Canoe rentals for the Black are available through **Partners Canoe Rental** (☎ 517-733-2877) or **Black River Canoe Outfitters** (☎ 517-733-8054).

Finally, a section of the **Sturgeon River's** upper reaches runs through the Green Timbers area of the state forest, but its navigable stretches lie outside the Pigeon River Forest's boundaries. For a description of the Sturgeon, see page 175.

Fishing

The Black River and the Pigeon River are major destinations for northern Michigan anglers. The **Black** (including its East Branch) is a premier fishing stream that supports trout, northern pike, walleye, bass, perch, and a variety of other fish. The **Pigeon**'s clear waters contain good numbers of brook, brown, and rainbow trout (more than 30 miles of the upper river have been designated as Michigan Blue Ribbon Trout Stream).

Pigeon River Country State Forest also contains several good fishing lakes. Popular spots include **Cornwall Creek Flooding** (bass, bluegill, and muskie), **Grass Lake** (bass and bluegill), and **Pickerel Lake** (bass, bluegill, and rainbow trout). Perhaps the best lake

Northern Lower Michigan

fishing in the forest, however, is at **South Blue Lake**, a glacier-carved kettle lake that holds large bluegill and largemouth bass.

On Snow

Cross-Country Skiing

After the snowflakes chase the hikers and mountain bikers off the trails for the year, Pigeon River Country State Forest becomes a playground for cross-country skiers and snowmobilers. Indeed, the region offers some of the most vigorous and remote cross-country skiing in the entire Lower Peninsula. The forest's dirt roads are not plowed, which means that skiers have to haul in all their gear from county roads. In addition, Pigeon River Country trails are not groomed. These factors should be given appropriate consideration when planning winter excursions into Pigeon River Country. Of course, the forest's rugged winter countenance does provide significant compensation. The **Shingle Mill Pathway**, for instance, offers great opportunities to see area wildlife. The pathway consists of five loops ranging in size from one to 11 miles; the first two loops are easy, but skiers who venture out into the longer loops will find the going tougher. These advanced trails boast fabulous scenery, including great views of the Pigeon River Valley. The trailhead is at the rear of the Pigeon River Bridge campground.

Another top attraction for cross-country skiers is the Green Timbers area. Closed to snowmobiling, the **Green Timbers tract** offers an oasis of quiet in the sea of snowmobiles that buzz through northern Michigan woodlands during the winter. The recreation area includes more than 20 miles of trails, and it has two shelters (Green Timbers Cabin and Honeymoon Cabin) for winter campers. The main trailhead for Green Timbers lies seven miles east of Vanderbilt on Sturgeon Valley Road.

Snowmobiling

Snowmobiling is permitted in all areas of Pigeon River Country State Forest except the Green Timbers unit. Trails within the forest's boundaries are not groomed, and major snowmobiling arteries on its eastern and western sides further relieve traffic, but the Pigeon River Valley remains popular..

Camping

Seven campgrounds containing a total of 125 sites can be found within the Pigeon River Country State Forest. These campgrounds, which feature primitive facilities, are sprinkled throughout the forest. They include **Pine Grove** (six sites), **Pickerel Lake** (39 sites; off Pickerel Lake Road), **Pigeon River** (19 sites), **Pigeon Bridge** (10 sites), **Town Corner** (12 sites), **Round Lake** (10 sites), and **Elk Hill** (12 sites, but primarily a trail camp for horses). All of these campgrounds are a short drive away from Vanderbilt or Wolverine. In addition, the Mackinaw State Forest – of which the Pigeon River Country State Forest is a part – maintains a number of other good campgrounds within its boundaries. Finally, campers have the option of rolling out their sleeping bags at **Clear Lake State Park**. Clear Lake features 200 nicely spaced lots, plenty of recreational options for kids, and modern amenities.

To Find Out More

Contact **Mackinaw State Forest headquarters** at 1732 West M-32, PO Box 667, Gaylord, MI 49735, ☎ 517-732-3541. For more information on the history of the region, see Dale Clarke Franz's *Pigeon River Country*.

■ Sleeping Bear Dunes National Lakeshore

9922 Front St.
Empire, MI 49630
☎ 616-326-5134

The photo albums of thousands of Michigan families include pictures of parents and children huffing and puffing their way up and down Sleeping Bear Dunes, the enormous piles of white sand that look out on Lake Michigan from the base of the state's Leelanau Peninsula. While the kids are apt to be sunburnt, exhausted, and crabby at the end of the day, memories of the area will remain lodged in their minds for years to come. But though the National Lakeshore is often seen primarily as a family destination, it also offers more challenging fare. Sleeping Bear Dunes and North and South Manitou Islands, which are offshore from the dunes but included within the National Lakeshore, all offer backcountry trekking opportunities, and the waters between the great dunes and the islands conceal the silent remains of an estimated 120 shipwrecks, many of which can be explored by divers. This area is known as the **Manitou Passage State Underwater Preserve.**

Getting There

The 35-mile Sleeping Bear Dunes National Lakeshore area is far up the northwestern coast of Michigan's Lower Peninsula, on the western edge of Benzie and Leelanau Counties. Travelers from the south can reach the Lakeshore by taking M-31 north to M-22 north or M-72 west. People journeying from the state's eastern sections can take either M-72 or M-115, the latter of which connects with M-31 at Frankfort.

North and South Manitou Islands can be reached via ferry from the town of Leland, or by privately owned vessel, though neither island offers long-term docking or fueling services for private boats. During the summer (June, July, August), the Leland ferry service makes trips to South Manitou Island every day, weather permitting. The schedule for South Manitou is a busy one in May, September, and October as well, with ferry service available five days a week (Tuesday and Thursday trips are eliminated). Call ahead for reservations on the ferry; you're likely to be left standing on Leland's shores if you show up without them. Journeys to North Manitou Island are less frequent. In July and August, ferry service to the island is available daily except on Tuesday and Thursday. Service in May, June, September, and October is less frequent. Visitors to North and South Manitou should bring extra provisions, as bad weather can delay ferry service by a day or more.

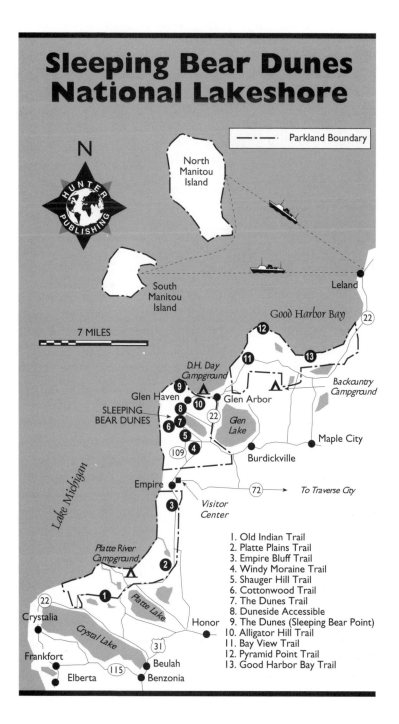

Sleeping Bear Dunes National Lakeshore

N

—··— Parkland Boundary

North Manitou Island

South Manitou Island

Leland

Good Harbor Bay

22

7 MILES

D.H. Day Campground

Backcountry Campground

Glen Haven

SLEEPING BEAR DUNES

Glen Arbor

Glen Lake

22

Maple City

109

Burdickville

Lake Michigan

Empire

Visitor Center

72 → To Traverse City

Platte River Campground

1. Old Indian Trail
2. Platte Plains Trail
3. Empire Bluff Trail
4. Windy Moraine Trail
5. Shauger Hill Trail
6. Cottonwood Trail
7. The Dunes Trail
8. Duneside Accessible
9. The Dunes (Sleeping Bear Point)
10. Alligator Hill Trail
11. Bay View Trail
12. Pyramid Point Trail
13. Good Harbor Bay Trail

Platte Lake

Honor

22

Crystalia

Crystal Lake

Frankfort

Elberta

115

31

Beulah

Benzonia

The idyllic coastline of Sleeping Bear Dunes National Lakeshore
(Robert De Jonge).

In addition to providing transportation to and from the islands, Manitou Island Transit offers charters for Great Lakes fishing or scuba diving in Manitou Passage. For more information on daily travel schedules, rates, and services, contact **Manitou Island Transit** at PO Box 591, Leland, MI 49654; ☎ 616-256-9061 or 616-271-4217.

Diving parties interested in the Manitou Preserve also can set out from three nearby harbors: **Leland** (☎ 616-256-9132), **Charlevoix** (☎ 616-547-3272), and **Frankfort** (☎ 616-352-9051). All three offer transient accommodations, but only Leland has a launch ramp. In addition, charter operators based in Traverse City offer scuba diving expeditions in the preserve. For more information, contact **Scuba North** (☎ 616-947-2520), **Great Lakes Scuba** (☎ 616-943-3483), or **T.C. Charters** (☎ 616-947-6612).

History

Both the Sleeping Bear Dunes area and the twin Manitou Islands owe their names to a Chippewa Indian legend. According to the Chippewas, a mother bear and two cubs once fled a monstrous forest fire on Lake Michigan's far western shores. The trio swam across cold Lake Michigan for days, buffeted by crashing waves and cruel winds, until finally the mother bear reached the Michigan shore. She clambered to a high bluff overlooking the lake to await her cubs, but they tired and drowned only a few miles offshore. The mother bear maintained her desperate vigil, but the cubs never arrived, and she finally died of sorrow at the spot where she had stood sentinel for so long. A nature spirit known as the Great Manitou was so moved by the sad turn of events that he decided to erect a monument to the mother bear's devotion. The spirit created a great mound of sand to mark where she had kept watch for her cubs, and formed two small islands offshore to mark the spots where her children finally succumbed to Lake Michigan's frigid waters.

Members of both the Chippewa and Ottawa Indian tribes were seasonal occupants of the region a few centuries ago, but their hold on the area began to weaken as early as the 1600s, when French traders moved in. The Sleeping Bear Dunes eventually emerged as a well-known landmark for vessels plying Lake Michigan, and the Manitou Passage became an established shipping lane.

South Manitou Island was utilized for Great Lakes shipping purposes as well. The island, 16 miles west of Leland, was settled in the 1830s by a mix of farmers, lumbermen, and workers charged with meeting the needs of the wood-burning steamers chugging up and down the lake. This included construction of a lighthouse in 1840 to mark the island's location and the entrance to the Manitou Passage. Eighteen years later a new tower was erected, but its life was a short one as well. In 1871 a massive 100-foot-high lighthouse was built on the island, and for decades its light showed the way for night-traveling freighters. The lighthouse was finally abandoned in 1958, but it remains a favorite destination for island visitors. North Manitou only recently passed out of private hands. Purchased by the National Park Service in 1984, the island, which lies 12 miles from Leland, has a ghostly aspect on certain evenings. Once the home of a small village of farming families, the island now offers only mute reminders of a bygone era in the form of crumbling cemetery headstones, wilding orchards, and the weathered skeletons of old homesteads. Today, the island is best known for the large numbers of deer hunters it attracts in the fall.

Flora & Fauna

Sleeping Bear is, of course, primarily associated with sand dunes, but other habitat types are also contained within its boundaries. Indeed, dune areas account for only a fraction of the National Lakeshore's 106 square miles. Old orchards and pastures have been transformed over the years into meadows that support spotted knapweed, orange hawkweed, black-eyed susan, and milkweed, while forests of red oak and red and white pine can be found in inland areas. The National Lakeshore also includes interdunal wetlands that nourish a wide range of plant life (including poison ivy, found throughout Sleeping Bear Dunes and the islands).

Many different animal species make their home within the Sleeping Bear area. Deer, raccoons, foxes, squirrels, woodchucks, beaver, and muskrats all romp through various areas of the park. Species of birds that are sighted in the Lakeshore include ruffled grouse, woodpecker, American goldfinch, blue jay, Canada goose, great blue heron, black and white warbler, evening grosbeak, red-tailed hawk, kestrel, great crested flycatcher, and brown thrasher. The islands also support wildlife, although their size and isolation limit the number of species there. Animals roaming South Manitou include squirrel, chipmunk, snowshoe hare, and fox.

The most visible animals on North Manitou are white-tailed deer and raccoons. The deer population, which was artificially introduced to the island back in the 1920s, grew to such enormous proportions that by the 1980s it had wreaked havoc with the vegetation. In recent years, however, hunters have culled the herd's size down to levels that the island can better support, and officials now say that North Manitou's vegetation is well on the way to recovery. Raccoons are a constant nuisance on the island, even by raccoon standards. Hang your food and trash or count on visitors. Finally, the southeastern tip of the island (Dimmick's Point) is a major nesting area for the endangered piping plover, and is thus closed to the public from May 1 to August 15.

Adventures

In The Air

Michigan's dunelands extend far beyond the boundaries of Sleeping Bear Dunes National Lakeshore. In fact, massive dune formations and sandy beaches can be found all along the state's western coastline, providing that side of the state with ideal settings for a variety of sun- and surf-related activities. One of the Midwest's premier hang gliding destinations lies just a few miles down M-22 from Sleeping Bear Dunes. Adorned with hulking dunes that look out on Lake Michigan's shining surface, the **Frankfort-Elberta area** is nirvana for paragliders and hang gliders. Hang gliding enthusiasts can launch from 400-foot launch points in this area, taking advantage of shoreline updrafts to soar thousands of feet in the air. A main gathering place is **Green Point Landing**, which can be reached by heading south out of Elberta and taking Green Point Road west off of M-22. For more information on hang gliding activity in the area, contact the **Benzie County Chamber of Commerce, ☎** 800-882-5801; **Traverse City Hang Gliders, ☎** 616-922-2844; or **Fly High** at **☎** 616-882-7169.

On Foot

The mainland has a dozen different scenic paths for day-hiking, but the only trail in the Sleeping Bear Dunes vicinity suitable for backpacking is the **Platte Plains Trail**. This trail, on the southern end of the Lakeshore between Otter Creek and the Platte River, consists of three loops totaling nearly 15 miles. It offers a blend of scenery, from stands of pine, oak, and aspen to open meadows, and features access to the beach at several points via short trail spurs. The Platte Plains Trail is not demanding; some of it follows the bed of an abandoned narrow gauge railroad track, and the terrain is relatively flat, except for the trail's hilly southern loop. The only backcountry campground is the five-site **White Pine Campground**, which features a community fire circle. The trail can be accessed from the **Platte River**

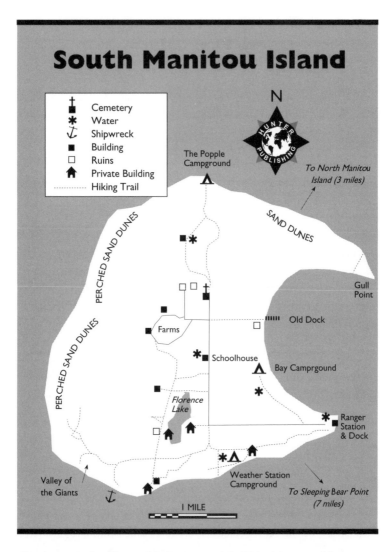

Campground – the park's largest, with 171 sites – and from two trailheads, the **Otter Creek Trailhead** and the **Trail's End Trailhead**. To reach the Otter Creek Trailhead, take M-22 to Esch Road and turn west; just before reaching the lake, an unpaved road will take you to the trailhead. The Trail's End Trailhead is at the end of Trail's End Road, six miles south of Empire, and is accessible via M-22.

South Manitou Island is the most popular destination in the park for backpackers. Possessed of three rustic campground areas,

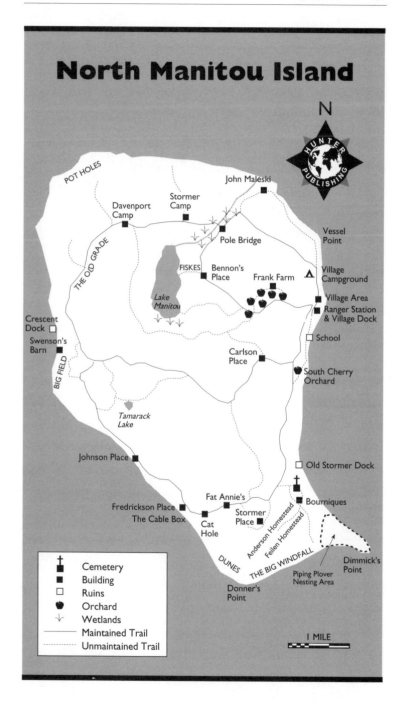

North Manitou Island

N

POT HOLES

John Maleski

Stormer
Camp

Davenport
Camp

THE OLD GRADE

Pole Bridge

Vessel
Point

FISKES

Bennon's
Place

Frank Farm

Village
Campground

Village Area

Lake
Manitou

Ranger Station
& Village Dock

Crescent
Dock

School

Swenson's
Barn

BIG FIELD

Carlson
Place

South Cherry
Orchard

Tamarack
Lake

Johnson Place

Old Stormer Dock

Bourniques

Fat Annie's

Fredrickson Place
The Cable Box

Stormer
Place

Cat
Hole

Anderson Homestead

Feilen Homestead

DUNES

THE BIG WINDFALL

Dimmick's
Point

Piping Plover
Nesting Area

Donner's
Point

✝	Cemetery
■	Building
☐	Ruins
🍎	Orchard
↓	Wetlands
——	Maintained Trail
·····	Unmaintained Trail

I MILE

The lighthouse on South Manitou Island (Travel Michigan).

a variety of dayhiking attractions – including a virgin grove of massive white cedars known as the **Valley of the Giants** – and a dozen miles of shoreline ideal for swimming, picturesque South Manitou attracts crowds, and reservations are now required for large groups. Weekend excursions are particularly popular – especially on holidays – so you may want to plan a mid-week visit if possible. Since the journey to South Manitou usually takes only about two hours, the island receives a fair number of people who arrive and depart on the same day. Those who stay overnight (or longer) are required to stay in the island's designated campground areas. **Weather Station Campground**, 1.2 miles from the dock, sits along the island's southern shores. The **Bay Campground**, 1.3 miles up the island's curving eastern shore, is another easily reached destination. The most distant of the island's camp-grounds is **Popple Campground**, perched 3½ miles from the dock on the island's northernmost point. All the campgrounds feature community fire rings, and most sites are equipped to handle as many as six campers (some sites, available on a reservation basis, can handle larger numbers). Water is available at several different places on the island, and both the Bay and Water Station Camp-grounds have nearby pumps (water for Popple campers is about one half-mile down the trail). The island occasionally sees visitors with heavy partying agendas; these folks, while a small minority, tend to favor the nearby Bay or Weather Station Campgrounds when they stumble off the ferry.

North Manitou Island has fewer visitors. No supplies are available on the island and potable water can be had only at the ferry docking area. These factors, coupled with the ferry service's emphasis on providing transportation to South Manitou, keep the crowds down. Those who do make the journey to North Manitou are permitted to camp anywhere on the 15,000-acre island with the exception of the old village, and explorers are free to follow or ignore the island's old roads and two-tracks as they see fit. It is a beautiful island, and well worth checking out.

Free permits are required for backcountry camping throughout the mainland areas of Sleeping Bear Dunes National Lakeshore.

On Water

Scuba Diving

 The **Manitou Passage State Underwater Preserve** is not officially included as part of the Sleeping Bear Dunes National Lakeshore, but it nonetheless draws many boaters and divers to the area. The preserve holds a number of treasures, from the wrecks of another era's freighters and schooners to the ruins of once-thriving docks and wharves.

 Those exploring here by boat need to exercise appropriate caution when cruising around the preserve's waters; several areas – South Manitou's Gull Point, Platte Bay's reefs, and others – can be treacherous.

Shipwrecks

The most notable of the shipwrecks in the preserve is a relatively recent addition to the Manitou Passage's dark collection. The *Francisco Morazan* is a 246-foot freighter that ran aground 300 yards south of South Manitou Island during a late 1960 snowstorm. A good portion of the *Morazan* remains above water, and it can be easily seen from shore. Lying in less than 20 feet of water,

Northern Lower Michigan

the freighter is easily accessible, but skin divers are discouraged from making it a destination because of enclosed sections and sharp shards of metal. Urges to explore the vessel's superstructure should be suppressed; cormorants and gulls nest there, and the *Morazan's* decks are covered with an unpleasant shellack of slippery guano.

Just a few hundred yards south of the *Morazan's* abandoned hulk lie the remains of another vessel, the **Walter L. Frost**. For years this wreck, a 235-foot steamer that ran aground in dense fog in 1905, remained largely intact, but it sustained heavy damage in 1960, when the *Francisco Morazan* landed on top of it. Still, sections of its hull, boilers, and other machinery remain. Another popular site is the wreck of the **Alva Bradley**, a small schooner that was discovered between North and South Manitou Islands in 1990. Artifacts from the vessel's last voyage abound on the lake floor, from rigging to remnants of its cargo of steel billets.

The most recent discovery in the preserve is the **Three Brothers**, a 162-foot steam barge that succumbed to Lake Michigan's heaving seas back in September of 1911. The vessel miraculously appeared off South Manitou's southeastern shores in the spring of 1996 as the Manitou Passage's shifting currents pushed away the shroud of sand that had concealed it for so many years. The *Three Brothers* lies at a depth of 45 feet, though its bow is only 10 feet under the surface. Area divers have welcomed the discovery, although they have lamented the speed with which its artifacts were stolen.

The most technically challenging wreck to explore is that of the **Congress**, a vessel that was set adrift from South Manitou Harbor in 1904 when its cargo of lumber became engulfed in flame. The ship, which features a largely intact hull and forward cabin (the latter can be penetrated), lies at the bottom of the harbor in 165 feet of water.

Skin Diving

The shallow depth in which most of the preserve's shipwrecks sit also makes the Manitou Passage Underwater Preserve attractive to skin divers. Vessels that can be explored in this fashion include the **J.S. Crouse**, a small freighter in 15 feet of water off Glen Haven; the **Rising Sun**, a steamer off the mainland's Pyramid Point in 10 feet of water; and the **James McBride**, a wreck visible from Sleeping Bear Point.

Finally, the Manitou Preserve contains the ruins of many docks and wharves (some of which reveal and conceal themselves with the floor's ever-shifting sands), and large schools of fish that make their home around its shoals of rock and sand.

On Snow

Cross-Country Skiing

The Sleeping Bear Dunes area is a popular spot for cross-country skiers and snowshoers during the winter. The backcountry campground at Platte Plains Trail is open year-round and is a favorite destination of Nordic skiers with a taste for winter camping, but other trails beckon as well. Indeed, the park has more than 50 miles of trails for skiers of all sizes and levels of skill. The best of these are the 3½-mile **Old Indian Trail**, which includes loops for both advanced and inexperienced skiers; the 10-mile **Scenic Drive Trail**, a relatively easy trail that offers great views of Glen Lake, the Manitou Islands, and Lake Michigan; the **Alligator Hill Trail**, which takes Nordic skiers through 8.6 miles of hilly hardwood forest and open fields; and the attractive **Bay View Trail**, a popular weekend destination that provides 10 miles of mostly easy skiing through old farm fields and beech-maple forest.

Camping

The Sleeping Bear Dunes area has two mainland campgrounds that are open from mid-April through November. Both are quite busy on summer weekends. The more rustic **D.H. Day Campground** (vault toilets, no trailer hookups) boasts 80 large sites in a nicely wooded area. The 171-site **Platte River Campground** features all the modern amenities, including hookups, restrooms, and coin-operated showers. A third campground, the **Valley View Campground** north of Glen Arbor, sits 1½ miles up the Valley View Trail and is reachable only on foot.

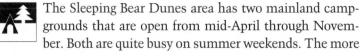
Northern Lower Michigan

Campsites can be reserved in the National Park by calling ☎ 800-365-2267.

To Find Out More
Contact **Park Headquarters** at 9922 Front St., Empire, MI 49630, ☎ 616-326-5134.

■ Thunder Bay Underwater Preserve

Alpena Convention and Visitors Bureau
PO Box 65
Alpena, MI 49707
☎ 800-582-1906 or 517-356-2151

The 288-square mile Thunder Bay Underwater Preserve serves as the final resting place for several of the hundreds of Great Lakes freighters and other vessels that have fallen victim to the ferocious storms and hidden reefs of those icy waters. In fact, the Thunder Bay Preserve, which is in Lake Huron, houses the carcasses of 80 vessels, including more than a dozen major freighters, schooners, steamers, and barges. This gives the region one of the highest densities of shipwrecks per square mile of any area of the Great Lakes. Notable wrecks include the **Nordmeer**, a 550-foot German steel steamer; the **Lucinda Van Valkenburg** (affectionately known to area divers as "Lucy"), a 128-foot schooner; and the **Grecian**, a 269-foot steamer that is often mentioned as an ideal dive site for inexperienced divers looking to hone their skills. But many other dive sites offer hours of interesting exploration as well, in part because of the clarity of the water. This clarity – which makes the preserve a favorite for divers with an interest in underwater photography – is often attributed to the high concentration of limestone on the lake floor. The Thunder Bay Underwater Preserve is a cornerstone of the proposed Thunder Bay National Marine Sanctuary.

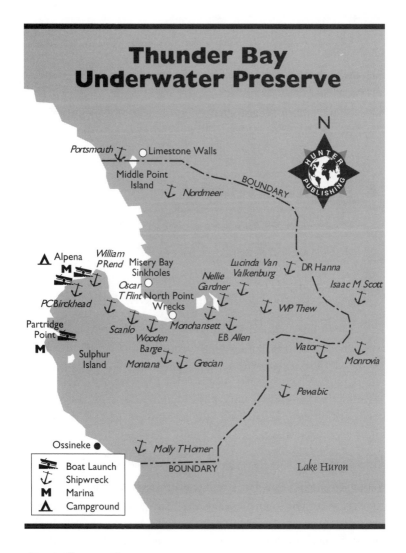

Thunder Bay Underwater Preserve

N

Portsmouth ⚓ ○ Limestone Walls

Middle Point Island ⚓ *Nordmeer*

BOUNDARY

▲ Alpena
M
William P Rend
Misery Bay Sinkholes
Lucinda Van Valkenburg ⚓ *DR Hanna*
Nellie Gardner ⚓
Isaac M Scott ⚓

Oscar T Flint ○
North Point Wrecks
⚓ *WP Thew*

PC Birckhead ⚓

Partridge Point
M
Scanlo ⚓ ⚓ *Monohansett* ⚓
EB Allen
Viator ⚓
Monrovia

Sulphur Island
Wooden Barge ⚓ ⚓ *Grecian*
Montana

⚓ *Pewabic*

Ossineke ●
⚓ *Molly T Horner*
BOUNDARY
Lake Huron

🚤	Boat Launch
⚓	Shipwreck
M	Marina
▲	Campground

Getting There

Thunder Bay Underwater Preserve is off the northeast coast of Michigan's Lower Peninsula. The city of **Alpena**, which is nestled in the northern corner of Thunder Bay, is the primary launching point for diving excursions in Thunder Bay Underwater Preserve. The city, which can be reached from the south or north via US-23 or from the west by M-28, boasts both a marina and a number of boat launch sites. In Alpena, Thunder Bay Divers (405 E.

Chisholm St., Alpena, MI 49707, ☎ 517-356-9336) provides guided explorations of area shipwrecks.

Marinas offering fuel and accommodations can also be found in **Presque Isle**, about 25 miles up the coast from Alpena, and on **Partridge Point**, a small peninsula just south of Alpena. Finally, the **Ossineke State Forest Campground**, a few miles further down US-23, has a boat launch with limited parking.

Boaters venturing out into Thunder Bay and Lake Huron proper should make sure that they equip themselves with a navigation chart that shows depths before venturing out, in order to avoid adding their own to the existing shipwrecks. Some areas of the Preserve are shallow, and the areas immediately surrounding several of the islands that dot the preserve can be particularly treacherous. Divers also need to remember that the limestone floor of the region can make anchoring a frustrating enterprise. Veterans urge newcomers to use the mooring buoys that are provided at some dive sites whenever possible.

History

Years ago, before interstate highways became an integral part of the American landscape, freighters and barges plied the waters of the Great Lakes in record numbers, carrying cargo to and fro all along that string of mighty lakes, from Duluth to Buffalo. But the lakes, which could be so placid on certain summer days, were not always so compliant. As Jacques Marquette, a 17th-century explorer of the Great Lakes, observed, "The winds from the Lake of the Illinois [Lake Michigan] no sooner subside than they are hurled back by the Lake of the Hurons, and those from Lake Superior are the fiercest of all. In the winter months there is a succession of storms; and with these mighty waters all about us, we seem to be living in the heart of a hurricane." Indeed, as the years passed, fierce storms battered hundreds of vessels into oblivion, killing thousands of sailors in the process.

Thunder Bay Underwater Preserve

One of nine underwater preserves covering approximately 1,900 square miles of bottomland off Michigan's coast, Thunder Bay houses a number of major shipwrecks within its boundaries. Many of these are scattered around Thunder Bay Island, which lies at the north end of the bay. A century ago, ship captains' efforts to navigate their vessels past the island and into the harbor of Alpena all too often failed, thwarted by fog, storms, and the formidable shoals that surrounded the island. The area thus came to be known as "Shipwreck Alley" among sailors of yesteryear.

Michigan's underwater preserve system was created in 1981, thanks in large measure to the efforts of the state's sizable sport diving community. The Thunder Bay Underwater Preserve was the first of the nine preserves to receive formal legal protection and recognition from the Michigan legislature. If Thunder Bay receives recognition as a National Marine Sanctuary, it would be the first freshwater and Great Lakes sanctuary to receive such protection (the other 12 are scattered along the shorelines of the Atlantic and Pacific Oceans and the Gulf of Mexico). It would also be the first Sanctuary to receive such a designation because of the area's cultural resources (shipwrecks) rather than its natural resources. Supporters of the plan note that sanctuary status would not restrict recreational access to the area; scuba divers, anglers, kayakers, and others would still be able to indulge their interests unimpeded, provided they adhere to already existing state and federal regulations. For more information on the proposed Thunder Bay National Marine Sanctuary, contact **Karen Brubeck, Public Outreach Coordinator**, 6893 Hedrick Rd., Harbor Springs, MI 49740, ☎ 616-526-8434 or **Ellen Brody, NOAA Project Coordinator**, 2205 Commonwealth Blvd., Ann Arbor, MI 48105, ☎ 734-741-2270.

Northern Lower Michigan

Adventures

On Water

Scuba Diving

 Divers exploring the Thunder Bay Underwater Preserve can choose from many fascinating and exciting underwater destinations. Of the approximately 80 ships at the bottom of Lake Huron in the area, several are particularly notable for one reason or another.

Shipwrecks

The **Nordmeer** is one of the most popular of the shipwrecks in Thunder Bay. It is also one of the easiest to spot, for a substantial portion of its superstructure remains above water. Located in the northern section of the preserve, seven miles east of Thunder Bay Island, the enormous German steel steamer became stranded on Thunder Bay Shoal in November 1966. It was abandoned nine days after hitting the shoal, as a harsh storm forced its captain and crew to retreat to the mainland. Resting at a depth of about 40 feet, the *Nordmeer* can be entered easily through its massive cargo hatches, which also allow light to penetrate portions of the ship's interior. A sunken barge lies close to the *Nordmeer*, and while the barge is dwarfed by its 550-foot neighbor, it too can be explored by divers. The *Nordmeer* is one dive site that does not typically have mooring buoys; instead, boats tie off alongside the wreck or throw a grappling hook into the hold.

Another popular destination for Thunder Bay divers is the **Montana**, a 235-foot sidewheel steamer that sank in 1914 in the wake of a crippling fire. Located five miles southwest of Thunder Bay Island, the vessel lies at a depth of about 70 feet. Despite the long-ago fire, the vessel's sides remain largely intact, which makes it possible for some exploration of its interior. The site is also known for its artifacts and large fish population. Like the *Nordmeer*, it is regarded as a good site for divers with basic to intermediate skills.

The **Grecian** is a short distance east of the *Montana*, approximately five miles south-southeast of Thunder Bay Island. The victim of a collision with another ship, the 269-foot steel-hulled *Grecian* sank in 105 feet of water in 1906. After an ill-fated attempt to retrieve the ship, it was finally abandoned. Ninety years later, it is an attractive site for recreational divers for several reasons, and is cited by supporters of the proposed sanctuary as one of the most notable shipwrecks in the region. Visibility in the area is excellent, despite the depth at which the ship lies (the deck lies at 75 feet), and much of the ship's interior can be investigated by experienced divers, provided they bring along the appropriate diving equipment (lines and lights).

Another ship that was laid low by an unlucky mid-lake encounter with another vessel was the 128-foot **Lucinda Van Valkenburg**. The "Lucy" is a wooden schooner that foundered in 1887 a few miles northeast of Thunder Bay Island. The Lucy sits in 70 feet of water and, while its stern has collapsed, the remainder of the ship can be explored by intermediate divers.

The **Monohansett** is another good dive site for inexperienced divers. Located only about 500 feet west of Thunder Bay Light (on the southern end of Thunder Bay Island), the 164-foot wooden schooner lies in about 20 feet of water. The *Monohansett* sank in 1907, after a fire erupted on board during a storm. Today, little of the ship's exterior has been preserved, but the vessel's innards – including its boiler, engine, and 114-foot propeller – can all be examined.

Of course, Thunder Bay Underwater Preserve also offers challenging excursions for more advanced divers. If shipping channel traffic does not faze you, then you might want to investigate the remains of the **W.P. Thew**, a steamer that sank in 90 feet of water in 1909. Its dark interior can be explored, but various obstructions make this a tricky – and potentially hazardous – venture. The *W.P. Thew* should be explored only by experienced divers.

Another site favored by advanced scuba divers is the **E.B. Allen**, a wooden schooner that was lost to the waves in 1871, less than three miles southeast of Thunder Bay Island. The ship, which remains largely intact, lies in about 100 feet of water, making it one

Northern Lower Michigan

of the deepest dive sites in Thunder Bay Underwater Preserve. A third shipwreck site available to experienced divers is near the eastern edge of the preserve, in 140 feet of water. There sits the hulk of the **D.R. Hanna**, a massive 552-foot freighter that sank in 1919 after being accidentally rammed by another ship in foggy conditions. The Thunder Bay region also holds the *Isaac M. Scott*, a huge steel-hulled freighter that was one of 11 ships lost during the "Great Storm of 1913." Twenty-eight sailors lost their lives on the *Scott*, which sank just outside the Preserve's boundaries but is included within the proposed National Sanctuary. It is about seven miles northeast of Thunder Bay Lighthouse. Investigation of the *Scott* should be made only by divers with advanced abilities.

Other Dive Sites

In addition to its many shipwrecks, the preserve contains a number of interesting geologic formations. The **Misery Bay Sinkholes**, north of Thunder Bay around North Point, offer cave diving opportunities for ambitious explorers. In recent years, however, concerns about high concentrations of corrosive natural gases in the area have convinced most divers to look elsewhere for their recreation.

Divers interested in exploring Thunder Bay's natural underwater beauty should turn their attention to the area's **limestone reefs** and **walls**. Both the southeast side of Thunder Bay Island and the mainland's South Point (located at the extreme southern edge of the preserve) are renowned for their limestone formations. Another is on the northern boundary of the preserve. This wall, just northeast of Middle Island, extends down 70 feet until it reaches a large depression in the lake floor. Finally, the waters south of Thunder Bay Island and its neighbors (Sugar Island, Gull Island) are known for supporting large schools of fish.

Skin Diving

Thunder Bay Underwater Preserve also offers many skin diving possibilities. A boat is required to reach dive sites within the preserve, but a number of shipwrecks are in relatively shallow water and can be investigated by skin divers. These include the **P.H. Birckhead**, a 156-foot wooden steamer that sank just south of the

Alpena marina, and the **William P. Rend**, a 287-foot freighter. Both of these sites are nestled near shore deep in Thunder Bay, and thus enjoy more shelter from rough weather than do sites further out in the lake. Another destination for skin divers is the wreck of the **Portsmouth**, which can be found out near Middle Island on the Preserve's northern boundary.

■ *Tips For A Greater Adventure* ■

Several of the dive sites in the preserve still hold large numbers of fascinating artifacts, and some divers might be tempted to abscond with such souvenirs, ethical qualms notwithstanding. Don't do it. The state of Michigan has the power to impose stiff legal penalties for unauthorized removal of artifacts. Repercussions for such illegal activity can range from confiscation of dive equipment (including boats) to imprisonment. Area divers don't look kindly on such thefts, either, so leave stuff where you find it.

To Find Out More

For information, contact the **Michigan Underwater Preserve Council**, 11 S. State St., St. Ignace, MI 49781, ☎ 800-338-6660. For additional information on efforts to establish the Thunder Bay National Marine Sanctuary, contact Ellen Brody, Project Coordinator, Proposed Thunder Bay National Marine Sanctuary, NOAA/GLERL, 2205 Commonwealth Blvd., Ann Arbor, MI 48105-2945, ☎ 734-741-2270; or Sherrard Foster, Atlantic, Great Lakes and Gulf Branch, Sanctuaries and Reserves Division, Office of Ocean and Coastal Resource Management, NOAA, 1305 East-West Highway - SSMC4, Silver Spring, MD 20910, ☎ 301-713-3125, ext. 127.

Northern Lower Michigan

■ Adventures Region-Wide

On Foot

Backpacking & Hiking

 Michigan's Upper Peninsula is a mecca for backpackers throughout the Midwest, and for good reason. But great trails have been forged in the state's northern Lower Peninsula as well, providing options ranging from month-long journeys to relaxing overnighters. Unfortunately, the proximity of these trails (when compared with UP destinations) to the state's southern population centers can cause an excess of traffic – both on the trails and on northbound freeways – over summer weekends. Once the schools reopen their doors, however, the scene improves dramatically. Quiet returns to the trails, and the North Country's rolling woodlands explode into leafy canopies of brilliant color. Fall, then, is in many ways the ideal time to plan a backpacking excursion in this region (but don't forget your stocking cap; autumn evenings in northern Michigan can get a wee bit chilly).

Michigan Shore-to-Shore Trail

This monstrous 219-mile trail (excluding spurs) cuts through the heart of the Lower Peninsula's northern reaches. It extends from the town of Oscoda, on Lake Huron, all the way to Empire, on the shores of Lake Michigan. In addition, backpackers can begin or end the eastern part of their excursion in Tawas City via a small trail spur, or take trail spurs that lead down into Cadillac or all the way up to the outskirts of Cheboygan. These options, coupled with the many access/resupply points along the main trail, make the Shore-to-Shore Trail a big attraction for backpackers with the time and inclination to lose themselves in the north woods for anywhere from a week to a month.

The main trail offers up a treasure trove of backcountry gems, from the Huron National Forest and its various attractions (the Au Sable River, etc.) in the east to the rolling woodlands and dunes of the state's western ramparts. But there are some sections

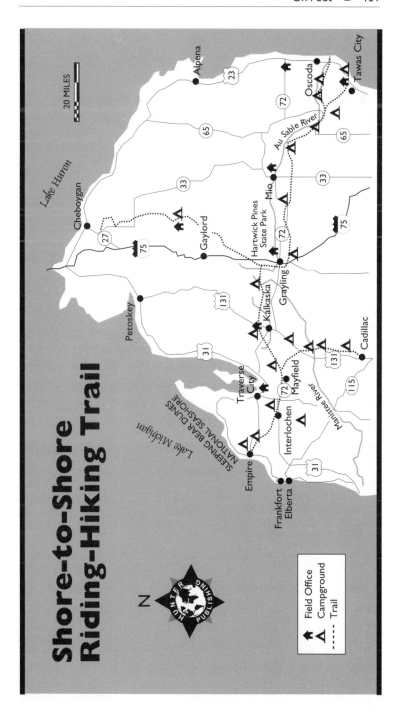

of the trail that amount to nothing more than gravel, dirt, or paved roads, and the terrain itself is flat for long stretches. Backcountry travelers are permitted to camp along the trail, provided they adhere to the various rules governing such camping (camp at least 200 feet from designated trails and bodies of water, etc.), but there are also a number of campgrounds spaced at intervals along the way. On occasion, backpackers may find themselves sharing a campground with equestrians, for the trail is also a favorite of Michigan riding enthusiasts (the Michigan Trail Riders Association organizes a number of trips down the main trail every year). For additional information on the main trail, see the section on *Huron National Forest,* page *99.*

The northern spur of the Shore-to-Shore extends into Crawford, Otsego, and Cheboygan Counties. It offers more consistently rolling terrain and secluded backcountry camping options than the main trail, and slices through parts of two state forests – the Mackinaw and Au Sable. The 44-mile southern spur winds its way through Grand Traverse, Missaukee, and Wexford Counties, cutting through Pere Marquette State Forest along the way. As with other sections of the Shore-to-Shore, the trail offers a pleasing mix of woodlands and fields, but in the springtime area wetlands make it a sometimes-soggy route.

Backpacker exploring the Jordan River Pathway.

Jordan River Pathway

One of the finest of the Lower Peninsula's many backpacking trails is the Jordan River Pathway, an 18-mile loop cradled in the heart of some of Michigan's most beautiful countryside. The trail cuts a swath through thick stands of maple, aspen, birch, elm, and white spruce that are home to white-tailed deer and other wildlife. The pathway's northern section meanders through woodlands and sunny meadows, occasionally swinging by the banks of the bustling Jordan River, while the loop's hillier southern side passes by scenic overlooks and over a couple of feeder streams that make for good lunch stops. Progress on the pathway can be measured by watching for the numbered markers interspersed along the route. These markers, which are sequentially numbered 1-25, are pretty handy, but DNR maps of the pathway do not always accurately reflect their true location (for instance, official maps place marker 10 equidistant from markers 9 and 11, when in reality marker 10 is far closer to marker 11). Backcountry camping in the valley is limited to the **Pinney Bridge Hike-In Campground**, a pretty meadow about eight miles into the loop. The campground sees a lot of day use, but its sites are widely spaced and include fire rings; it also has a water pump (the trail does not provide hikers with a source of water, so come with full bottles). To reach the trail, take US-131 to Dead Man's Hill Road, six miles north of the town of Alba. Turn west and go two miles to the parking area.

Beaver Island

Backpackers in Michigan and neighboring states have long enjoyed exploring a number of the islands that lie off the state's mainland, most notably Isle Royale National Park and the Manitou Islands. Beaver Island is yet another option for hikers, albeit a somewhat odd one in several respects. Unlike Isle Royale and the Manitous, which remain almost entirely undeveloped, Beaver Island actually houses an assortment of shops, restaurants, and other accommodations in the small village of St. James, around which most of its 450 year-round residents live. Moreover, Beaver Island has a history that is, well, pretty weird. The island's most notable historical figure is undoubtedly James Strang, a controversial Mormon who established a prosperous religious commu-

Northern Lower Michigan

nity on the island and subsequently declared himself its king; his strange reign ended in 1856 when he was murdered by a follower, and the Mormons were subsequently forced off the island.

But while the 55-square-mile Beaver Island has many of the trappings of civilization that one might see on the mainland, it does offer treats for hikers. Much of the island's southern half is part of the Mackinaw State Forest, and its many old logging trails and hiking paths allow backpackers to explore most of the island in relative solitude. In addition to the Beaver Island State Forest Campground, which is on the island's eastern shoreline off East Side Drive, backpackers can also camp off-trail in certain other areas of the island, including its southern reaches and stretches of the western shoreline; contact the **Mackinaw State Forest** at ☎ 517-732-3541 for more details on backcountry camping restrictions. Since the island lies more than 30 miles from the Michigan mainland, both visitors and residents must make the journey by air or water. **Island Airways** makes regularly scheduled flights throughout the year; ☎ 616-547-2141. To reach the island via ferry, contact the **Beaver Island Boat Company** in Charlevoix, ☎ 616-547-2311. Boaters also have the option of embarking on their own voyage out to the island; St. James has a recreational harbor with two marinas offering transient accommodations.

Green Pine Lake Trail

If you are searching for a trail that seems a million miles away from the frenzied work-a-day world, then the 11-mile Green Pine Lake Trail in Clare County is apt to be a disappointment. Although it runs through a portion of Au Sable State Forest, hikers encounter a number of roads and power line towers along the route, and the size of the Pike Lake Campground on its eastern end (33 sites) draws crowds. But the area's rolling woodlands and numerous bogs and marshes do support a wide variety of plant and animal life, and the pathway's easygoing character makes it an attractive option for parties with young or less-athletic members. Backpackers hoping to elude the crowds at Pike Lake should begin their hike there and work westward to the Mud Lake campground, which offers eight tent sites.

The Mud Lake sites are accessible by car and, because of this, may be hard to come by on summer weekends.

The Pike Lake campground and trailhead is 9½ miles northwest of Farwell off M-115, while the trail's western trailhead at Mud Lake can be reached by taking M-66 north out of Barrytown to Browns Road. Turn east on Browns to Campground Drive south.

Sand Lakes Trail

This modest trail network, which sprawls out amid the woodlands of the 2,800-acre Sand Lakes Quiet Area, offers hikers a variety of route and activity options. Old dirt roads and unmarked trails criss-cross the area, and the pathway itself includes several optional loops. The scenery along the Sand Lakes Trail will not knock your socks off; it boasts no spectacular views, and users have beaten the area up a bit in recent years. But it does offer ample opportunities for quiet and secluded backwoods camping, and both Big Guernsey Lake and the nearby Boardman River attract backpacking anglers as well as afternoon fishermen. Camping is permitted anywhere in the area, providing overnight visitors adhere to the usual guidelines. A campground is also on the northeast side of Big Guernsey Lake. It can be reached by taking Island Lake Road eight miles west out of Kalkaska to Guernsey Lake Road. Turn south and follow the posted signs to the campground and trailhead.

North Country National Scenic Trail

When the North Country Trail is completed, it will provide backpackers with a trail extending all the way from upstate New York to North Dakota's Lake Sakakawea. Nearly a quarter of the trail's length – 875 of an estimated 4,000 miles – will thread its way through Michigan's Lower and Upper Peninsulas. While progress on the trail has been fitful in southern Michigan due to the lack of public land, large sections have already been certified in northern Lower Michigan and the UP. See page 111 for Lower Peninsula trail information. For the UP segment of the trail, see page 281.

These backpacking trails are supplemented by an abundance of trails that are ideal for day hiking. Many of the state parks in

Northern Lower Michigan

northern Michigan include hiking trails within their boundaries that can be tackled in an afternoon or a full day, and most state forests and recreation areas are similarly equipped. These range from leisurely lakeside strolls past towering dunes to journeys through thick stands of northern forest. Among the most attractive of these day hikes is the **Orange Trail**, at Wakeley Lake; the **South Point Trail**, at Negwegon State Park; the **South Point area** of Negwegon State Park; the **Marl Lake Trail** in South Higgins Lake State Park; the **Ridge, Island**, and **Lighthouse Trails** of Ludington State Park; and the challenging **Rifle River Trail** in the Rifle River Recreation Area.

In addition to the trails discussed above, great backpacking and day hiking experiences can be had in a number of other areas of Michigan's northern Lower Peninsula, including Huron National Forest, Manistee National Forest, Sleeping Bear Dunes National Lakeshore (which includes both South and North Manitou Islands), and the Pigeon River Country State Forest Area. Trails and other aspects of these areas are described in the specific sections on these attractions above.

On Wheels

Mountain Biking – Northwest Lower Peninsula

 Northwestern Lower Michigan has emerged as a hotbed of mountain biking activity in recent years. The region features many rugged and challenging trails set in largely unspoiled regions of the countryside, as well as milder trails for less experienced riders. Cool woodlands, ruffling meadows, and rippling rivers are abundant along many of these pathways, and several trails run through areas that still hold healthy populations of wildlife.

NORBA Trail

The NORBA Trail, at the Schuss Mountain-Shanty Creek Ski Resort in Antrim County, is the most famous of Michigan's mountain biking trails. Until 1997 it was the site of the prestigious **Sleeping Bear Mountain Bike Race**, which drew the country's top riders and crowds of 30,000 or more. In addition, the 1996 race was the decisive one in determining the roster of the US Olympic mountain biking team. But disputes between the race's promoters and NORBA (National Off Road Bicycling Association) resulted in the cancellation of the 1997 race.

Despite this loss, the NORBA Trail is certain to play host to major mountain biking races for years to come. Certainly, its popularity with area bikers has not dimmed. Armed with a technically daunting layout and scenic backdrops of forest and meadow, the NORBA Trail draws mountain bikers from all over Michigan. The 13-mile trail is divided into four loops, ranging from the seven-mile Michigan loop – the cornerstone of the network – to the .8-mile Erie Loop. A mixture of single-track and two-track, the Michigan loop offers a tough, sometimes muddy roller-coaster ride featuring notorious stretches known by such colorful nicknames as Tom's Tango, Tim's Remorse, and The Water Hole. The NORBA network's other loops are single-track. Of these, the three-mile Superior Loop is particularly popular. The Schuss Mountain-Shanty Creek Ski Resort is five miles west of Mancelona on M-88. Contact the resort at ☎ 800-678-4111.

VASA Trail

Another trail well-known for its pretty surroundings and challenging layout is the VASA Trail, cradled in the rolling countryside southeast of Grand Traverse Bay. As with so many other mountain biking trails, the VASA Trail originated as a cross-country skiing trail, but the enormous surge in mountain biking's popularity – and the efforts of local volunteers – quickly transformed it into a major destination for bikers as well. The primary trail at VASA is the 25-Kilometer Loop, a 15½-mile journey through demanding forest terrain. The trail, which is quite wide, includes swift descents, leg-straining uphill climbs (such as The Wall, a brutal stretch about one-third of the way through the loop), and winding turns; it will demoralize inexperienced and/or unfit bikers. In 1997 an adjacent loop, the 14-mile VASA Single Track, was made available to mountain bikers for the first time, and future expansions of the VASA network appear likely. To reach VASA Trail from the west, take US-31 east through Traverse City to Bunker Hill Road east. After a mile, turn south on

Northern Lower Michigan

VASA Trail

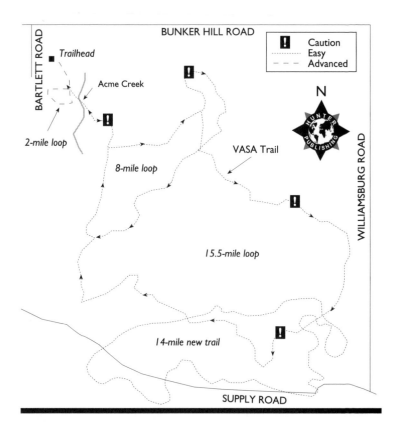

Bartlett Road and follow it to the trailhead. From the east, take M-72 westbound to Lautner Road southbound to Bunker Hill Road. Go west on Bunker Hill Road to Bartlett Road and head south to the trailhead. For more information, ☎ 616-938-4400.

The NORBA and VASA Trails are among the state's best-known mountain biking paths, but many other northwest Michigan trails are quite popular as well.

Bois Blanc Island

This 27-mile loop circumnavigates the island, providing good views of thriving woodlands and Lake Huron. The tour, which traverses level terrain for most of its length, consists of a mix of gravel road, smooth dirt road, and worn double-track. It is an ideal destination for fat-tire fans looking for a scenic respite from more teeth-rattling routes.

Cadillac Pathway

For those seeking an easily accessible, less demanding mountain biking trail, the 10-mile Cadillac Pathway is ideal. Composed of mostly rolling single-track, its many loops allow users to put together personalized routes in accordance with their abilities. The trail's eastern loops are considerably easier than its western sections, many of which are surrounded by private land. Still, the pathway runs through pretty forests of pine and hardwood, and Cadillac-area riders only have a short way to go to reach its trailheads. The main trailhead is 3½ miles east of US-131 on Boon Road, while a second trailhead can be found on 13th Street east of US-131, off the parking lot of a vocational school.

Crystal Mountain Trails

Located at Crystal Mountain Resort, the trail provides options for mountain bikers of varying degrees of experience and fitness. The **Aspen Trail**, which accounts for 4½ miles of the Crystal Mountain Trails' 11-mile total, is a mellow trail that is largely two-track. The **Glacier Valley Loop** is more than three miles long and offers nerve-wracking descents, wicked climbs, and hairpin curves. **Crystal Mountain Resort** is west of Thompsonville on M-115. Contact the resort at ☎ 800-968-7686.

Lake Ann Pathway

The five-mile Lake Ann Pathway charts a course through a grand mix of hardwood forest garnished with healthy side courses of water. The trail bobs and weaves its way past the shorelines of Lake Ann, Shavenaugh Lake, and Mary's Lake, while also paying brief visits to spots along the Platte River. This natural scenery, coupled with the trail's many loops, make it a favorite among area mountain biking enthusiasts. Lake Ann Pathway can be reached by taking US-31 14 miles west out of Traverse City to Reynolds Road. Turn north on Reynolds for four miles, until you reach the trailhead parking lot on the east side of the road.

Northern Lower Michigan

Muncie Lakes Pathway

Another of the many quality mountain biking trails in the Traverse City area, the Muncie Lakes Pathway offers nearly 10 miles of challenging single-track through open meadows and pine and hardwood forests (though some clear cutting detracts from the area's beauty); at several junctures loops within the network provide great views of the Boardman River, which runs along the pathway's southern border. The trail itself is a mixed bag; parts of it are sandy, while others still show the effects of equestrian traffic from earlier years. The trailhead to Muncie Lakes Pathway can be reached by taking M-72 east out of Traverse City to Williamsburg Road (CR-605) south until it merges with Supply Road (CR-660). Turn off Supply Road at Brown Bridge Road and go west for two miles, then north on Ranch Rudolf Road. The trailhead is a short distance up Ranch Rudolf Road.

Pine Haven Trails

Midland County's Pine Haven Recreation Area offers eight miles of trails for beginner-to-intermediate riders. They run through pretty woodlands, but they do not dry well, and can be a real mess in the spring. To reach the park, take West River Road off US-10 to Maynard Road. Turn right on Maynard and follow to the entrance. For more info, ☎ 517-832-6870.

Sand Lakes Quiet Area Trails

This Pere Marquette State Forest single-track, a popular cross-country trail in winter, offers about 10 miles of fairly tough riding over moderately steep terrain. The trail is firm, though, and it cuts through a nice mix of northern hardwoods. To reach the trailhead, take M-72 east to Broomhead Road and turn south. The well-marked parking lot lies half a dozen miles down the road.

Wildwood Hills Trail

This 11-mile trail offers mountain bikers up in the tip of the mitten a solid workout. Composed of a mix of single-track, two-track, and dirt road, the trail goes through rolling woodlands and valleys mixed with meadows that erupt with wildflowers in summer. The area is a terrifically scenic one, but it also attracts a fair amount of ATV traffic. To reach the trail, take I-75 to M-68 west, then quickly get off on southbound Old US-27. Take that to Wildwood Road; the trailhead is four miles west on Wildwood.

In addition, the Manistee National Forest is home to three popular mountain biking trails – **Big M, Mackenzie**, and **Hungerford Lake**. For information on these trails, see the *Manistee National Forest* section, page 107. Finally, several area resorts – including **Boyne Mountain Resort, Sugar Loaf Resort**, and **Grand Traverse Resort** – have recently established mountain biking trails.

Mountain Biking - Northeast Lower Peninsula

These mountain biking trails, while lacking some of the thrills and spills of some other regions of the state, nonetheless offer attractive challenges for knobbies of all experience levels (often within the same trail system). Many of the trails, such as scenic Buttles Road Pathway, are comprised of loops ideal for basic to intermediate mountain bikers. But the region also includes punishing trails – with steep and tough terrain – at such places as the Black Mountain Forest and Rifle River Recreation Areas. Following are some of the best and most popular trails.

Beaver Creek Trail

Located in North Higgins Lake State Park, the Beaver Creek Trail is an ideal course for weekend mountain bikers looking to work up a sweat without leaving flesh on the trail. About 6½ miles long, the trail winds through thick forests of pine, oak, and other hardwoods. The trailhead is only a few hundred feet from the park's Civilian Conservation Corps (CCC) Museum. To reach the park, take Higgins Lake Road eastbound from US-27 or Higgins Lake Road westbound from I-75. ☎ 517-821-6125.

Black Mountain Forest Recreation Area Trails

One of the toughest of northeastern Michigan's mountain biking trail systems is here, nestled west of Rogers City, between Black Lake and Lake Huron. Knobbies can easily spend an entire weekend tearing around the area, for in addition to more than 30 miles of mountain biking trails, there are also several dirt roads. Serious mountain bikers spend part of every visit on the **Black Mountain Challenge**, a six-mile loop of scenic double-track that features a dizzying flurry of grinding ascents and white-knuckle descents. Another favorite is the **Top of the Mountain Ride**, a 12-mile loop of two track and rough forest roads. The recreation area also includes two nice campgrounds – **Black Lake Campground** and **Onaway State Park** – that are sometimes used by bikers looking to hit the trails early. The presence of these campgrounds, however, also contributes to the primary drawback associated with the Black Mountain Recreation Area: crowds. Black Mountain's trail system is popular with hikers and equestrians, and other parts of Black Mountain swarm with riders of ATVs and motorcycles (the recreation area includes an extensive network of ORV trails). To reach the Black Mountain Forest Recreation Area, take M-211 north out of Onaway to CR-489, continuing north. The southernmost of the trailheads is right off 489, less than 10 miles out of Onaway, but other trailheads lie off Doriva Beach Road, Black Mountain Road, and Twin Lakes Road, all of which lie on the north end of Black Lake.

Chippewa Hills Pathway

A trail popular with Nordic skiers as well as mountain bikers, the eight-mile Chippewa Hills Pathway offers rides of moderate difficulty through hilly forest areas and along the edge of deep valleys. Primarily single-track, it has a pleasing mix of climbs and downhill runs throughout much of its length. An underrated trail, the pathway is particularly pretty in the fall, when its woodlands erupt with color. It is in the southernmost part of Alpena County, due west from the small town of South Ossineke, which lies south of Alpena on US-23. It is accessible from two different trailheads, which can be reached by taking Nicholson Road 12 miles west out of South Ossineke to Kissau Road. Both trailheads are on Kissau, the first near the juncture of Kissau and Nicholson, the second a little farther south.

Hartwick Pines Trails

The mountain biking trail system at Hartwick Pines State Park is one of the Lower Peninsula's most scenic. Situated next to the beautiful Au Sable River valley, the big park is blessed with rolling hills and thriving forestlands. Hartwick Pines maintains a number of trails, but only one of these is open to mountain bikes.

This loop, known as the **Weary Legs Trail**, is an eight-mile route that also includes two spurs linking its western and eastern lengths at two different points – thus giving riders the option of shortening or lengthening the rides. The three-mile loop created by the southernmost of these spurs is called the **Aspen Trail**, while the five-mile loop that lies between the two spurs is known as the **Deer Run Trail**. None of these loops is particularly difficult or crowded. To reach Hartwick Pines State Park, take M-93 north off of I-75 to the park entrance. ☎ 517-348-7068.

Marl Lake Trails

Housed in the bustling South Higgins Lake State Park, the Marl Lake Trail system offers a respite from the cacophony that marks other areas of the park during the summer. Cool forest and peaceful shoreline views lie only a few minutes' bike ride away from the hot gleam of suntan lotion-shellacked skin and scorching car upholstery. The network itself is an easy one, though exposed roots will rattle inexperienced teeth in a few early sections. It is composed mostly of flat single- and double-track, and includes two connecting spurs that divide the trail into three loops. The longest of these – which are often populated with hikers on weekends – is 5½ miles. To reach South Higgins Lake State Park, take CR-104 eastbound from US-27 to CR-100. Take CR-100 northbound to the park entrance. The trailhead to Marl Lake Trail is across the road from the entrance. If entering from the east, take I-75 to M-18 south to Robinson Road (CR-103). Take Robinson to CR-100 and turn south, to park entrance. ☎ 517-821-6374.

Ocqueoc Falls Pathway

Presque Isle County's Ocqueoc Falls Pathway is one of the most scenic trails in the Lower Peninsula. It snakes along the ridges of the Ocqueoc River valley for the first three miles of its six-mile length, winding among vibrant stands of hardwood and pine, with grand views up and down the valley. The route then descends into the valley and the banks of the Ocqueoc River itself, which can be followed back to the trailhead. The trail gets its name from Ocqueoc Falls, a scenic waterfall near the trailhead (and one of only two in the Lower Peninsula). The area is also home to Ocqueoc Falls Campground, a beautiful campground that overlooks the river. To reach Ocqueoc Falls Pathway, take M-68 to Ocqueoc Falls Road; the parking area is just west of the junction of those two roads.

Rifle River Trails

The Rifle River Recreation Area lures mountain bikers from all over northeast Michigan with its enticing combination of scenic woodlands, sparkling lakes, and varied single-track trails, which can be enjoyed by everyone from first-timers to diehard knobbies. Winding among 10 lakes that dot the region, the system boasts loops that range from sweaty climbs over rolling hills and breezy ridgetops down into the fields and woodlands that shelter under those ridges. The most difficult trail loops are in the system's northern sections, where most of the lakes and ponds lie, while the easier southern loops go along the banks of the Rifle and through pretty open fields. To reach the Rifle River Recreation Area, take M-33 to CR-F-28; the park entrance lies 4½ miles east on F-28. ☎ 517-473-2258.

Pigeon River Country State Forest also offers mountain biking trails. For further information on these trails, see the section on *Pigeon River Country State Forest*, page 125.

To Find Out More

Most of the state's mountain biking trails are on public land. For further information on mountain biking in state forests, contact the state DNR's **Forest Management Division, Recreation and Trails Section** at ☎ 517-373-4175. For information on mountain biking in state parks, contact the DNR's **Parks and Recreation Division** at ☎ 517-373-1270. In addition, DNR district offices provide maps and information on specific trails contained within their boundaries.

Cycling

Michigan's northern Lower Peninsula provides cyclists with a variety of options, ranging from multi-day treks to afternoon affairs. These journeys include forays on everything from automobile-cluttered roadways to shady bike paths to dusty backcountry roads, and the more ambitious routes often include some hybrid of all three types.

For true cycling adventurers, Michigan's scenic coastline provides eye-popping inspiration if you want to disappear on your bike for three or four days (or even longer). Both the eastern and western shorelines of the Lower Peninsula's northern reaches are studded with attractive routes and well-maintained state parks (as well as civilized lodging if you are dispirited by inclement weather or your legs crave the nearest hot tub). Blessed with such assets, shoreline-hugging multi-day routes of enduring popularity have emerged on both sides of the state (Frankfort to Mackinac City and Alpena to Cheboygan are favorites).

Great single-day treks are plentiful as well. Shaped by natural attractions (lakes, meadows, forests, shoreline dunes, etc.), the allure of many of the region's small villages and towns, the routes of organized tours and races, and the ever-thickening grid of roadways that lace the state, these routes are among Michigan's most scenic and popular, and well worth seeking out. In addition, a number of these treks begin and end at state parks, providing cyclists with the opportunity to infuse a dose of camping into their excursions. But while the circuits detailed below are a great way to sample northern Michigan's many charms, you might ponder the benefits of leaving the maps behind on an autumn weekend and charting your own course through the region's cottage-speckled towns and rolling countryside.

Alpena-Long Lake Tour

Bicyclists seeking quiet roadways and pleasing surroundings would do well to chart a course for northeast Michigan's Thunder Bay area. One of the region's finest tours flows right out of Alpena, passing by the Long Lake shoreline and through a mix of open fields and woodlands before returning to town.

The first few miles of this 35-mile circuit are not the most peaceful of the trip, and require you to keep to the shoulder of northbound US-23 until reaching Long Lake Road. Once you reach the shores of Long Lake, however, the ride assumes a decidedly more relaxed feel. Turn left on Long Lake Road and follow for eight miles, then turn south on Bolton Road. Bolton will eventually merge into Long Rapids Road, which will take you back into Alpena.

Big Mac Shoreline Tour

This long-time favorite goes along Lake Michigan's sparkling shoreline and through acres of thriving farmland. One of northern Michigan's less demanding routes, the Big Mac loop traverses relatively flat terrain for much of its length. Many bicyclists choose to extend the ride with a jaunt down Wilderness Park Drive to Big Stone Bay, the crown jewel of the state's beautiful **Wilderness State Park** (the tour is about 29 miles, including the Wilderness State Park option).

To begin the Big Mac loop, take Central St. (which becomes Country Road 81) west out of Mackinac City and follow to Gill Road (note that CR-81 is also known as Cecil Bay Road after Wilderness Park Drive). Turn east on Gill and take to M-108 north, which will bring you back into town.

Crystal-Platte Loop

This Benzie County favorite takes you around both Crystal and Platte Lakes, two gems separated from Lake Michigan by an immense ridge of dune and woodland. This undemanding loop past pretty shorelines and picturesque cottages is about 40 miles long.

The loop can be picked up at various spots along the route, but the ideal location to begin and end the ride is at the Platte River Campground, a large, modern campground in Sleeping Bear Dunes National Lakeshore. Cyclists embarking from there take M-22 north to CR-706 east to M-31 south. The road will take you into Benzonia, where you can pick up M-115 westbound. M-115 meets up with M-22 near Frankfort, and from there you can peddle north back up to the campground. All in all, a very nice excursion, especially if busy summer weekends are avoided.

Harbor Springs Loop

This tough but rewarding Emmet County circuit takes you through some of Michigan's most spectacular fall foliage. More than half of the 38-mile circuit, which can be launched from either Cross Village or Harbor Springs, runs along M-119. The road attracts relatively little traffic, however, even during the summer season, and it slices through some of the prettiest woods in all of Michigan. Indeed, the array of hardwoods that line the road provides a seemingly endless shade canopy. The many thigh-busting ascents that mark this route lead some riders to shorten the circuit by cutting across Robinson or Stutsmanville Roads. These roads bisect M-119 and CR-77 (State Road), the inland road that connects Cross Village and Harbor Springs.

Hart-Montague Bicycle Trail

This 22-mile asphalt pathway marks the first triumph of the Rails-to-Trails Conservancy in Michigan. Years ago the trail, which runs from Hart to Montague, rumbled with the roar of Chesapeake and Ohio locomotives, and the presence of old train depots along its length still conjure up echoes of those bygone days. Today, it's a favorite of west Michigan cyclists. The winding pathway, which begins in Hart's John Gurney Park and leads past open meadows, gurgling streams, and scenic woodlands, is a growing favorite with families, drawn both by its setting and its flat, wide surface.

Leelanau Lakeshore Loop

This scenic tour follows the route laid out by an annual charitable event. The 33-mile tour begins at Sugar Loaf Resort (six miles north of Cedar, off M-22) and covers a loop that offers a little bit of everything. The gently rolling route skirts the Sleeping Bear Dunes National Lakeshore, trundles through the village of Glen Arbor, and follows the southern shoreline of Glen Lake before returning to the resort. It's an easy one to follow: take M-22 west for 12 miles, then take M-109 south to CR-616 east; follow to CR-669, and turn north until you return to Sugar Loaf Mountain Rd.

Old Mission Peninsula

A favorite of Traverse City-area bicyclists, the Old Mission Peninsula loop follows the shoreline of the narrow peninsula's entire length. The peninsula, which divides Grand Traverse Bay into its eastern and western sections, is festooned with vast cherry orchards, wineries, and other alluring attractions (from fruit mar-

Northern Lower Michigan

kets to the lighthouse that adorns the peninsula's northern tip) sure to draw bicyclists who wish to make a full day of it.

The main cycling loop is about 40 miles long, and while reminders of civilization are never far off (the circuit includes several miles on the wide shoulder of M-37, a busy roadway during the summer), the undemanding terrain, brisk breeze, and great shoreline views make it a perennial hot spot. Most cyclists start from Bryant Park, at the southwest base of the peninsula, but those interested in shorter trips can jump on the loop from any number of places further in.

Torch Lake Circuit

This loop around Antrim County's Torch Lake is one of the most aesthetically pleasing in the entire state. Torch Lake is a real beauty, a slender lake well-known for its exceptionally clear waters and attractive shoreline. The circuit follows Torch's shores for most of its length, departing only for a brief dalliance with Elk Lake for a few miles of the loop's southwestern portion. The route passes through a couple of quaint small towns on the way as well, providing an opportunity to replenish with ice cream, pop, or even a brew or two. The circuit begins and ends just outside of Eastport, at Barnes County Park. The park is off US-31, at the lake's northern tip.

Most of the circuits listed above can be easily shortened or lengthened in accordance with your appetite for sightseeing and the level of comfort your cycling shorts provide. Of course, many other areas of northern Michigan offer great bicycling as well. The areas surrounding **Frankfort, Petoskey, Gaylord**, and **Tawas**, among others, offer plenty of options for cyclists. Organized rides of all shapes and sizes have proliferated in recent years. Contact local chambers of commerce or regional bicycling clubs for additional information.

To Find Out More

For additional information, contact the **Michigan Department of Natural Resources' Parks Division** at ☎ 517-373-1270. Bicycles are also allowed on many trails in the Michigan's state and national forests. For information on **state forest trails**, contact the Michigan Department of Natural Resources, Forest Management Division, PO Box 30028, Lansing, MI 48909, ☎ 517-373-1275; contact individual forest service offices for information on national forest trails. For information on the **Rails-to-Trails Conservancy**, contact the organization's Michigan chapter at PO Box 23032, Lansing, MI 48909, ☎ 517-393-6022. Finally, **Michigan Bicycle Touring, Inc.** offers a series of multi-day touring packages for riders; contact them at 3512 Red School Road, Kingsley, MI 49649, ☎ 616-263-5885 (www.bikembt.com).

On Water

Canoeing & Kayaking

The northern half of Lower Michigan houses some of the state's most pristine and well-loved rivers, from the "Mighty Manistee" to the "Awesome Au Sable." These rivers, while not as fierce as some in the Upper Peninsula, nonetheless possess a wild quality that attracts paddlers at all levels of ability.

> **✳ TIP** *Several Michigan rivers have been besieged in recent years with swarms of canoers, some distressingly ignorant of both basic paddling maneuvers and basic river etiquette. This has caused friction between those who are on the rivers to party and those who came there to fish or paddle in peace. If you are in the latter camp, you might want to consider making a mid-week or off-season trip.*

Most Michigan rivers do still offer rewarding canoeing and kayaking, even on summer weekends. This is especially true of the Lower Peninsula's northern parts. Descriptions of some of the region's finest rivers can be found in the northern Lower Michigan sections devoted to specific regional attractions. The essay on Huron National Forest, for example, covers both the Au Sable and the Au Sable South Branch, while the essay on Manistee National

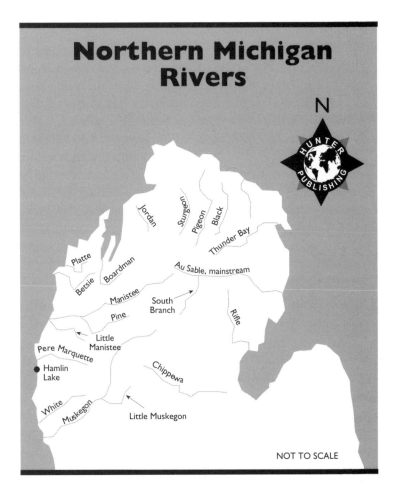

Forest provides canoeing and kayaking information on the Manistee, the Little Manistee, the Pere Marquette, the Pine, and the White. Finally, coverage of the Pigeon River Country State Forest includes information on paddling the Black and Pigeon rivers. But there are lots of quality paddling options in other parts of northern Michigan, too. Here's a rundown of some of the best:

Betsie River (Class I-II)

This river offers a variety of great paddling options, from afternoon jaunts to weekend trips. For kayakers and canoers interested in a leisurely paddle through a serene landscape fairly bursting with wildlife, the **Grass Lake Marsh** area is an ideal destination. The marsh holds a wide assortment of wildlife – beaver, mink, river otter, black bear, deer, waterfowl, and birds, including a thriving bald eagle contingent. Paddlers can count on a slow current in the Betsie's upper reaches. It quickens west of Wallin Road Bridge, though, transforming itself into a quick, twisting river that will provide hours of enjoyment for capable paddlers. Those who take the river its entire 45-mile length to Lake Michigan (take out in Elberta at the M-22 Bridge) will find their campground options limited, but the Betsie runs through a fair amount of state land, with camping opportunities for overnighters. Most visitors equipped with their own kayaks or canoes start from **Grass Lake State Forest Campground**, on Grass Lake outside of Thompsonville. Liveries providing services on the Betsie include **Alvina's Canoe and Boat Livery (☎ 616-276-9514)** and **Vacation Trailer Park (☎ 616-882-5101)**.

Boardman River (Class I-II)

A long-time favorite of knowledgeable Michigan paddlers, the Boardman originates in Kalkaska County in two branches before uniting in Grand Traverse County. From there it ambles placidly through a valley of muscular hillsides and vibrant woodlands on its way to Grand Traverse Bay. The river's upper sections are its most remote, despite the presence of anglers; its shoreline has become a thicket of cottages in its middle reaches. Its last few miles have become popular with weekend tubing enthusiasts. This latter area, though, also holds the river's most challenging water. Traverse-area kayakers swarm to the water below Beitner Bridge, a narrow channel festooned with small boulders that churn up good whitewater. The river has a few portages (several dams and the odd fallen tree in its upper stretches) along its length, but nothing too daunting. Paddlers can disembark at Boardman Lake or any number of places further upriver.

Canoeists and kayakers en route to the Boardman should begin their journey in Grand Traverse County. While the shores of the river's northern and southern branches have ample camping options, these stretches are more suitable for anglers than canoers (indeed, the Boardman is renowned for its trout fishing). Better to put in further down at Forks Campground or Scheck's Place, two primitive camping sites. From there paddlers can enjoy about 25 miles of good water. Both spots can be reached by taking M-37 north to its juncture with US-31. Where the two highways meet, take Beitner Road east to River Road. Turn right (south) and follow the road – which turns into Brown Bridge Road – for a dozen miles or so.

Chippewa River (Class I-II)

This long, shallow tributary of the Tittabawassee River cuts across Lower Michigan's midsection, winding all the way from its beginnings in Clare County to the Saginaw Valley. For canoers, the river begins in earnest south of Barryton, in Mecosta County. From there it moves at a moderate pace across low country woodlands and farm country, alternating between deep stretches and shallow bottom-scrapers, especially during dry years. Several spots on the river should be portaged by most paddlers; a fast chute at Drew Dam, for instance, is apt to be big trouble for non-experts. The river has multiple access points along its length, but camping options are limited. This leads many river travelers to take day-long bites out of the river rather than attempt overnight or weekend trips. Canoe liveries offering services on the Chippewa include **Buckley's Mountainside Canoes** (☎ 517-772-5437), **Chippewa River Outfitters** (☎ 517-772-5474), and **Chippewa Valley Canoe Livery** (☎ 800-686-2447).

Hamlin Lake (Class I)

This lake, which can be found in the hugely popular **Ludington State Park**, is home to the only marked canoe trail in the entire state park system. The three-mile route goes through a relatively easy mix of ponds and marshes that support a great variety of wildlife. The trail system features five portages, but these are short and easy and should not deter anyone from spending an afternoon on its placid waters. The beginning and ending stages of the trail – which necessitate traveling on open water – can get dicey on windy days, but the bulk of the trail winds through protected waters. Canoe rentals are available through the park. ☎ 616-843-2193.

Jordan River (Class I-II)

This small but spirited river cuts through one of Michigan's most gorgeous valleys. The river's moderate pace and remote setting make it a prime destination in any season for afternoon paddlers, but it is during the fall, when winter's distant footfalls begin to be heard, that the stream becomes truly stunning. The maple, aspen, and birch forests that line its banks flame up in a riot of colors, and the river's surface glows with reflected color on clear autumn afternoons. Paddlers generally put in at Graves Crossing Road, which lies just off M-66, about 18 miles north of Mancelona (those who put in further up can expect miserable encounters with fallen trees and other obstacles). The three-to-four-hour trip concludes at M-32's Webster Bridge, just before the river ends in Lake Charlevoix. Area canoe liveries include **Swiss Hideaway** (☎ 616-536-2341) and **Jordan Valley Outfitters** (☎ 616-536-0006).

Muskegon River (Class I-II)

The brawny Muskegon offers something for everyone along its 227-mile length. Much of the big river is suitable for families, but a stretch outside of Big Rapids can conjure up Class II-III conditions during high water periods (this makes the Big Rapids area an alluring one for kayakers). In addition, reservoirs behind the river's infrequent dams attract large numbers of boaters and can get very choppy, and the portages around a couple of those dams are a pain. On the whole, though, the Muskegon is a mild-mannered stream. Blessed with good access sites, a variety of campgrounds, and miles of placid countryside, it is a nice river for overnight trips.

Not surprisingly, the river undergoes a gradual transformation as it runs from its Houghton Lake-area headwaters to its mouth on Muskegon Lake. The Muskegon's upper reaches are shallow (one to five feet) and 30-75 feet wide, but as the miles pass the river widens (to more than 200 feet in places) and deepens (two to eight feet, with deeper pools). Whereas the dimensions of the river change considerably, the river's shoreline does not. The stream offers a consistently pleasing blend of woodlands and fields as it meanders through the state's midsection. Liveries offering serv-

Northern Lower Michigan

ices to Muskegon River paddlers include **Duggan's Canoe Livery** (☎ 517-539-1798), **Muskegon River Camp and Canoe** (☎ 616-734-3808), **Old Log Resort** (☎ 616-743-2775), **Sawmill Tube and Canoe Livery** (☎ 616-796-6408), **Vic's Canoes** (☎ 616-834-5494), and **White Birch Canoe Livery** (☎ 616-328-4547).

Platte River (Class I)

Although Benzie County's Platte River is 30 miles long, only the latter half is really suitable for canoeing; its upper reaches, while scenic, are brushy and extremely shallow. Conditions improve past the US-31 Bridge at Veteran's Memorial Campground (though canoes carrying a lot of weight will still bottom out in some areas), and it is here that most paddlers begin their journey down the Platte. The river is clear and quick and winds through rolling forestland for the next 10 miles or so, but watch out for anglers; this stretch of river is a hotbed of trout fishing activity. After swinging through Platte Lake, the river passes under the M-22 Bridge – a popular access point for afternoon canoers – on its way to Lake Michigan, passing dunes, woodlands, and cottages along the way. Canoe rentals for the Platte are available through **Riverside Canoes** (☎ 616-325-5622).

Rifle River (Class I-II)

This 60-mile river is one of eastern Michigan's premier canoeing attractions. Bracketed by pretty woodlands for much of its length, the Rifle offers clear water, a moderate current, and a couple of spicy little runs. In addition, campsites along a good portion of its length make it a natural for extended trips. For those planning a multi-day trip, the upper river is accessible at several points, including Sage Lake Road east of M-33 (take M-33 south out of Rose City), Ballard Bridge (take Peters Road east from M-33) and Ladd's Landing (take Greenwood Road east off of M-33; turn north on Rifle River Trail to the Landing). Canoe liveries providing services on the Rifle are numerous and include **Cedar Springs Campground** (☎ 800-986-4646), **Riverbend Canoe Rental** (☎ 517-653-2576), **River View Campground and Canoe Livery** (☎ 517-654-2447), **Russell Canoes** (☎ 517-653-2644), **Troll Landing Canoe Livery** (☎ 517-345-7260), and **White's Canoe Livery** (☎ 517-654-2654).

Anglers enjoy a clear autumn day on the Sturgeon River (Travel Michigan).

Sturgeon River (Class I-II)

This Cheboygan County river offers one of the finest paddling experiences in the entire Lower Peninsula. Threading its way through stately public forestlands for much of its length, the fast-paced Sturgeon hits you with sharp turns, light rapids, sweepers and other obstructions at an exhilarating pace. None of this stuff will engender panic in experienced canoers or kayakers, but beginners will likely find themselves retrieving their gear further downstream (in other words, novices should find another stream on which to hone their skills). Good campsites are plentiful along its shores, too. Put in at the bridge on Trowbridge Road south of Wolverine or in the town itself, at Wolverine Park. Good take-out spots can be found at Fisher Woods Road or on the left shoreline of Burt Lake, in Burt Lake State Park. Canoe liveries providing services for the Sturgeon include **Tomahawk Trails Canoe Livery** (☎ 616-238-8181) and **Sturgeon & Pigeon River Outfitters** (☎ 616-238-8703).

Thunder Bay River (Class I)

The Thunder Bay River offers a mellow glide through a mixed hardwood forest for much of its 57-mile length before emptying into Lake Huron. High-water periods could prove troublesome for novice paddlers, but the river usually reflects a very laid-back attitude. A good portion passes through public land, making overnight excursions possible, but high riverbanks and thick brush do limit your options. You can put in at a couple of different spots in the Atlanta area, including the Atlanta Dam or Eichorn Bridge (on McMurphy Road, south of M-32), while afternoon canoers usually hop in at the M-65 Bridge, just south of Long Rapids.

The last dozen or so miles of the river are a drag, with a couple of unpleasant portages and heavy shoreline development; you should consider taking out at Orchard Bridge (north of M-32 on Herron Road).

Other Options

Kayaking opportunities are plentiful along the northern Lower Peninsula's **Great Lakes shorelines** as well. On the western side of the state, small bays **(Suttons Bay, Omena Bay, Northport Bay)** and sheltered areas along both the east and west arms of **Grand Traverse Bay** draw kayakers, as do the protected waters of **Little Traverse Bay**. **Beaver Island** has attracted growing numbers of kayakers in recent years as well. Lower Michigan's northeastern shoreline includes **Thunder Bay** and **Presque Isle County's North Bay, Presque Isle Harbor**, and **Tawas Bay**, all of which offer sheltered waters for kayakers. The shallow Tawas Bay area is a particularly good locale for novice kayakers to learn the ropes.

Fishing

So many fishing spots, so little time. This lament – a common one among northern Michigan fishermen – underscores the region's reputation for terrific fishing. Blessed with the Great Lakes, numerous inland lakes and reservoirs, and an abundance of top-notch trout streams, Michigan's northern Lower Peninsula attracts droves of anglers every year.

Rivers

Several of northern Michigan's rivers rank among the best in the entire country for fishing. Indeed, legendary rivers such as the Pere Marquette, the Au Sable, and the Muskegon beckon anglers from all over the Midwest and beyond. Over on the west side of the state, the shorelines of major streams like the Pere Marquette (trout, chinook and coho salmon, northern pike), Muskegon (trout, walleye, smallmouth bass, northern pike), **Baldwin** (trout and chinook salmon), **White** (trout, smallmouth bass, northern pike, walleye, and panfish), **Betsie** (trout, salmon, and walleye), **Pine** (brown, brook, and rainbow trout), **Platte** (trout and coho salmon), **Little Manistee** (trout, walleye, panfish, and northern pike), and **Manistee** (trout, walleye, bass, and chinook salmon) all bristle with

Michigan offers some of the best fishing in the country (Travel Michigan).

flyfishermen and spincasters during fishing season. Countless smaller creeks and streams in the area, many of them tributaries of the region's big rivers, also get a lot of attention.

The Lower Peninsula's northernmost ramparts receive plenty of fishing action as well, as anglers flock to the **Black** (trout, muskie, northern pike, and walleye), **Pigeon** (trout and walleye), **Ocqueoc** (trout), and **Bear** (trout and salmon) rivers, among others.

Over on the northeastern side of the state, any discussion of fishing streams inevitably begins with the **Au Sable**, the storied river that has drawn trout and salmon fishermen to its shores for generations. Other streams are noteworthy, too, however (and less crowded). These include the **Thunder Bay** (trout, walleye, northern pike, and panfish), **Rifle** (trout, chinook salmon, walleye, smallmouth bass, and panfish), and **Tobacco** (brown and brook trout) rivers.

Northern Lower Michigan

Inland Lakes

Northern Michigan holds many of the state's most highly prized inland fishing lakes. Top attractions include **Houghton Lake** (the state's largest inland lake and a major source of northern pike, bluegills, walleye, and bass), **Mitchell Lake** (walleye, bluegill, perch), **Portage Lake** (salmon, northern pike, and smallmouth bass), **Big Platte Lake** (panfish, walleye, northern pike, steelhead), **Long Lake** (smallmouth bass, walleye), **Elk Lake** (perch, bass, lake trout), **Black Lake** (sturgeon, northern pike, yellow perch, walleye), **Mullett Lake** (sturgeon, northern pike, walleye), and **Burt Lake** (walleye, perch, bass, northern pike, muskellunge, trout). Other notable fishing lakes in northern Lower Michigan include **Manistee Lake**, **Crystal Lake**, **Otsego Lake**, **Fletcher Pond**, **Torch Lake**, **Lake Charlevoix**, and **Skegemog Lake**.

Ice Fishing

During the wintertime, hundreds of little ice fishing shanties spring up on area lakes and ponds. Top winter fishing destinations in northern Lower Michigan include **Muskegon Lake, Crystal Lake, Crooked Lake, Bear Lake, Long Lake, Higgins Lake, Hamlin Lake, Mitchell Lake, Fletcher Pond, Mullett Lake, Lake Charlevoix**, and **Lake Cadillac** (home of Tip-Up Town, USA – a major ice fishing/snowmobiling festival).

Great Lakes

Trout and salmon (especially chinook) fishing in **Lake Huron** has been superb in the mid-1990s, although the state DNR expects a drop in brown trout fishing over the next few years. Walleye fishing in the lake is also thriving, bolstered by the presence of a healthy fishery in Saginaw Bay. Over in **Lake Michigan** anglers have in recent years enjoyed fishing reminiscent of the lake's tremendous mid-1980s period. The lake supports large populations of coho and king salmon, steelhead, brown trout, lake trout, walleye, and other popular fish, and those fisheries are expected to remain steady or improve over the next couple of years.

Scuba Diving

Straits of Mackinac Underwater Preserve

The preserve lies between Michigan's Lower and Upper Peninsulas under the shadow of the state's massive Mackinac Bridge. The preserve, which is 148 square miles in size, contains the remains of nine major wrecks, several of which offer exciting dives.

Most of the vessels lie in relatively deep water and the region's limited visibility and sometimes treacherous currents have the potential to wreak havoc on inexperienced underwater explorers. Divers with little experience should, at the very least, secure knowledgeable diving companions before venturing into the Straits Preserve's more perilous realms.

Boat operators need to stay alert when taking diving parties out into the preserve. A shipping channel runs through the area, and the Straits of Mackinac are also utilized by large numbers of recreational boaters and passenger ferries. But the region's popularity with tourists during the summer season does have its upside: there is a wide selection of marinas and boat launch facilities. **St. Ignace, Mackinac Island, Cheboygan**, and **Mackinaw City** all have marinas that offer full transient accommodations, while streamlined services can be found at the marina at **Bois Blanc Island**. Boaters should keep in mind that the region's popularity has created a big demand for slips; call ahead for reservations. Boat launches can be found in **Mackinaw City, St. Ignace, Presque Isle**, and both **Sturgeon Bay** (on the state's west side) and **Hammond Bay** (on the east side).

Shipwrecks

The headliner among the shipwrecks that dot the bottom of the Straits Preserve is the *Cedarville*, a 588-foot freighter that sank in 1965 after colliding with another vessel in a fog bank. Ten of the *Cedarville*'s 35 crew members drowned as its captain scrambled to evacuate the fast-sinking ship (the vessel's cargo of limestone

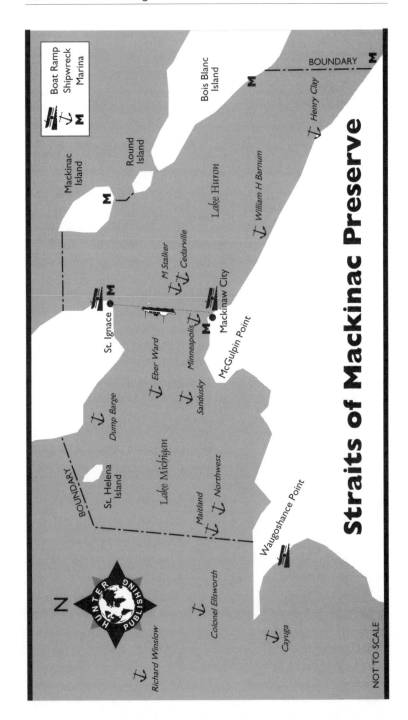

Straits of Mackinac Preserve

accelerated its descent into the Straits' murky depths). Today, the ship lies on its side in more than 100 feet of water, though its hull is less than 40 feet from the surface. The superstructure and cabins can be accessed at about 70 feet, but penetration should be undertaken only by experienced divers with adequate equipment for such exploration. The ship lies approximately 2½ miles east of Mackinaw City, less than a mile south of the **M. Stalker**, a 19th-century schooner that also attracts divers unfazed by its proximity to the shipping channel. The 135-foot vessel lies in about 90 feet of water. As is the case with most other wreck dive sites within the preserve, both the *Cedarville* and the *M. Stalker* are marked by mooring buoys that include posted summaries of the vessels' histories.

Another big preserve attraction is the wreck of the **William H. Barnum**, a 218-foot wooden steamer that sank in Lake Huron in 1894. The vessel lies in about 75 feet of water and is upright and largely intact, though its steam engine, boilers, and props are all exposed in the stern. A favorite of experienced divers, the *Barnum* lies a mile off the Lower Peninsula's north coast near the small village of Freedom.

The 110-foot **Sandusky** is one of the older attractions for divers in the Great Lakes. The sailing vessel was struck down by a vicious storm more than 140 years ago, and it is the only wreck in the preserve with a carved figurehead. This figurehead, of a ram's head, has had a troubled history in recent years. Back in the late 1980s, concerns about vandals led members of the Michigan diving community to add it to the collection of South Haven's Lake Michigan Maritime Museum and replace the original with a carved replica. The *Sandusky* sits upright in about 90 feet of water. The interior of the ship, which has been well-preserved by the Straits' frigid waters, can be explored by veteran divers.

Other wrecks within the preserve include the **Northwest**, the **Maitland**, the **C.H. Johnson**, the **Eber Ward**, the **St. Andrew**, the **J.H. Outhwaite**, the **Albermarle**, and the **Minneapolis**. The latter is a particularly treacherous dive, because of both the depth at which the 226-foot steamer lies (125 feet) and the heavy currents that swirl around its resting place; dives to the *Minneapolis* should only be undertaken by experienced divers.

Northern Lower Michigan

Other Sites

The Straits Preserve also contains attractions that can be reached from shore. The waters of **St. Ignace Harbor** contain dock ruins, discarded nautical equipment, and a variety of other items at both its northern and southern ends. The primary harbor dive site off the bay's northern shores lies at the end of Hazelton Street, while the major shore-access site along its southern length is off State Street, in a local park.

 If exploring the harbor, stay out of the ferry lanes and display a diver-down flag.

Finally, an unusual rock formation just a few hundred yards east of Mackinac Island has emerged as a popular dive site in recent years. The area around this formation, dubbed the "**Rock Maze**," houses large schools of fish, but boaters should approach with caution, for rocky shoals dot the vicinity.

Thunder Bay Underwater Preserve

In addition to the Straits of Mackinac Underwater Preserve, the waters off the Lower Peninsula's northern shorelines house two other major bottomland preserves. The 288-square-mile Thunder Bay Underwater Preserve, off the shores of Alpena, contains a number of wrecks that are ideal for scuba diving, including the *Nordmeer*, the *Lucinda Van Valkenburg*, the *Montana*, and the *Grecian*. See page 146.

Manitou Passage State Underwater Preserve

The other major Great Lakes scuba diving mecca in northern Michigan lies between North and South Manitou Islands and the sprawling sands of the Sleeping Bear Dunes National Lakeshore. The preserve includes several notable shipwrecks, including the *Francisco Morazan*, the *Congress*, and the *Three Brothers* (the remains of the latter were discovered in 1996). For additional information on the Manitou Passage Preserve, check out the section on Sleeping Bear Dunes, page 129. Finally, **Grand Traverse Bay** is a popular destination for area divers.

Inland Lakes

Several inland lakes in the northern Lower Peninsula also attract divers. These include **Higgins Lake, Hart Lake**, and **Hardy Pond**.

To Find Out More

To find out more about the Straits of Mackinac Underwater Preserve, contact the **St. Ignace Chamber of Commerce** at 560 N. State St., St. Ignace, MI 49781, ☎ 800-338-6660. For information on all the Michigan underwater preserves, contact the **Michigan Underwater Preserve Council** at 560 N. State St., St. Ignace, MI 49781.

Outfits offering charter services in the Straits Preserve include the **Macomb Scuba Center** at 13465 E. 12 Mile, Warren, MI 48093, ☎ 810-558-9922. The center also maintains offices with limited hours in St. Ignace; contact the **Straits Scuba Center**, 587 N. State St., St. Ignace, MI 49781, ☎ 906-643-7009. For diving in Grand Traverse Bay, contact **Scuba North** at 13380 W. Bay Shore Drive, Traverse City, MI 49684, ☎ 616-947-2520.

Boating & Sailing

A smorgasbord of options await recreational boaters in northern Lower Michigan. Whether voyaging on the Great Lakes or cruising through more protected waterways, both pristine wilderness and congenial city lights lie within the grasp of Michigan boaters. Of course, many cruising itineraries seek a balance between the two, alternating dinners at harbor-area pubs with evening meals on remote moonlit bays. Whatever your cruising tastes, northern Michigan can meet your needs.

Lake Michigan Cruising

The vast waters of Lake Michigan attract a wide variety of recreational boaters, from charter fishing boats drawn by the huge fish that roam its depths to sailboats seeking to take advantage of its often potent afternoon breezes. The lake's size and grandeur allow boaters to prowl some stretches of its shoreline in solitude for

Sailboats anchored in the waters of Harbor Springs (Randall McCune).

hours at a time, alone but for the gulls wheeling overhead and the distant silhouette of an occasional freighter.

This solitude is most likely to be attained off Michigan's central shoreline (though Great Lakes fishing is big through this area). Whereas the southern and northern shorelines of Michigan's Lower Peninsula are dotted with popular cruising destinations, the state's central coastline has relatively few harbors. Villages and towns equipped with recreational harbors along this stretch of the lake include **Pentwater**, a pretty resort village, and **Ludington**, an appealing little town that uses Pere Marquette Lake for its harbor. Boaters working their way up the coastline, which features both high bluffs and stretches of sand dunes, can also find recreational harbors in **Manistee, Arcadia**, and **Frankfort**. Boat traffic gets considerably heavier from here on out for cruisers and sailboats working their way northward to the Leelanau Peninsula/Grand Traverse Bay regions.

Northwest Michigan is a mecca for Great Lakes boaters. Protected waters (Grand Traverse Bay, Little Traverse Bay, Lake Charlevoix), clusters of summer cottages, and a heavy sprinkling of tourist-friendly towns and villages all combine to make the region immensely popular with summer vacationers. The area's many harbors, marinas, and public boat launch sites make it easy for operators of sailboats, cabin cruisers, and fishing boats alike to sample its varied attractions. Boaters cruising up and around the tip of the **Leelanau Peninsula** can find harbors in the villages of **Leland, Northport**, and **Suttons Bay**. At the base of the West Arm of Grand Traverse Bay lies **Traverse City**, the unofficial capital of northern Michigan. Marinas and recreational harbors can be found all along the shores of Traverse City and the Old Mission Peninsula, the long spear of land that separates Grand Traverse Bay into its two arms. The next major destination for boaters working their way up to the top of the mitten is **Charlevoix**, a resort community nestled between Lake Michigan, Round Lake (site of its main harbor), and Lake Charlevoix. Nearby **Petoskey** and **Harbor Springs** maintain lovely harbors as well, and are perennially among the hottest destinations for boaters who like to water down their nautical adventures with a splash of shopping or fine dining.

These mainland ports get the lion's share of attention on Lake Michigan, but boaters with an appetite for more adventurous excursions also have the option of setting course for one or more of the lake's rugged islands. **Beaver Island**, which lies 30 miles off the Michigan mainland, is the most popular of these. It is the largest of a cluster of islands commonly known as the Beaver archipelago. Beaver Island's one town is St. James, a small village that features restaurants, antique shops, and other markings of civilization. It also maintains a harbor that fills up on summer weekends, but boaters unable to find room at the dock have the option of anchoring off the harbor's northern end. Travelers who weary of the genial but crowded harbor atmosphere at St. James can always go off and explore one or more of Beaver's sister islands. Three moderately sized islands – **High, Garden**, and **Hog** – sit off Beaver's northern shores, each of them equipped with coves that can assume idyllic qualities on warm summer evenings.

Boaters should exercise caution when exploring any of these outlying islands, however, because of the presence of extensive reefs and the varying levels of protection that each island provides from inclement weather (charters offering

exploration of the outer islands are available in St. James). Indeed, up-to-date charts are essential when piloting through the archipelago.

North and South Manitou Islands, which lie further down the coastline, are also popular with boaters. For additional information on these islands, see the section on Sleeping Bear Dunes National Lakeshore, page 129.

Lake Huron Cruising

Many boaters regard the Mackinac Bridge, the massive thoroughfare that straddles the Straits of Mackinac, connecting Michigan's Upper and Lower Peninsulas, as the dividing line between Lake Michigan and Lake Huron. This abrupt line of demarcation, while somewhat arbitrary, is fitting in this case, for the cruising experiences offered by the two lakes are different. A great number of the vessels that ply Lake Michigan's waters are engaged in relatively short journeys, bound for salmon hot spots or popular resort communities. Those that rove across Huron's shining surface, though, are often midway through lengthy summer voyages, drawn by the lake's wilderness beauty and variety. The most fabled of Huron's wilderness treasures lie in **Georgian Bay** and the **North Channel**, both of which belong to Ontario. In fact, those areas are among the top cruising grounds in the entire world, for they offer a stunning blend of wilderness anchorages and delightful harbors. But Michigan's shoreline has considerable charms as well, and many long-distance cruisers who traverse Huron's waters spend significant time working their way up or down the state's northeastern coast.

The northernmost of Lake Huron's Michigan harbors actually lies in the Straits of Mackinac, under the shadow of the mighty bridge. This harbor serves as a gateway to **Mackinaw City's** many tourist attractions. Fifteen miles further down the coastline lies Cheboygan, the hub of a great deal of Great Lakes cruising. A popular destination in its own right, **Cheboygan** is also a common launching point for recreational boaters setting forth for Mackinac Island, Bois Blanc Island, and Les Cheneaux Islands. In addition, it serves as a gateway to both the Straits of Mackinac and the Inland Waterway.

The **Inland Waterway** is a remarkable chain of interconnected lakes and rivers that extends 36 miles in from Cheboygan. This waterway – Cheboygan River to Mullett Lake to Indian River to Burt Lake to Crooked River to Crooked Lake – is tremendously popular with Michigan boaters. Festooned with restaurants, beaches, full-service marinas, and campgrounds (both private and state-operated), the area hosts all manner of recreational vessels, including sailboats, houseboats, power boats, and waverunners. Indeed, the character of the waterway varies with the area. Much of the waterway shoreline has been built up with summer cottages and tourist businesses, and traffic in some areas can get quite heavy. But boaters in search of quieter surroundings can still find coves suitable for anchorage, and mornings on the waterway still belong to anglers.

Boaters working their way south from Cheboygan can find recreational harbors at **Hammond Bay** and **Rogers City** and glimpses of shoreline cottages, but a good deal of this northeastern stretch features undeveloped shoreline, a pleasing mix of deep woodlands and sandy beaches. Popular anchorages in this area include **Presque Isle Harbor** (keep to the south side of the bay), **False Presque Isle** (which offers fine protection from prevailing winds), and the area between **Thunder Bay Island** and **Sugar Island**. Many boaters, however, prefer to work their way all the way down to **Alpena**. Located in Thunder Bay, Alpena is the primary port destination on Michigan's northeastern shores.

 Boat operators should be aware of the area's many shoals and its dearth of protected anchorages.

South of Alpena, ports can be found in **Harrisville, Oscoda**, and **East Tawas**. The latter harbor attracts large numbers of cruising boats and features multiple docking options. The town itself offers a variety of entertainment, including an array of restaurants and shops. South of East Tawas lies Michigan's "Thumb" area; for a description of cruising opportunities in this region, see page 63.

Inland Lakes

In addition to Great Lakes cruising, Michigan boating enthusiasts have a mind-boggling array of inland lakes to explore and enjoy. **Houghton Lake, Torch Lake, Lake Charlevoix, Higgins Lake**, and **Hubbard Lake** are among the largest and most popular destinations, but countless smaller lakes offer fine boating opportunities as well.

To Find Out More

For additional information on Michigan boating, contact the **Michigan Department of Natural Resources**, Recreation Division, PO Box 30257, Lansing, MI 48909, ☎ 517-335-4837.

On Snow

Cross-Country Skiing

Cross-country skiing enthusiasts in northern Michigan have a terrific array of options. Blessed with plentiful snow, gorgeous woodlands, and miles of quiet trails, the Lower Peninsula's northern reaches are a true winter wonderland for skiers. Following is a list of some of the region's most popular trails.

Black Mountain Pathway

This relatively new option (it opened in the early 1990s) has been an immense hit with area skiers. Situated on a heavily wooded ridgeline looking over Lake Huron's steel-grey waters, the Black Mountain Pathway offers both beautiful scenery and a smorgasbord of loops to please everyone from beginners to daredevils. The well-groomed, well-marked system is more than 30 miles long and lies within the larger Black Mountain Recreation Area. The pathway can be accessed from four different trailheads. Inexperienced skiers should keep to the pathway's more southern loops; advanced skiers generally gravitate to the trail's northern section, which features big hills and ample opportunities to tear down the mountain's flanks. The Black Mountain Recreation Area sprawls across Cheboygan and Presque Isle Counties, between Black Lake and the Huron shoreline. To reach it, go north out of Onaway on M-211 for six miles. Turn west on Bonz Beach Highway for half a mile before turning north on CR-489, which takes you into the area.

Boyne Nordican

Boyne ranks as one of the best resorts in the Midwest for cross-country skiing. Its nicely groomed trail system rolls through thick stands of pine forest and offers loops for all skill levels. The 15-mile pathway also includes a section of lighted trail for night skiing. **Boyne USA Resorts** (which includes both Boyne Mountain and Boyne Highlands) is headquartered just west of US-131, near Boyne Falls. ☎ 800-GO-BOYNE for more info.

Cadillac Pathway

This trail, which is groomed for track skiing only, offers half a dozen loops over rolling hillsides festooned with pines and hardwoods. Most of the loops, which range in length from less than two miles to about 10 miles, are suitable for skiers of intermediate skill; beginners may have trouble negotiating some of the pathway's many hills. To reach the trailhead, take US-131 north out of Cadillac to Boon Road. Turn east and go 3½ miles to the parking lot.

Chippewa Hills Pathway

An ideal trail for mid-range skiers, the Chippewa Hills Pathway system contains four interconnected loops that swoop up and around forested hillsides and pretty valleys. Tucked away in northeast Michigan's upper corner, the pathway offers greater opportunities for solitude (especially mid-week) than do some other area trails. To reach the trailhead, take Nicholson Road west from US-23 for 12 miles and follow the signs.

Crystal Mountain Trail

Benzie County's Crystal Mountain Resort maintains 32 kilometers of groomed trails roughly divided into lower (for inexperienced skiers) and upper (for more advanced skiers) portions, and offers night skiing as well. Scenic highlights include good views of the Betsie River Valley. The Crystal cross-country trail system is also adjacent to the 30-acre **Michigan Legacy Art Park**, which features 15 outdoor sculptures and carvings that fit in nicely with the surrounding woods. The resort is off US-115, just west of Thompsonville. ☎ 616-378-2000 for more details.

Forbush Corners

This private touring center offers 24 miles of meticulously groomed trails for various experience levels, and includes access to the Hartwick Pines cross-country trail. Forbush Corners is approximately 10 miles north of Grayling on CR-612, just off I-75.

Garland

The Garland Resort features 25 miles of finely manicured trails for cross-country skiers, from the hilly Wolverine Trail (5.3 miles) to the easy Beavertail (2.8 miles) and Black Squirrel (4.4 miles) loops. It is also home to a rustic lodge of truly mammoth proportions, and some of the finest – and most atmospheric – dining available anywhere. Among the options at the lodge are combination sleigh ride/gourmet dinner evenings that routinely get rave reviews. Garland (☎ 800-968-0042) is five miles south of Lewiston on CR-489.

Hanson Hills Recreational Area Trail

This Grayling-area beauty is attracting growing numbers of experienced Nordic skiers. Hanson Hills boasts more than 20 miles of groomed trails that cut through beautiful woodlands.

 The loops are color-coded to help you find routes that match your abilities, but be warned: even the easier green and blue loops provide significant tests for inexperienced skiers.

The three-mile brown loop and 7½-mile red loop are the toughest in the network. The brown trail features killer climbs and screaming descents that are sure to plant some folks in snowbanks, while the red loop is a constant up-and-down affair through some of the prettiest country around. To reach the Hanson Hills Recreation Area, take I-75 to Exit 251 (Four Mile Road). Go west until you reach Military Road. Turn north on Military until you reach M-93. Turn right on M-93 for about two miles, until you hit a paved road on the right, which will take you into the parking lot.

Loud Creek Trails

This Oscoda County system is a favorite of experienced skiers, but the exceedingly hilly terrain will be a bummer for beginners and even some intermediate-level skiers. The network offers up a steady diet of grinding climbs and pulse-quickening descents on most of its loops, which wind through a pleasing mix of marsh and forest. Several streams thread through the area as well, adding to its charm. The system is just southeast of Mio, off Cauchy Road.

Ludington State Park Trails

This beautiful and spacious park offers nearly 17 miles of groomed trails, mostly over fairly level terrain. The absence of snowmobiles from most of its 5,200 acres adds to the park's appeal for Nordic skiers, but you should note that its scenic trails have no warming shelters and that equipment can not be rented at the park. Ludington State Park is 8½ miles north of Ludington at the end of M-116. ☎ 616-843-2423.

Muncie Lakes Pathway

This is one of northern Michigan's busiest networks, drawing large numbers of skiers from nearby Traverse City. It offers something for everyone, from easy little loops to longer jaunts out to its namesake lakes. Much of the trail system is quite scenic, although scabbed-over clearcut areas mar a couple of sections. The Muncie Lakes system can be reached by any number of different routes; one way is to take Garfield Road south out of Traverse City to Hobbs Highway. Take Hobbs east to Rennie Lake Road, which will lead you to the trailhead parking lot.

North Higgins Lake State Park Trails

Thirteen miles of attractive Nordic skiing trails await in North Higgins Lake State Park. Centered around the park's interpretive center, the trail system goes through peaceful corridors of forestland. It is groomed and tracked and includes segments for all

Northern Lower Michigan

levels of ability. To reach the park, take Exit 244 off I-75 and go west for 4½ miles to the entrance. of the park. ☎ 517-821-6125.

Ocqueoc Bicentennial Pathway

This seldom-groomed trail takes skiers past the Ocqueoc River and its waterfalls. The pathway, which winds through a mix of pine and hardwood forests, consists of three interconnected loops, ranging in size from three to six miles. The trailhead lies 11 miles west of Rogers City on M-68.

Ogemaw Hills Pathway

This trail doesn't get as much attention as some of its northern cousins, but it ranks as one of the Lower Peninsula's prettiest and more varied systems. It features more than 15 miles of wide trails that snake through thick pine and hardwood forests, and includes loops suitable for everyone from children to advanced skiers. The pathway can be reached by taking Business I-75 through West Branch to Fairview Road. Turn north on Fairview and go about five miles to the trailhead parking lot.

Sand Lakes Quiet Area

Another busy Traverse City-area trail. The Sand Lakes system offers loops for all skill levels and a picturesque setting that attracts winter campers. To reach the trailhead, take M-72 east to Broomhead Road and turn south. The parking lot lies half a dozen miles down the road.

VASA Pathway

The popularity of this tremendously appealing trail (it has averaged more than 10,000 skiers a season in past years) will no doubt increase with North American VASA's decision to purchase a powerful new groomer. This acquisition, made in response to one of the few gripes that skiers had about the pathway, further solidified the VASA Pathway's place at the top of northern Michigan cross-country skiing destinations. Long known as one of the state's finest cross country race trails, it is also a favorite of recreational skiers. It consists of three loops, ranging from an easy two-mile loop to the pathway's famed 25-kilometer (16-mile) loop, which takes skiers through demanding but beautiful terrain. This trail throws everything but the kitchen sink at skiers, interspersing screaming downhills with brutal uphill climbs and hairpin turns. To reach the VASA Pathway from the west, take US-31 east through Traverse City to Bunker Hill Road east. After a mile, turn south on Bartlett Road and follow it to the trailhead. From the east, take M-72 westbound to Lautner Road southbound to Bunker Hill Road. Go west on Bunker Hill Road to Bartlett Road and head south to trailhead.

Wilderness State Park Trails

This park is tailor-made for rugged skiers who want to shuck it all for a few days and lose themselves in Michigan's winter wonderland. The park has about a dozen miles of cross-country trails that run through cedar swamps and atop heavily forested ridges. But these remote trails are only part of the park's allure; Wilderness State Park also maintains five rustic cabins that can be reserved by backwoods explorers. Keep in mind, though, that a couple of the cabins are primarily used by snowmobilers because of their proximity to a trail, and that the other three – Nebo Cabin, Sturgeon Cabin, and Waugoshance – are immensely popular. In other words, call for reservations well in advance if you hope to get your mitts on one. You can reach the park at ☎ 616-436-5381. The park lies eight miles west of Mackinaw City; take CR-81 west onto westbound Wilderness Park Drive, or take Gill Road west off of US-31.

Other notable cross-country skiing trails in northern Lower Michigan include the **Lake Ann Pathway** (outside of Traverse City), the **Buttles Road Pathway** (near Lewiston), the **Tisdale Triangle Pathway** (near Roscommon), the rugged **Wakeley Lake Trail** (near Grayling); the trail systems at **Leelanau State Park, South Higgins Lake State Park, Hartwick Pines State Park**, and **Roscommon's Cross Country Ski Headquarters**; and pathways maintained by the region's other major resorts (Shanty Creek, Sugar Loaf, Grand Traverse Resort, the Homestead, Marsh Ridge, Treetops/Sylvan Resort, etc.). In addition, this section's coverage of **Huron National Forest, Manistee National Forest**, and **Sleeping Bear Dunes National Lakeshore** include cross-country skiing information for those regions.

Northern Lower Michigan

Downhill Skiing & Snowboarding

On the slopes in Northern Michigan (Randell McCune/Boyne Resorts).

Weather systems moving over Lake Michigan dump between 120 and 170 inches of snow annually on the steep moraines and towering sand dunes that make up the northwest corner of the state. This creates some of the best ski conditions in the Midwest – so it is little wonder that 25 of Michigan's 42 ski areas are in the northern Lower Peninsula, most of them clustered around the Grand Traverse area. In addition to challenging slopes and outstanding ski schools, many area resorts offer top-notch restaurants and lodging, along with a wide range of other activities – from cross-country skiing, snowshoeing, ice skating, and sleigh rides to dips in heated outdoor hot tubs and pools. While "black diamond" may not mean quite the same thing as it does in Aspen or Jackson Hole, northern Lower Michigan still has a great deal to offer skiers – and it's within 4-5 hours' drive of Detroit and Chicago.

Boyne Highlands

Located in Harbor Springs – 25 miles north of its sister resort, Boyne Mountain – Boyne Highlands features the highest vertical drop in the region at 550 feet and a longest run measuring more than a mile. Many of its 42 runs provide a stunning view of Little Traverse Bay (some say you can even see the Mackinac Bridge on a clear day). With a high percentage of intermediate runs and nice accommodations, it is considered an ideal place for beginners and families, though there are enough steeps and moguls to keep experts happy as well. Weekend/holiday adult lift ticket prices are $39, which gives skiers access to both Boyne resorts. ☎ 800-GO-BOYNE.

Boyne Mountain

Boyne Mountain, near Petoskey, was one of the state's first ski areas, established in 1948. It has remained on the cutting edge ever since, and even installed the nation's first high-speed six-person chair. With a vertical drop of 500 feet and longest run of 5,280 feet, Boyne offers a wide selection of steep hills and mogul fields to challenge more experienced skiers. Its 40 runs include icy Hemlock – which is topped by the Eagle's Nest restaurant – and newly opened Devil's Dive – which is the steepest in the state with a 61% grade. But Boyne has something for everyone, with a new 20-acre beginner area and 15 miles of premier cross-country ski trails. Off the slopes, Eriksen's Restaurant is the only three-star slopeside dining room in Michigan. The $39 adult weekend lift ticket is interchangeable with sister resort Boyne Highlands. ☎ 800-GO-BOYNE.

Caberfae Peaks

Located 15 miles west of Cadillac on M-55, Caberfae is not as fancy as some of the other resorts, with a modest lodge, restaurant, and ski shop the only amenities at the base of the slopes. But it does offer good skiing, with 23 runs – the longest nearly 4,000 feet – and a 490-foot vertical drop. New for 1997 is a snowboard park featuring a quarter-pipe and ridges. ☎ 616-779-0685 for more information (additional coverage of Caberfae can be found in the section on Manistee National Forest, page 117).

Crystal Mountain

Crystal has earned a reputation as an outstanding family resort, with top-notch instruction, four different programs for children, and a wide range of off-slope activities. Located 40 miles northwest of Cadillac on M-115, the resort features 25 downhill runs and a 375-foot vertical drop, with a terrain park for snowboarders. Nearly all of the runs are lighted and open for night skiing, even during the week. There are also 30 kilometers of cross-country trails, 1,500 acres of backcountry to explore on snowshoes, an ice skating rink, and sleigh rides. The $37 adult weekend lift ticket price includes night and cross-country skiing. ☎ 800-968-7686.

Northern Lower Michigan

The Homestead

Located off M-22 near Glen Arbor, 25 miles west of Traverse City, the Homestead resort features 14 downhill runs with spectacular views of Lake Michigan and the Leelanau Peninsula. It is the only ski area in the state to limit the number of lift tickets sold in order to reduce crowds and lines. A full-service resort, it offers restaurants, shops, and a variety of accommodations. An adult weekend lift ticket is $22. ☎ 616-334-5000.

Mount Holiday

Less well-known than other Traverse City-area resorts, Mount Holiday features 15 runs and a 200-foot vertical drop. It maintains a hands-off policy in its snowboard area, which attracts large numbers of shredders who like to create their own radical bumps and jumps. Lift tickets are $22 for adults on weekends. ☎ 616-938-2500 for more information.

Nub's Nob

Across the road from Boyne Mountain in Harbor Springs, Nub's is known for its excellent snow conditions and many expert hills. Since developing 12-run Pintail Peak for 1997, it features 38 runs – the longest of which is 5,000 feet – and a vertical drop of 150 feet. There are two half-pipes for snowboarders, one intermediate and one advanced, as well as a terrain park. Groomers are at work all night long tending to the output of the ski area's 108 patented snow guns, which produce some of the best artificial snow in the country. Though there are few other amenities on site, Nub's slopeside cafeteria offers sandwiches and burgers made to order, along with fresh soups and pies. An adult weekend lift ticket is $39. ☎ 616-526-2131.

Schuss Mountain/Shanty Creek

Shanty Creek Resort, near Torch Lake and Little Traverse Bay, consists of two downhill ski areas four miles apart with a regular shuttle running between them. Summit Slope features mostly beginner and intermediate terrain, while Schuss Mountain is somewhat more demanding. Together they include 41 runs – the longest of which is 5,280 feet – and a 450-foot vertical drop. Children enjoy learning to ski in the Gandyland area, which features mini-slalom courses and large cartoon cutouts. There is also an obstacle-strewn alpine terrain run for adults. The two ski areas offer different accommodations, ranging from Bavarian-style inns in Schuss Village to condominiums overlooking Lake Bellaire in Summit Village. An adult weekend lift ticket is $35. ☎ 800-678-4111.

Sugar Loaf

Near Cedar on the Leelanau Peninsula, on a 500-foot dune overlooking Lake Michigan, Sugar Loaf has some of the best scenery of any ski area. On a clear day, there are views of the Manitou and Fox islands, Sleeping Bear Dunes National Lakeshore, and two inland lakes. The ski area features 25 runs – the longest of which is 5,280 feet – and a 500-foot vertical drop. There is an excellent ski school for novices, as well as good steep stuff for experts, like icy Awful Awful. The snowboard area gives shredders the thrill of performing tricks on the carpeted roof of a half-buried VW Beetle. Lift tickets are $35 for adults on weekends. ☎ 616-228-5461.

Treetops/Sylvan Resort

This full-service resort near Gaylord offers 19 runs and a 225-foot vertical drop. An adult weekend lift ticket costs $28. ☎ 800-444-6711.

Snowmobiling

Northern Lower Michigan crawls with snowmobiles during the winter. The region's heavy snowfall, combined with its plentiful public lands and light winter population, make it a mecca for snowmobiling fans from around the Great Lakes. For many year-round residents, snowmobiles are the preferred mode of transportation during the winter season (as a quick pass through the parking lots of many northern Michigan breakfast diners will confirm). And as the numbers of snowmobilers continues to grow (officials estimate that the number of snowmobilers zooming around Michigan has nearly tripled over the past two decades), Michigan ski resorts are beginning to offer mid-week dining and lodging packages specifically designed to attract snowmobilers.

Hundreds of miles of nicely groomed trails run through the rolling hills and valleys of the northern Lower Peninsula. Major

Northern Lower Michigan

The northern Lower Peninsula is a haven for snowmobilers (Ski-Doo).

snowmobiling networks can be found near the region's larger towns, including Alpena, Cadillac, Gaylord, Grayling, Manistee, and Traverse City. In addition, a number of specific trails have emerged as particular favorites with locals and visitors.

Popular trails in the northwestern part of the state include the **Blood Creek Trail** (23 miles; southeast of Baldwin); **Little Manistee Trail** (45 miles; 4½ miles north of Baldwin on M-37); **Irons Trail System** (a 90-mile network of trails; runs out of Irons); **White Pine Trail** (62 miles; runs from Cadillac to Reed City to Baldwin to Clare); **Stony Lake Trail** (35 miles; out of Mears); **Newaygo County Trails** (61 miles; groomed trails start from Winter Sports Park); **Betsie River Trail** (38 miles in Pere Marquette State Forest); **Chandler Hills-Wolverine Trail** (51 miles; west of Boyne Falls on CR-626); **Tin Cup Trail** (19 miles; five miles northwest of Nirvana); **Grayling-Lovells Trail System** (45 miles; two miles north of Grayling on Old US-27); **Blue Bear Trail** (40 miles in Pere Marquette State Forest east of Kalkaska); **Boardman Valley Trail** (78 miles in Pere Marquette State Forest); and **Chandler Hill Trail** (34 miles; in Jordan River Valley area).

In northeastern Lower Michigan – which sees less snowmobiling action than the other side of the state – the premier snowmobiling attraction lies in the **Black Mountain Recreation Area**. This 9,000-acre area of Presque Isle County is one of the most rugged areas in all of Michigan, and the trail system that runs through it reflects that reality. The 80-mile system, which also includes the **Silver Creek Trail**, offers stunning scenic views and exhilarating twists and turns.

Other notable trails on the "sunrise" side of the state include the **Roscommon-St. Helen Trail** (25 miles; one mile southeast of Roscommon); **Oscoda Trails** (64-mile network; off M-72, five miles west of the Alcona County line); **Mackinaw City-Cheboygan Trail** (16 miles); **Bush Creek Trail** (30 miles; two miles north of Atlanta on M-33); **Muskrat Lake Trail** (25 miles; from Muskrat Lake, near Fairview); **Devil's Lake Trail** (17 miles; four miles south of Alpena on Piper Road); **Millersburg Trail** (35 miles, from Millersburg or Atlanta); and the **Ogemaw Hills Trail** (30 miles; three miles east of St. Helen on Beaver Lake Road).

To Find Out More

For detailed maps and information about Michigan's snowmobile trail system, contact the **Michigan Snowmobiling Association** at ☎ 616-361-2285 or the **DNR's Forest Management Division** at ☎ 517-373-1275.

Snowmobilers wishing to ride public trails need to purchase a permit. These annual permits cost $10 and are valid from October 1 to September 30. Contact the state **Department of Natural Resources**, ☎ 517-335-4837.

■ Where To Sleep

 The northern Lower Peninsula holds a lot of options for travelers. Chain hotels of varying quality are, of course, abundant in Cadillac, Traverse City, Gaylord, and other larger towns. In addition, ski resorts (Boyne, Grand Traverse Resort, Crystal Mountain, The Homestead, Treetops/Sylvan Resort, Schuss Mountain/Shanty Creek, etc.) are favorite destinations during the winter months, and cozy B&Bs and country inns attract folks year-round. Here's a sampling of attractive spots.

Price Guide

$	up to $50 per night
$$	$50-$100
$$$	$100-$175
$$$$	more than $175

Northwest Michigan

Chimney Corners (1602 Crystal Drive, Frankfort, MI 49635, ☎ 616-352-7522, $$). This rustic lodge offers quality, country-style accommodations. Stone fireplaces, a warm library/sitting room, and great food in a deep woods setting.

Garland Resort (Route 1, Box 364-M, CR-489, Lewiston, MI 49756, ☎ 517-786-2211, $$$-$$$$). This pricy resort is primarily known for its incredible golf facilities, but it also includes tennis courts, a complete weight/exercise room, a large pool, ornate public areas, and tastefully decorated guest rooms.

Lamplighter Bed and Breakfast (Ludington, MI 49431, ☎ 616-843-9792, $$-$$$). Spacious rooms and 19th-century elegance are the hallmarks of this Ludington inn.

Manistee Inn and Marina (378 River St., Manistee, MI 49660, ☎ 616-723-4000, $$). Accessible by car or boat, this hotel is in the heart of town on the Manistee River. It has 25 modern rooms.

Perry Hotel (Bay and Lewis Sts., Petoskey, MI 49770, ☎ 616-347-4000, $$-$$$$). Stationed next to the Gas Light District, this historic 19th-century hotel maintains 81 rooms and a nice dining room/cocktail lounge.

Pointes North Inn (101 Michigan Ave., Charlevoix, MI 49720, ☎ 616-547-0055, $$-$$$). This nicely appointed hotel offers a variety of accommodations, from basic rooms to one- and two-bedroom suites with lofts, mini and full kitchens, and balconies.

Terrace Inn (216 Fairview, PO Box 1478, Bay View, MI 49770, ☎ 616-347-2410, $$). A popular destination during all four seasons, the Inn has 44 individually decorated rooms, each with a private bath, and attractive common areas, including a nice dining room that serves excellent fare.

Northeast Michigan

Fireside Inn (18730 Fireside Highway, Alpena, MI 49707, ☎ 517-595-6369, $-$$). A rugged, comfortable place in pretty country surroundings, this laid-back spot includes great rustic-flavored rooms (including the Fireside Room, which boasts a massive stone fireplace), a variety of outdoor options (from canoeing to horseshoes to walking trails), and an all-around pleasant atmosphere. The Inn has 16 rooms and offers breakfast and dinner during the summer.

Penrod's Resort (100 Maple St., PO Box 432, Grayling, MI 49738, ☎ 517-348-2910, $$). This resort maintains modern log cottages on the Au Sable River that sleep from two to six people. A family-oriented resort, it offers mountain bike, canoe, and kayak rentals.

Wyandotte Lodge (1320 McMasters Bridge Rd., Grayling, MI 49738, ☎ 517-348-8354, $-$$). On the scenic Au Sable River, about 15 miles east of Grayling, this backcountry spot offers rooms in the lodge itself, as well as five cabins that overlook the river.

■ Where To Eat

Given northern Michigan's popularity as a year-round weekend and vacation destination it should come as no surprise that many communities in the region are able to support a diverse range of restaurants, from burger-and-fries joints to breakfast diners to steakhouses.

Price Guide
$ . . . . inexpensive
$$ . . . . moderately priced
$$$ . . . . expensive

Alpena

The Anchorage (1000 US-23 N., Alpena, MI, ☎ 517-356-2151, $$). Located in the Alpena Holiday Inn, this steakhouse packs 'em in, especially during the summer.

Jon A Lau Saloon (414 North Second Ave., Alpena, MI, ☎ 517-354-6898, $$). This historic watering hole offers a menu of solid pub fare, including tasty barbecue ribs.

Northern Lower Michigan

Someplace in Alpena (817 West Chisholm, Alpena, MI, ☎ 517-354-8325, $). Travelers with a hankering for some home cooking would do well to stop here. Fresh baked pies and breads and fabulous soups made from scratch are among the delights.

Cadillac

Hermann's European Café (214 N. Mitchell, Cadillac, MI, ☎ 616-775-9563, $$). The menu changes but the quality does not. This popular eatery features international dishes, great desserts, and an extensive wine list.

Lakeside Charlie's (301 S. Lake Mitchell, Cadillac, MI, ☎ 616-775-5332, $$). Flavorful burgers, steaks, pasta, and seafood in a casual setting.

Terrace Room Restaurant (Mackinaw Trail, Cadillac, MI, ☎ 616-775-9947, $$). Northern Michigan cuisine served in a roomy dining area that overlooks the rolling hills of McGuire's Resort. Saturday buffet and Sunday brunch bring in big crowds.

Charlevoix, Petoskey, Harbor Springs

Andante (321 Bay St., Petoskey, MI, ☎ 616-348-3321, $$$). Nestled on the shores of Little Traverse Bay, Andante offers delicious cuisine in an intimate setting for well-heeled boaters and cottagers.

Nanny's (219 Ferry Ave., Charlevoix, MI, ☎ 616-547-2960, $$). This eatery's Sunday brunch and Tuesday/Friday/Saturday dinner buffets pack folks in. Good burgers for the lunch crowd, too.

Stafford's Weathervane (106 Pine River Lane, Charlevoix, MI, ☎ 616-547-4311, $$). Located on the Pine River inlet, the Weathervane offers classic American fare.

Teddy Griffin Roadhouse (Pleasantview Rd., Harbor Springs, MI, ☎ 616-526-7805, $$). Pizza, Great Lakes seafood, steaks, and BBQ ribs are offered at this bustling eatery.

Villa Ristorante Italiano (US-131 S., Petoskey, MI, ☎ 616-347-1440, $$). Great Italian food in a friendly setting.

Cheboygan

The Boathouse (106 Pine Street, Cheboygan, MI, ☎ 616-627-4316, $$). Steak and seafood cuisine in a casual setting.

Chateau Lodge (10621 Twin Lakes Rd., Cheboygan, MI, ☎ 616-625-9322, $$). In the heart of the Black Mountain Recreation Area, this restaurant is a big favorite with snowmobilers and other winter visitors.

Hack-Ma-Tack Inn (8131 Beebe Rd., Cheboygan, MI, ☎ 616-625-2919, $$). This seasonal favorite (closed from November to April) attracts lots of attention from voyagers on the Inland Waterway. Housed in a historic 19th-century hunting lodge, the Inn is best known for its prime rib and whitefish dishes.

East Tawas, Tawas City

Pier 23 Supper Club (821 W. Bay, East Tawas, MI, ☎ 517-362-8856, $$). Great regional cuisine overlooking Tawas Bay. During the summer, its roomy deck attracts large numbers of boaters.

Frankfort

Art's Tavern (M-22, Glen Arbor, MI, ☎ 616-334-3754, $). Great pub and grub spot with an extensive menu that includes burgers, whitefish, and Mexican fare.

Coho Café (320 Main St., Frankfort, MI, ☎ 616-352-6053, $). Contemporary cuisine overlooking Frankfort Harbor.

Hotel Frankfort (231 Main St., Frankfort, MI, ☎ 616-352-9671, $$). This handsome downtown eatery offers intimate casual dining. Menu runs toward seafood, pasta, and prime rib.

Main Sail (Main St., Frankfort, MI, ☎ 616-352-7107, $$). The main restaurant offers steaks, whitefish, prime rib, and pork chops, while its Chart Room Lounge is a good spot to quaff a brew or two.

Northern Lower Michigan

Gaylord

Busia's Polish Kitchen (2782 Old 27 South, Gaylord, MI, ☎ 517-732-2790, $$). This family-owned restaurant furnishes authentic Polish fare as well as steak, seafood, and other staples in a comfortable, congenial atmosphere.

Diana's Delights (143 W. Main St., Gaylord, MI, ☎ 517-732-6564, $). Excellent homestyle breakfasts and lunches made from scratch.

Hidden Valley (East Main St., Gaylord, MI, ☎ 517-732-5181, $$$). A satisfying variety of regional and international cuisine in a lodge with scenic views of the Sturgeon River Valley.

Sugar Bowl (216 W. Main, Gaylord, MI, ☎ 517-732-5524, $$). Family-oriented restaurant features a full menu, including a variety of Greek-American dishes.

Grayling

Albie's (105 Fred Bear Dr., Grayling, MI, ☎ 517-348-2240, $). Hearty appetites will appreciate Albie's, which features monster subs, juicy burgers, and giant pasties.

Stevens Family Circle (E. Michigan Ave., Grayling, MI, ☎ 517-348-2111, $). This cozy spot features homemade soups and sandwiches and an authentic 1950 soda fountain.

Midland, Mt. Pleasant

Café Edward (5010 Bay City Rd., Midland, MI, ☎ 517-496-3351, $$). Nice bistro serving a variety of continental fare.

The Embers (1217 S. Mission, Mt. Pleasant, MI, ☎ 517-773-5007, $$$). An elegant refuge on Mt. Pleasant's hectic main drag, the cavernous Embers maintains a nice repertoire of fine dining options.

Omelettes & More (112 E. Main, Midland, MI, ☎ 517-839-0930, $). Hearty breakfasts are served any time at this popular local eatery.

Traverse City

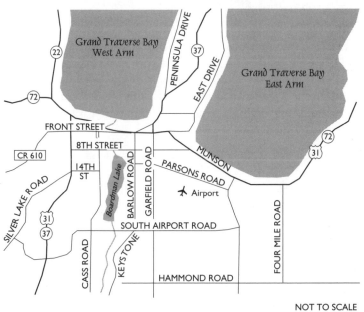

Grand Traverse Bay West Arm

Grand Traverse Bay East Arm

PENINSULA DRIVE

EAST DRIVE

FRONT STREET

8TH STREET

CR 610

14TH ST

SILVER LAKE ROAD

Boardman Lake

BARLOW ROAD

GARFIELD ROAD

PARSONS ROAD

MUNSON

Airport

SOUTH AIRPORT ROAD

CASS ROAD

KEYSTONE

HAMMOND ROAD

FOUR MILE ROAD

NOT TO SCALE

Traverse City

Bluebird (102 River, Leland, MI, ☎ 616-256-9081, $$). This perennial favorite brings folks back with its tasty Great Lakes seafood dishes and extensive wine list.

Boathouse Blue Water Bistro (14039 Peninsula Dr., Traverse City, MI, ☎ 616-223-4030, $$). This relative newcomer to the Traverse City area made an immediate splash, winning *Traverse Magazine*'s People's Choice Award for Best New Restaurant of 1996. Great Lakes seafood, pasta, and steaks served in a casual atmosphere.

Boone's Long Lake Inn (7208 Secor Rd., Traverse City, MI, ☎ 616-946-3991, $$). Prime rib and steak dishes are the mainstays at this country-flavored restaurant.

Key to the County (104 Main St., Lake Leelanau, MI, ☎ 616-256-KEYS, $$). A new addition to the region, this tavern and grill offers a variety of good food in a warm, comfortable atmosphere. Live music offered on some evenings.

Omelette Shoppe and Bakery (124 Cass, Traverse City, MI, ☎ 616-946-0912, $). The top breakfast spot in the city, hands down.

Poppycock's (128 East Front, Traverse City, MI, ☎ 616-941-7632, $$). Vegetarians flock to this top-flight restaurant, which features a wide range of inventive meatless dishes. But meat lovers won't be left out in the cold, for the eatery also offers tasty burgers, steaks, and more.

Tapawingo (9502 Lake, Ellsworth, MI, ☎ 616-588-7971, $$$). Long a giant of Traverse City's restaurant community, Tapawingo continues to offer superb cuisine in an elegant setting overlooking St. Clair Lake.

Windows (7677 West Bay Shore Dr., Traverse City, MI, ☎ 616-941-0100, $$$). Accolades abound for this restaurant, which features gourmet French-American cuisine with a dash of Cajun spice. A *Wine Spectator* Award recipient, Windows also was named the region's top restaurant in 1997 by *Traverse Magazine* readers.

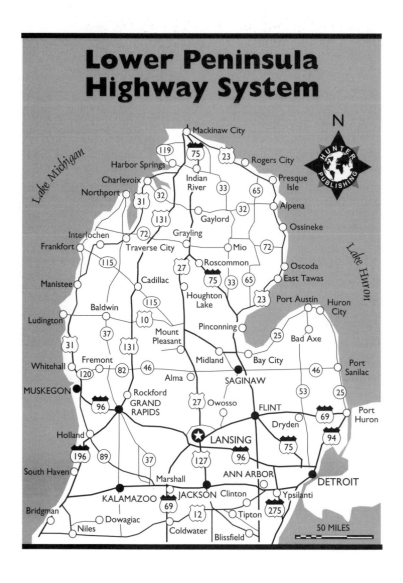

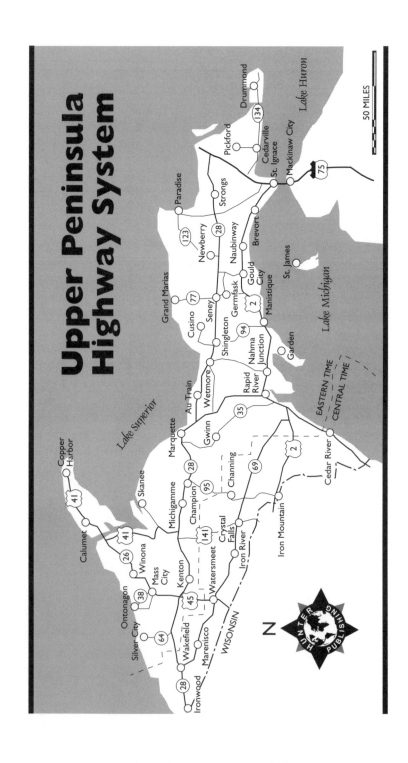

The Upper Peninsula

Michigan's UP has the feel of a lost and wild continent. Blessed with more than 1,700 miles of shoreline on three Great Lakes, approximately 4,300 inland lakes, and an estimated 12,000 miles of clear streams, the sparsely populated peninsula retains the aura of unspoiled majesty that it had in earlier centuries. A land of dense timber, trackless marshes, swift rivers, crashing waterfalls, stony hills, and glittering lakes, the Upper Peninsula is a paradise for adventurers of every stripe, from backpackers, kayakers, canoeists, and scuba divers to snowmobilers, skiers, cycling enthusiasts, and fat tire devotees.

Getting Around

As befits such a place, travel in the UP tends to proceed at a fairly unhurried pace. Even its major roadways (US-2, US-41) feature long stretches of two-lane, and the small communities scattered across the peninsula operate at a more relaxed pace than do the towns and villages of Michigan's Lower Peninsula. But all in all, the UP is adequately equipped for visitors. It maintains 29 recreational harbors, and is serviced by airports in Escanaba, Houghton, Iron Mountain, Ironwood, Kinross, Marquette, and Menominee, with rental cars available at all of these places.

■ Hiawatha National Forest

2727 North Lincoln Road
Escanaba, MI 49829
☎ 906-786-4062

Hiawatha is the only national forest to border three Great Lakes (Huron, Michigan, and Superior). The forest is comprised of two separate sections totaling over 893,000 acres – one in the eastern Upper Peninsula (in Chippewa and Mackinac Counties) and one in the central UP (in Alger, Delta, and Schoolcraft Counties). The eastern section provides easy access to Tahquamenon Falls State Park, while the central section borders Pictured Rocks National Lakeshore.

Hiawatha itself features 777 miles of rivers and streams, 418 inland lakes, and 104 miles of Great Lakes shoreline for the enjoyment of paddlers, fishermen, swimmers, sunbathers, and scuba divers. There are also a number of hiking trails leading from the forest's 20 developed campgrounds to a variety of historic sites, waterfalls, and dramatic lakeshore views. And with up to 240 inches of annual snowfall, Hiawatha provides ample opportunities for snowmobiling, cross-country skiing, and snowshoeing. As if this weren't enough, the Munising District of Hiawatha National Forest administers Grand Island Recreation Area – a 21-square-mile island across from Munising that features towering sandstone cliffs, waterfalls, caves, inland lakes, numerous trails for mountain biking and hiking, and two historic lighthouses.

Getting There

To get to the eastern section of Hiawatha National Forest, simply cross the Mackinac Bridge from Michigan's Lower Peninsula. It lies mostly to the west of I-75 and stretches from Lakes Michigan and Huron in the south to Whitefish Bay on Lake Superior in the north. The central UP section of Hiawatha can be reached via either US-2 or M-28. It stretches from Big Bay de Noc on Lake Michigan to Munising on Lake Superior.

History

The forest was named for the Native American hero of Longfellow's famous poem "Song of Hiawatha." Its eastern unit, which was initially known as the Marquette National Forest, was dedicated in 1909, nearly two decades after the passage of the Forest Reserve Act. The western unit of the forest was established in 1931, during the height of the Depression.

Flora & Fauna

The lands of Hiawatha National Forest consist of 46% wetlands, including several distinctive bogs and sand dune/swale areas. This environment supports numerous endangered, threatened, and rare plants, including the dwarf lake iris, hart's tongue fern, monkey flower, and pitchers thistle. Hiawatha is also home to 30 varieties of trees – including aspen, beech, birch, cedar, hemlock, maple, oak, pine, and spruce – which put on an impressive color display in the fall. There are six designated wilderness areas within the forest that protect stands of virgin timber, delicate wetlands, pristine lakes, and sweeping sand dunes. Fauna in the area includes hundreds of bird species, as well as black bears, moose, bobcats, and deer. Some of the less appealing creatures include mosquitoes and black flies, which can be particularly problematic in the spring.

Adventures

On Foot

A 77-mile section of the **North Country National Scenic Trail** crosses the length of the eastern section of Hiawatha, from the Mackinac Bridge to Tahquamenon Falls State Park. Free primitive campsites are scattered along the route, which also passes through the Brevoort Lake and Soldier Lake developed campgrounds. For a detailed description of the trail, see the *UP Hiking/Backpacking* section, page 281.

The central UP section of Hiawatha is home to the 40-mile **Bay de Noc-Grand Island Trail**, which is traveled by hikers and horseback riders alike. It follows a historic Indian portage route between Lake Michigan and Lake Superior. In the south, it begins at Little Bay de Noc, which was named after the Noquet (or Noc, for short) Indians who inhabited the region from the mid-1600s. The trailhead is two miles north of US-2 on CR-509. The trail passes through rolling wooded areas of jack pine, poplar, birch, and beech, as well as open meadows and old lumber sites. Back-country camping is allowed along the way, and the trail also

Bay de Noc – Grand Island Trail

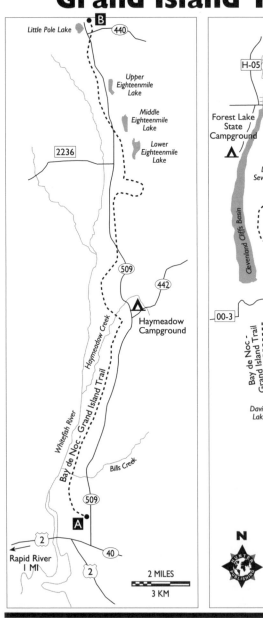

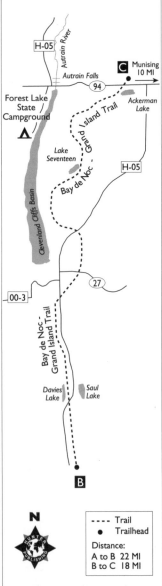

passes through the developed Haymeadow Creek campground, which is known for its plentiful supply of wild strawberries and blueberries. About five miles later, the trail enters the Whitefish River Valley and follows the river into a maple forest towering above a dense understory of trillium. The trail ends at the intersection of M-94 near Ackerman Lake, but from there hikers can continue on a section of the North Country Trail to Munising, on the shore of Lake Superior across from Grand Island.

Hiawatha also offers many opportunities for shorter hikes. Interpretive trails beginning at many of the campgrounds lead to points of historic, natural, or scenic interest.

A nine-mile loop known as **Bruno's Run** is accessible from both the Pete's Lake and Widewaters campgrounds in the central UP section of Hiawatha. The trail passes numerous small lakes, skirts the Indian River, winds through valleys and over hills, and goes through a dense grove of mature hemlock trees. Camping is allowed along the way.

Northwest of Manistique off CR-440 is the 26-mile **Pine Marten Run Trail**, which is also open to horseback riders. It consists of five loops that wind through a series of inland lakes. Camping is permitted along the trail, and Adirondack shelters are available near Rim and Rumble Lakes.

In the eastern part of Hiawatha, a two-mile trail at **Monocle Lake** crosses a beaver dam on its way to a high bluff with a scenic overlook. At Foley Creek, the one-mile **Horseshoe Bay Trail** leads through a white cedar forest to a secluded beach on Lake Huron.

On Wheels

Mountain Biking

 Hundreds of miles of unmarked (and often unmapped) logging roads wind through Hiawatha, making it a popular destination for adventurous mountain bikers. But Hiawatha also contains a good portion of one of the state's best rail trails, the 33-mile **Haywire Rail Trail**. This rugged trail, which also takes you through a good section of neighboring Lake Superior State Forest, traverses some of the state's prettiest woodlands. But the pathway does not surrender its charms easily; the handiwork of area beavers has transformed the trail into one of the wettest in the UP, and sand traps can bedevil bikers. The northern trailhead is just south of Shingleton, on the east side of M-94. The pathway's southern trailhead is off Riverview Road, in Manistique.

Other significant mountain biking areas in Hiawatha include **Bruno's Run**, a 27-mile network called the **Valley Spur**, and **Grand Island** (see *On Grand Island* section, page 218).

On Water

Canoeing & Kayaking

Hiawatha is a paradise for boaters, canoeists, kayakers, and fishermen, offering almost endless possibilities. The forest features 163 miles of designated canoe routes along several mild-mannered rivers, facilitating trips ranging in length from a few hours to a few days. The **Au Train canoe route** begins in the Au Train Lake Campground and meanders 10 miles through forests and wildlife-filled backwaters to Lake Superior. Several resorts in the Au Train area offer canoes for rent – call the **Au Train Tourist Association** at ☎ 906-892-8144. Paddlers may enjoy a longer but equally relaxing trip on the 25-mile **Carp River canoe route**, which begins off Forest Road 3458 and ends in St. Martin Bay on Lake Huron. Camping is permitted along the way, and the route passes Carp River Campground two miles before its end point. The scenic, 35-mile **Indian River canoe route** runs from Fish Lake, one-half mile upstream from Widewaters Campground, past the Indian River Campground to Indian Lake. It passes through remote forests and wildlife-filled marshes, with only a few easy stretches of fast water along the way. The 44-mile **Sturgeon River canoe route** is best suited to more experienced paddlers, as two stretches of rapids and frequent fallen trees create challenges. It begins at CR-440, south of Munising, and continues past the Flowing Well Campground to Big Bay de Noc.

In addition to these river routes, Hiawatha offers fine opportunities for lake canoeing at **Big Island Lake Wilderness Area**, 15 miles southeast of Munising off H-13. The area has 23 secluded

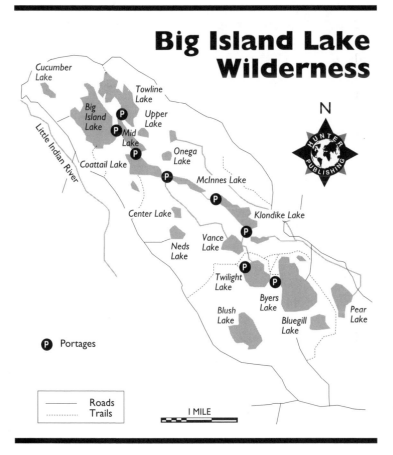

Big Island Lake Wilderness

- Cucumber Lake
- Towline Lake
- Big Island Lake
- Upper Lake
- Mid Lake
- Coattail Lake
- Onega Lake
- McInnes Lake
- Center Lake
- Klondike Lake
- Vance Lake
- Neds Lake
- Twilight Lake
- Byers Lake
- Blush Lake
- Bluegill Lake
- Pear Lake
- Little Indian River

P Portages

--- Roads

.... Trails

1 MILE

N

inland lakes linked by eight portage trails ranging from 100 to 1,800 feet in length. The lakes are surrounded by rolling hills covered in aspen, birch, and maple trees, as well as wildflowers and berries. It is not unusual to see bald eagles, loons, great blue herons, beavers, and pine martens in the area. Minimum-impact backcountry camping is allowed, but there are no developed campsites. Kayakers can enjoy peaceful floats down Hiawatha's rivers or explore the sand dunes along the Lake Michigan shore, the islands off the Lake Huron coast, or the sandstone cliffs of Grand Island.

Fishing

Hiawatha offers diverse fishing opportunities in its many rivers and inland lakes, as well as along the Great Lakes shorelines. Most of the inland lakes hold crappie, walleye, perch, large- and smallmouth bass, and pike, while the rivers and streams tend to support rainbow trout, brook trout, brown trout, and salmon. The 4,200-acre **Brevoort Lake** in the eastern section of the National Forest is a popular spot for walleye, as it includes a spawning reef that was constructed in 1985. In the central UP section of Hiawatha, **Au Train, Corner, Moccasin, Gooseneck**, and **Thunder Lakes** are all noted for their walleye. **Jackpine** and **Pete's Lakes** are popular for smallmouth bass, while **McKeever Lake** is known for its pike.

On Snow

Cross-Country Skiing

Hiawatha National Forest maintains many groomed trails for cross-country skiing and snowshoeing. In the central UP section of the forest, the seven-mile **Bruno's Run** hiking trail is made available for skiing. In addition, six miles southwest of Munising, off M-94, is the **Valley Spur ski area**. Here Nordic fans will find 12 miles of trails ranging from easy one-milers to hilly longer routes and a seven-mile skating loop. The **Buckhorn trail system** provides 17 miles of groomed trails, including a 3½-mile skating loop. The trailhead is near the Buckhorn Lodge on Forest Road 2254, off M-94 south of Munising. The eight-mile **McKeever Hills trail system**, on H-13 south of Munising, includes three scenic and hilly loops. There is also a rustic log cabin on McKeever Lake that can be rented by contacting Hiawatha's Munising Ranger District (☎ 906-387-2512). At 39 miles, **Rapid River** is the longest groomed trail system in the area. It passes through flat valleys and over steep ridges. The trailhead is on US-41, seven miles north of Rapid River.

Hiawatha's eastern section also offers several possibilities for Nordic enthusiasts. The **Sand Dunes ski area**, off H-57 just north of US-2, passes through some old Lake Michigan dunes. There are seven loops ranging from 1½ to 15 miles, all clearly marked and some with descriptive names like "Holy Cow!" and "Omigosh!" Alternate routes bypass some of the bigger hills, making the trail suitable for beginners as well as for more experienced skiers. The nine-mile **McNearney ski trail** – at the junction of M-28 and Salt Point Road, five miles north of Strongs Corners – offers several easy loops plus the three-mile Forester's Loop, which includes steep hills for advanced skiers. This trail system passes through white spruce and virgin hemlock forests and skirts nine inland lakes.

Dogsledding

During the winter months the woodlands of Hiawatha National Forest come alive with the sound of barking dogs and jangling harnesses. Dogsledding is an increasingly popular pastime in the UP, and nowhere is this growth more evident than in Hiawatha. In recent years the national forest has emerged as the state's primary destination for mushers and their teams. Hiawatha's bountiful snow, coupled with its network of old logging roads and firecutting trails, make it an ideal environment for mushers seeking to train their dogs for racing, guided adventures, or their own pleasure. Consequently, it is not unusual to find a dozen different dogteams galloping through the forest's snow-laden hills and valleys on crisp winter afternoons.

The most heavily used dogsledding trails sprout out from **Chatham**, a small town on the border of Hiawatha that is home to a number of mushers. The network of trails range up to the Lake Superior shoreline in the north and run about 30 miles eastward deep into Hiawatha. Dogsledding teams share some of these trails with snowmobilers. Perhaps the most popular dogsledding trail in the UP is the **Bay de Noc-Grand Island Trail** (known by local mushers as the Ackerman Trail). Snowmobiles are forbidden from using the 40-mile trail, which begins near the shores of Lake Superior and slices through the heart of the forest to the peninsula's southern coastline. A portion of the famed UP 200 Sled Dog Race follows this trail.

Wilderness dogsledding adventures are available through several outfitters. These businesses offer excursions that vary in length from an afternoon to a week or more. For information on trips and destinations, contact **Caribou Creek** (☎ 906-439-5747), **Triple Creek Kennels** (☎ 906-249-3470), **Side Treks** (☎ 906-228-8735), or **Buckstop Bed and Breakfast** (☎ 906-446-3360).

Snowmobiling

Snowmobiles provide one of the main forms of transportation during the long winter. The 31-mile **Nahma Grade Trail**, accessible from CR-40 east of Rapid River, follows an old railroad track that was used by the Nahma and Northern Railroad from 1901 until the 1940s. Groomed and marked, it goes through swamps, over rolling, forested hills, and across Mormon Creek and the Sturgeon River.

Ice Climbing

The 4,640-acre **Rock River Canyon Wilderness Area**, off H-01 west of Munising, features two 150-foot-deep sandstone canyons. In the wintertime, water seeping out of the canyon walls freezes into spectacular ice formations that are very popular with ice climbers.

Climbing the sandstone walls is discouraged in the summertime because they are so fragile.

On Grand Island

With 13,500 wooded acres and over 30 miles of picturesque coastline, Grand Island Recreation Area is a popular destination for hikers, mountain bikers, sea kayakers, and snowmobilers. The island is less than a mile offshore from Munising, and ferry service is provided throughout the summer by **Pictured Rocks Cruises**. The boats make two round trips daily in spring and fall, and three during July and August. ☎ 906-387-2379 for schedules and rate information.

Grand Island was one of the few sites on Lake Superior that housed a permanent Native American village. Artifacts suggest that the Ojibwa lived there over 2,000 years ago. The first white settlers – Abraham Williams and his family – were allowed to set up a fur trading post in 1840. A small cemetery on the island testi-

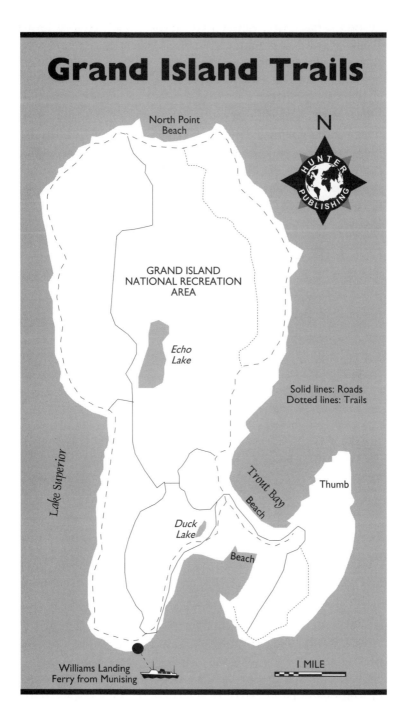

Grand Island Trails

N

HUNTER PUBLISHING

North Point Beach

GRAND ISLAND NATIONAL RECREATION AREA

Echo Lake

Solid lines: Roads
Dotted lines: Trails

Lake Superior

Trout Bay Beach

Thumb

Duck Lake

Beach

Williams Landing
Ferry from Munising

1 MILE

fies to the hardships they suffered in these early days. In 1900, Grand Island was purchased by the Cleveland Cliffs Iron Company, whose owner imported elk, moose, caribou, and deer in the hopes of creating a game preserve. The US Forest Service purchased Grand Island in 1990 and made it part of Hiawatha National Forest, with the exception of one small parcel of private property and several buildings.

The wild character of the island remains intact today. Its shoreline ranges from imposing sandstone cliffs and caves – resembling the nearby Pictured Rocks – to appealing sand beaches. Further inland, rugged hills are parted by rushing streams and marshy inland lakes. Though most of the non-native wildlife that was imported around the turn of the century eventually died off or crossed the ice to the mainland, the island is still home to black bear, deer, grouse, and a wide variety of waterfowl. Unfortunately, it is also notorious for its population of mosquitoes and black flies, particularly in the spring and early summer.

A 122-mile network of old logging roads – mostly rough and unmaintained – crisscross Grand Island, making it a mecca for both **mountain bikers** and **backpackers**. In fact, the **24-mile loop** around Grand Island is considered one of the best mountain biking trails in the entire Midwest (☎ 906-387-2512 for a detailed map). It consists mostly of single-track through the woods, traversing scenic cliffs and climbing several challenging hills. There are a total of seven rustic campsites, all near the south end of the island – three on Murray Bay and four on Trout Bay. Backcountry camping is allowed everywhere except on private property and in the ecologically sensitive North Beach area.

The scenic, relatively protected coastline of Grand Island also attracts many **sea kayakers** from the mainland. Some choose to begin their trips at Hiawatha's Bay Furnace Campground west of Munising. It takes at least two days to paddle around the island, and kayakers must exercise care in navigating the cold and unpredictable waters of Lake Superior. For those with a sense of adventure but without their own kayaks, **Northern Waters** (☎ 906-387-2323) offers guided day trips to the high points of Grand Island and the surrounding area. No experience is necessary.

Private motorboats are also allowed to visit the island, but they are advised to obtain a good weather forecast before venturing out since fog can pose a significant hazard. Boaters must obtain a free permit from Hiawatha National Forest Headquarters (☎ 906-786-4062) to moor overnight in the protected waters of Murray or Trout Bays. The latter bay offers **anglers** good opportunities to catch lake trout and coho salmon. Bass and northern pike are plentiful in Grand Island's inland lakes, but the shore areas tend to be marshy and portage routes for canoes are difficult.

Other popular attractions of the Grand Island area are the ship-wrecks of the **Alger Underwater Preserve.** Many charter boats are available to take scuba divers to the well-preserved wrecks (call the Alger County Chamber of Commerce at ☎ 906-387-2138 for a listing). Non-divers can view some of the shallower wrecks aboard a semi-glass-bottomed boat operated by **Grand Island Charters** (☎ 906-387-4477). Included in the 2½-hour tour are the *Bermuda*, a 150-foot wooden schooner that went down in Murray Bay in the late 1800s, and the *Hetler*, a 210-foot steamer that sank off the eastern side of the island in 1926. These and several other wrecks are easily visible from the surface thanks to the clear water of Lake Superior. The tour costs $15 per person, with children under 12 half-price.

Camping

Hiawatha National Forest offers more than 20 developed campgrounds, ranging in size from one to 70 sites. Most of them are on the shores of lakes and feature rustic, wooded sites with picnic tables, fire rings, and pit toilets, though a few offer flush toilets and electrical hookups. The campgrounds in the central UP section of the forest include: **Camp 7 Lake**, 41 sites on a 60-acre recreational lake eight miles east of Forest Road 13 on CR-442; **Colwell Lake**, 32 sites (a few with electrical hook-ups) and a nice beach, 20 miles southeast of Munising on M-94; **Corner Lake**, nine sites and a large beach, on CR-440 two miles east of Forest Road 13; **Indian River**, 12 sites on a bluff overlooking the river, 20 miles north of Manistique on M-94; **Little Bass Lake**, 12 sites, off CR-437 west of M-94; **Little Bay de Noc**, 38 sites and boat access to the bay, on CR-513; **Flowing Well**, 10 sites along the Sturgeon River, three miles north of US-2 on H-13; **Au Train Lake**, 37 sites on a large lake, 10 miles west of Munising on Forest Road 2596; **Bay Furnace**, 50 sites on the shore of Lake Superior, five miles west of Munising on M-28; **Island Lake**, 45 sites, 10 miles south of Munising on Forest Road 2268; **Pete's Lake**, 41 sites on a clear lake, 12 miles south of Munising off H-13; and **Widewaters**, 34 sites, canoe access to the Indian River, 13 miles south of Munising on Forest Road 2262.

Developed campgrounds in the eastern UP section of the forest include: **Bay View**, 24 sites, sunsets over Whitefish Bay, 35 miles west of Sault St. Marie on Forest Road 3150; **Monocle Lake**, 44 sites, access to the historic Point Iroquois Lighthouse, seven miles west of Brimley off Forest Road 3150; **Soldier Lake**, 44 sites, a sandy beach, off M-28 at Forest Road 3138; **Three Lakes**, 28 sites on a peaceful lake, two miles south of M-28 off Forest Road 3142; **Brevoort Lake**, 70 sites on a popular 4,200-acre walleye lake, 20 miles west of St. Ignace, north of US-2; **Carp River**, 44 sites along a popular fishing stream, eight miles north of St. Ignace off H-63; **Foley Creek**, 54 sites and a sandy beach on Lake Huron, six miles north of St. Ignace off H-63; and **Lake Michigan**, 35 sites nestled among the sand dunes, 18 miles west of St. Ignace off US-2. There are also a number of primitive campsites available on the smaller lakes within Hiawatha, including 10 sites on Lyman Lake and four each on Swan Lake, Steuben Lake, Gooseneck Lake, Chicago Lake, and Carr Lake.

To Find Out More

Contact **Hiawatha National Forest headquarters** at 2727 North Lincoln Road, Escanaba, MI 49829, ☎ 906-786-4062.

■ Isle Royale National Park

800 East Lakeshore Dr.
Houghton, MI 49931
☎ 906-482-0984

Isle Royale National Park is an isolated wilderness paradise surrounded by the formidable waters of Lake Superior. It is in the
northeast corner of the largest of the Great Lakes, over 50 miles
from the tip of Michigan's Upper Peninsula and only 15 miles
from the Canadian shoreline. The island itself is 45 miles long
and nine miles wide, but the park boundaries extend several miles
out from shore and encompass some 200 smaller islands.

Accessible only by boat or seaplane and open only from mid-April
through the end of October, Isle Royale is the least-visited spot in
the national park system, attracting fewer visitors in a year
(16,000) than Yellowstone does in an average day. Nevertheless,
the island's rugged beauty and overwhelming sense of solitude attract an inordinate number of repeat visitors, and the average stay
is four days, compared to four hours in other national parks.
Wheeled vehicles of any kind are prohibited on the island, but
there are many opportunities for exploration on foot or by boat.

Getting There

Simply getting to Isle Royale can be a challenge. Ferry boats and
seaplanes make the trip across unpredictable Lake Superior only
in good weather, so arrivals and departures can sometimes be de-
layed by hours or even days due to poor conditions.

 *Since six-foot rollers are common on the lake
even under sunny skies, boat passengers are
advised to take precautions against
seasickness (as you might imagine, the
journey can become mighty unpleasant if you
begin to feel nauseous after the first hour).*

Reservations for both boats and seaplanes should be made at least
a month in advance. Beginning in 1997, the park instituted an entry fee of $4 per person per day.

The main point of access to the island is **Rock Harbor**, a developed area on the southeastern shore featuring a visitor center,
camp store, gift shop, lodge, restaurant, laundry, shower facility,
and full-service marina. It is the destination of the major boat and
seaplane services operating out of Michigan. From Rock Harbor

Isle Royale National Park

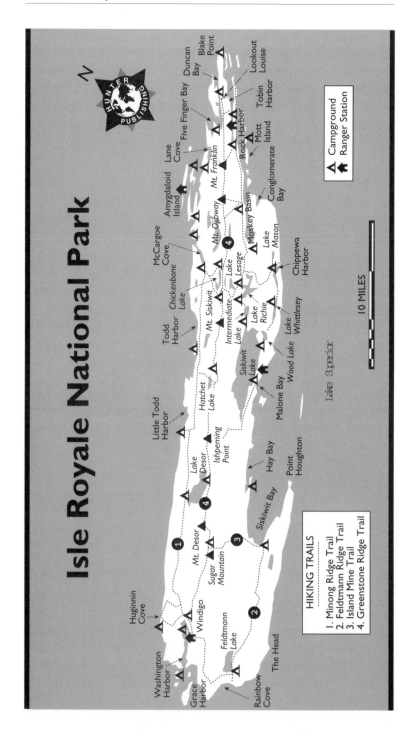

marina, charter boat service is available to other parts of the island. The other main launching point for Isle Royale excursions is **Windigo**, on the western end of the island. Windigo, though significantly less developed than Rock Harbor, has a ranger station and sells boat gas and other supplies.

The National Park Service operates the largest of the Isle Royale passenger boats out of Houghton, Michigan, in the Keweenaw Peninsula. In addition to 120 passengers, the 165-foot *Ranger III* can transport canoes, kayaks, and motorboats under 20 feet in length. It makes the 6½-hour trip to the island two days per week, spends a night at Rock Harbor, and returns the following day. There is a snack bar on board, and during smooth crossings the NPS rangers give informational talks and show videotapes. Fees start at $92 per person round-trip, with additional charges for boats or gear in excess of 100 pounds. Contact the park headquarters for further information.

A concessionaire runs a smaller passenger vessel, the 81-foot *Island Queen III*, to Rock Harbor from Copper Harbor, Michigan. The journey to Isle Royale is a bit shorter at 4½ hours, but travelers must make up part of the difference by driving an extra hour from Houghton to the tip of the Keweenaw Peninsula. And at half the length of the *Ranger III,* the *Island Queen III* is not an ideal choice for the queasy. Rates are $76 per person round-trip. Contact the *Island Queen III,* Copper Harbor, MI 49918, ☎ 906-289-4437 in summer or 906-482-4950 in winter.

Another boat option is the ***Wenonah,*** out of Grand Portage, Minnesota. This 65-foot vessel makes the three-hour trip to Windigo daily and returns the same day. A sister ship, the ***Voyageur II,*** travels clockwise from Windigo to Rock Harbor three days per week, remains at Rock Harbor overnight, then continues back to Windigo, dropping off and picking up passengers at pre-arranged spots along the way. Rates for the *Wenonah* are $60 per person round-trip, and a jaunt around the island on the *Voyageur II* costs $40. Contact **GPIR Transport Lines**, 1507 N. First St., Superior, WI 54880, ☎ 715-392-2100.

Seaplane service to Isle Royale is more expensive and dependent on the weather, yet considerably faster. Each plane can transport six people and their gear from Houghton to Rock Harbor in about an hour, at a cost of $200 per person round-trip. For information contact **Isle Royale Seaplane Service**, Box 371, Houghton, MI 49931, or call ☎ 906-482-8850 in summer.

History

Beginning around 2000 B.C., Isle Royale was the site of the earliest mining activity in North America. Prehistoric miners of unknown origin pounded on rocky outcroppings with hammerstones to extract the pure copper that was often visible near the surface. The mineral was fashioned into decorative objects that were traded throughout the eastern United States.

Isle Royale became part of the United States in 1783 when Ben Franklin, negotiating the Treaty of Paris with the British, used an inaccurate map that showed the island far closer to the middle of Lake Superior than it actually is. Shortly thereafter, it became the site of larger mining efforts and a commercial fishery. Though most of this activity ended by the late 1800s, several old mine sites, abandoned mining equipment, and the former fishery can still be seen. Isle Royale first became a popular destination for tourists around the turn of the century. Due to its unusually pristine air and water, it attracted a large number of allergy sufferers from midwestern cities. Several resorts were built during the 1920s, but of these only Rock Harbor Lodge remains today.

Isle Royale became a national park in 1946, and 30 years later it was added to the National Wilderness Preservation System. In 1980, the island was designated as an International Biosphere Reserve by the United Nations in recognition of its potential for ecological research of global importance.

Flora & Fauna

Isle Royale is perhaps most famous for its wolf and moose populations. The island's many moose are ancestors of a small group that swam from Canada around the turn of the century. You may catch a glimpse of one or more of the large, gangly creatures during your stay. Though moose are generally wary and a bit shy around people, park rangers advise visitors to quietly move out of their way. In a few rare instances, hikers have been chased or treed by amorous but nearsighted bull moose or by cow moose protecting their calves.

The moose population is held in check by three small packs of eastern timber wolves, the descendants of animals that walked across a frozen Lake Superior during a particularly cold winter in 1948-49. Few visitors to the park ever see a wolf, though many hear the nighttime howls that provide an eerie reminder of their presence. The island's isolation makes it an ideal "outdoor laboratory," and wildlife biologists from Purdue University have been studying the predator-prey relationship in the park since 1958 – the longest continuous study of large mammals ever conducted. The researchers' findings have influenced wolf conservation efforts around the world.

Isle Royale is also home to a wide variety of other wildlife, including red squirrels, snowshoe hares, beavers, red foxes, and otters. "Camp foxes" are particularly plentiful around the bustling Rock Harbor Campground and cottages. On a leisurely evening stroll, you're likely to see several of the playful critters bounding through the woods and wrestling with each other. Over 120 species of birds regularly inhabit the island, and another 100 species can been spotted occasionally. Some of the regulars include loons, ducks, mergansers, osprey, and bald eagles.

The island's unusual climate and relative isolation have contributed to a great diversity in plant life, making Isle Royale a popular destination for botanical researchers and armchair gardeners alike. In fact, more than 700 species of plants can be found in the park, including some that are typical of the Arctic tundra and others that are common to the Black Hills of South Dakota. The cool and humid northeastern part of the island supports a boreal forest, consisting mainly of balsam fir and white spruce, while the warmer and drier southern part of the island is a northern hardwood forest made up of sugar maple and yellow birch. Beneath the towering canopy of trees is an often-dense undergrowth that includes thimbleberry, alder, 32 kinds of orchids, and 525 species of fungi.

Adventures

On Foot

Isle Royale is a hiker's dream, offering an extensive system of trails, predominantly cool weather, moderate elevation changes, and frequent opportunities to view wildlife. Over 166 miles of hiking trails crisscross the island, leading to 36 established campgrounds and innumerable spots of historic or aesthetic interest. Many of the trails require hikers to negotiate rocks, roots, and mud, so sturdy, well-broken-in boots are a must. Average temperatures range from 40 to 70° during the summer, and rain is always a possibility. In late summer, hikers can snack on plentiful thimbleberries and blueberries along the trail (these sweet treats can be addictive – pursuit of thimbleberries has been known to add hours to hikes).

The main east-west artery on Isle Royale is the 40-mile **Greenstone Ridge Trail**, which runs along the island's rocky spine from Windigo to Lookout Louise. Of moderate difficulty, it climbs to

Hiking one of Isle Royale's heavily wooded trails.

the best vantage points on the island and also skirts a number of secluded inland lakes. It takes most backpackers about five days to hike the length of the trail. Many through-hikers opt to travel part of Isle Royale's length on the 28-mile **Minong Ridge Trail**, which begins at Windigo and connects up with the Greenstone Ridge Trail in the middle of the island, near Chickenbone Lake. Rugged and unmaintained, this strenuous route is for experienced hikers (with sound knees and ankles) only, and traveling its length can take the better part of a week. But Minong Ridge also holds the promise of wonderful views of northern Lake Superior and the Canadian mainland, and it has a reputation for great wildlife viewing.

A favorite excursion in the western end of the park is a circuit that encompasses panoramic views from Greenstone Ridge and Feldtmann Ridge, Feldtmann Lake's angler-friendly waters, and the Siskiwit Marsh, an historical haunt of both moose and wolves. The loop – which combines the nine-mile **Feldtmann Lake Trail**, 10-mile **Feldtmann Ridge Trail**, and 4.8-mile **Island Mine Trail** with six miles of the Greenstone Ridge Trail – is of moderate difficulty and requires about three days to complete.

Numerous popular trails originate in the Rock Harbor area as well. The 13-mile **Rock Harbor Trail** follows the island's southern shoreline over rocks and through woods to Daisy Farm and Moskey Basin, pleasant but busy campgrounds on a scenic, protected bay of Lake Superior. A favorite day-hike from Rock Harbor is the **Stoll Trail**, an easy, four-mile loop that passes evidence of some of the earliest mining efforts on the island.

Many other trails of various lengths are carved into the island as well, ranging from the cluster of short trails on Isle Royale's east end to the 10-mile **Indian Portage Trail**, a north-south trail that cuts across the island's midsection and is commonly used by canoers (for portaging among the inland lakes) and hikers (who use it to splice together trips featuring portions of both the Minong Ridge and Greenstone Ridge Trails).

On Water

Canoeing & Kayaking

 Water is one of the main attractions at Isle Royale, from the clear, cold, blue-green waters of Lake Superior to the serene beauty of the island's numerous inland lakes. Boaters and experienced sea kayakers can travel along the spectacular, rocky shoreline, explore the numerous offshore islands, or take shelter in one of many secluded natural harbors.

The NPS discourages canoeists from tackling the open waters of Lake Superior, which has a mercurial temperament and rarely tops a numbing 45° even in summer.

Most canoeists gravitate to a series of scenic lakes in the island's central interior for their paddling and fishing pleasure. These lakes – **Lake Whittlesey, Wood Lake, Siskiwit Lake, Intermediate Lake, Lake Richie, Lake LeSage, Lake Livermore**, and **Chickenbone Lake** – are connected to one another by a system of portages, most of which are less than half a mile in length. Quiet and uncrowded, these pristine lakes offer hours of solitude and good fishing to those who make the effort to reach them. This network of lakes can be accessed from Moskey Basin, McCargoe Cove, Chippewa Harbor, and Malone Bay via portages that range from 0.3 miles (Malone Bay) to two miles (Moskey Basin).

 Inland paddlers would do well to remember that, while the lakes offer top-notch fishing and blissfully quiet surroundings, they are not suitable swimming holes; a number of the inland lakes contain disconcertingly large leeches.

Sea kayakers can roam the island's outer fringes, exploring Isle Royale's many beautiful coves and craggy satellite islands. Given the rugged appeal of the island, the considerable mystique that shrouds Lake Superior, and the presence of attractive shoreline campsites, it is little wonder that Isle Royale's shores have emerged as a favorite destination of veteran sea kayakers over the last several years.

 Make no mistake, the park is no place for inexperienced paddlers. Superior's icy and unpredictable waters should be explored only by experienced kayakers armed with appropriate storm gear and the ability to recognize and adapt to changing weather conditions.

Kayakers visiting Isle Royale have two primary options: they can head westward down the island's southern coastline or they can light out for the so-called "Five Fingers" region that crowns the mainland's eastern end. Those who head westward when they embark from the Rock Harbor area will find shelter from outlying islands for the first half-dozen miles. This stretch also features a number of campgrounds that are often crowded with backpackers and powerboaters. Kayakers moving on from picturesque Moskey Basin (nine miles from Rock Harbor) will encounter a hardy southern shoreline rippling with low cliff faces, rocky beaches, and dense forest. The dearth of sheltering islands along Isle Royale's southern flanks can make for choppy going, but there are several bays in which paddlers can seek refuge, principally Conglomerate Bay, Chippewa Harbor, Blueberry Cove, and Malone Bay (22 miles from Rock Harbor). Kayakers following the shoreline westward will then hit Hay Bay, a pretty little slot in the side of the much larger Siskiwit Bay. A thin reef of islands provide Siskiwit Bay with a meager measure of protection from Superior, but paddlers should still be prepared for rough water through this stretch. The bay offers a couple different camping options, at Hay Bay and Siskiwit Bay Campground (the latter lies 31 miles from Rock Harbor).

Isle Royale's wild shores make the park a favorite destination for canoeists and sea kayakers.

After passing around Point Houghton, kayakers will find themselves on Lake Superior proper, with nothing but endless waves on their left flank. Small coves and beaches dot the wild shoreline along this stretch. Three jutting pieces of land – Long Point, The Head, and Rainbow Point – mark the southwest corner of the island. From there the shoreline banks to the north and, after passing by two exceptionally pretty coves (Rainbow Cove and Grace Harbor), sidles into Washington Harbor and Windigo park headquarters (52 nautical miles from Rock Harbor). This is the end of the line for most paddlers. The only kayakers who brave Isle Royale's northwestern side are usually circumnavigating the entire island. Others, mindful of that unprotected shoreline's reputation for dangerous seas and poor landing options, either conclude their journeys at Windigo or take *Voyageur* to the park's Five Fingers area.

The **Five Fingers** is an island-speckled paradise for kayakers and canoeists, and a substantial number of paddlers who visit Isle Royale spend all their time there. A maze of fjord-like waterways, grizzled islands, and dazzling natural harbors, the area is an incredibly atmospheric and evocative one to paddle through. Five Fingers can be approached from either Rock Harbor or McCargoe Cove, on the island's north side. The latter is a prized launching spot for kayakers, but paddlers will face several miles of unprotected paddling along the park's northern coastline before reaching the safety of Herring Bay (canoeists should use extreme caution here). Once in Herring Bay, a short portage leads to Pickerel Cove, a lovely waterway that opens out into the heart of Five Fingers. Adventurers heading out from Rock Harbor can either cruise around Blake Point, the park's far northeastern point, or take a 0.8-mile portage from Tobin Harbor into Duncan Bay. Both routes have their drawbacks. Blake Point can get mean, and canoeists should not try it under any circumstances. The Tobin Harbor-Duncan Bay portage is not a barrel of laughs, either. To be perfectly blunt, it stinks. This portage is extremely steep on the north side of Greenstone Ridge, and mishaps can and do occur.

Once safely ensconced in the Five Fingers' calm waters, you can put such hassles behind you and enjoy miles of breathtaking scenery. A spectacular patchwork of secluded coves and strangely misshapen islands (several of which still hold the decaying skeletons of old cabins on their tangled shores), the Five Fingers region should be savored; give yourself at least three or four days to explore its secrets.

Boating & Sailing

Isle Royale's numerous hideaway harbors – and limitless opportunities for fishing, hiking, and scuba diving – attract many boaters. The park service ferry will carry small boats across from Houghton for a fee, while larger vessels can make the crossing themselves. The marina at Rock Harbor can accommodate boats up to 65 feet in length, and full services are available. All boaters should stop in one of the ranger stations to obtain a permit upon arrival. Over the course of a 100-mile circumnavigation of the main island, boaters will find many sheltered areas equipped with small docks that provide access to the park's campgrounds and hiking trails. In order to protect the island's wildlife, no pets are allowed within the park boundaries, even if they are kept onboard at all times.

Fishing

Many canoeists (and hikers) pack a rod and reel. The waters of Isle Royale provide excellent opportunities for anglers, with significant populations of rainbow, brook, and lake trout, northern pike, yellow perch, and walleye. A Michigan fishing license is required in Lake Superior, but no license is needed to fish the inland lakes and streams. Michigan catch limits apply and the use of live bait is not allowed. (Fishing licenses can be obtained at most stores that sell fishing gear or bait.)

Scuba Diving

Shipwrecks

Ten major shipwrecks dot the waters near Isle Royale, making the park a mecca for scuba divers. Many of the wrecks are exceptionally well-preserved due to the cold waters of Lake Superior, a factor that only increases the allure of the region.

The 164-foot *America* is perhaps the best known of Isle Royale's shipwrecks. The vessel, which was lost during a 1928 storm after hitting a reef, lies just north of Washington Harbor in the North Gap, a narrow passage between Thompson Island and the mainland. The stern of the *America* lies at about 70 feet, but its bow is in just a few feet of water and can be seen from the surface. This is an excellent dive that offers extensive penetration of the ship's ballroom, galley, kitchen, and engine room. Given the level of boat traffic that passes through the North Gap, though, divers are urged to deploy floating diver-down flags here in addition to the standard dive flag that they fly on their boat.

Further west, about three miles off Washington Island, lie the remains of three other Great Lakes vessels – the **Cumberland**, the **Henry Chisholm**, and the **George M. Cox**. The latter two ships are favorite dive sites. Both vessels lie near the Rock of Ages Lighthouse (built in 1908), which looms over the notorious Rock of Ages Reef. This reef struck down both the *Cox* and the *Chisholm*. Blinded by a fogbank, the 259-foot *George M. Cox* sank in 1933 on its maiden voyage after being refitted as a luxury liner. It lies keel-up at a depth of 15-95 feet. The 256-foot *Chisholm* ran aground on the reef in 1898, 10 years before the lighthouse was built. Its remains are scattered across the lake floor at depths ranging from 25 to well over 100 feet (the steam engine lies at 140 feet). This is an advanced dive with no penetration opportunities.

The northern end of the park features a couple of popular wreck diving sites as well. The 532-foot **Chester Congdon** lies two miles northeast of Hill Point. It rests in two pieces, for the reef on which it ran aground in 1918 snapped the vessel in two. The *Congdon*'s bow sits in 70-110 feet of water, while its stern lies at 30-180 feet. This is an advanced dive. The **Emperor** lies about one mile to the east. The 525-foot ship, which was lost in 1947, offers diving for a variety of ability levels. Less experienced divers can explore the boat's bow, which lies in relatively shallow water, while advanced divers can descend to its stern, which sits at 170 feet.

Divers must obtain a free permit from one of the ranger stations on the island before setting out. Removal of artifacts from the water is prohibited. Licensed sport diving charter operators in Isle Royale's waters include **Superior Diver** (PO Box 388, Grand Portage, MN 55605, ☎ 218-475-2316), **Superior Trips** (7348 Symphony St. NE, Fridley, MN 55432, ☎ 612-854-1165), **Lake**

Superior Excursions (PO Box 448, Mile 52, Highway 61, Beaver Bay, MN 55601, ☎ 218-226-4100), and The Royale Diver (3444 White Bear Ave., White Bear Lake, MN 55110, ☎612-773-8710).

Camping & Accommodations

A free permit, available on the National Park Service boat or at the visitor centers on the island, is required for camping. The park's 36 campgrounds are spaced at convenient intervals of three to seven miles, and most are near water and have a pit toilet. Many also feature a limited number of three-sided shelters – a blessing in wet weather – but few allow campfires. Campsites are first-come, first-served, but early birds are usually willing to make room for weary travelers who arrive late in the day. Precautions should be taken when storing food, as the squirrels and foxes are persistent and ingenious camp robbers. All water must be filtered or boiled before use – chemical treatments are ineffective against the tapeworm and intestinal bacteria that often infect it. Black flies and mosquitos can be problematic, especially in June and July, so bring plenty of insect repellent.

The only accommodations on Isle Royale are found at Rock Harbor Lodge. Many of the lodge's 60 rustic but comfortable rooms overlook Lake Superior, and there are also 20 housekeeping cabins available in the woods nearby. Rates for the lodge itself are $162 per night, double occupancy, which includes all meals. The cabins with kitchenettes are $98 per night, double occupancy. The Rock Harbor Lodge dining room offers a breakfast buffet, as well as a choice of three or four entrées at lunch and dinner. The dinner specialty is delicious, fresh-caught Lake Superior trout. The restaurant is also the only place on the island to enjoy a well-deserved cold beer after you emerge from the wilderness.

Guests at the Rock Harbor Lodge can shop at the visitor center or the nearby gift shop. The Rock Harbor area also provides easy access to trails for day-hikes or picnics, and canoes or charter boats are available for rent at the Rock Harbor marina. Boat tours depart from the harbor to six historic and scenic locations around the island, including the 1840s Edisen Fishery. Park rangers run guided nature hikes during the day and present informational programs at night. For further information, contact Rock Harbor Lodge, PO Box 405, Houghton, MI 49931. ☎ 906-337-4993 (May-September); 502-773-2191 (October-April).

■ *Tips For A Greater Adventure* ■

As you might expect, the trails and campgrounds near the major dropoff points at Rock Harbor and Windigo tend to be relatively crowded. To ensure greater seclusion on a backpacking trip, and to avoid having to retrace your steps, make arrangements ahead of time to have a water taxi service take you to a more distant trailhead, like McCargoe Cove, to begin your hike. Isle Royale has many campgrounds and trailheads that are accessible by water, and most of them connect to the major trails back to Rock Harbor and Windigo. This strategy will allow you to make the most of your limited time on the island.

The Rock Harbor Lodge offers two water taxi options, both dependent on weather and lake conditions. The *Sandy* offers scheduled scenic cruises Monday through Saturday at a cost ranging from $9.25 to $14.50 for adults. It will drop off and pick up hikers at its regular destinations according to its cruise schedule. The other water taxi service provides significantly greater flexibility. For an initial cost of $60, plus $10 per person, it will drop off or pick up as many as six passengers at a number of locations around the island, seven days per week. Contact **National Park Concession Service**, Mammoth Cave, KY 42259-0027, ☎ 502-773-2191.

The Rock Harbor area becomes particularly crowded the evening before the *Ranger III* departs for the mainland, because everyone wants to be close by so they don't miss the 9 AM boat. If you plan to stay at the Rock Harbor Campground that night, and especially if you have hopes of nabbing a shelter, try to get there before noon. There are plenty of day-hikes and other activities (renting a canoe, browsing the gift shops, giving newly arrived visitors the benefit of your advice, etc.) to keep you busy as you readjust to civilization.

To Find Out More

The National Park Service has pamphlets describing many aspects of Isle Royale. Contact the park headquarters for specifics. In addition, an enthusiastic visitor has copied much of the Park Service information onto the Internet at http://www.nyx.net/~sjhoward/Isle_Royale.

■ Mackinac Island State Park

Mackinac Island, MI 48757
☎ 906-847-3328

Located in the Straits of Mackinac between Michigan's Upper and Lower Peninsulas, Mackinac Island has attracted tourists for more than a century with its unique combination of scenic beauty, historic landmarks, and quaint Victorian atmosphere. Three miles long and two miles wide, the island is accessible only by boat or plane. No cars are allowed (with the exception of a few emergency and construction vehicles), so the main streets of town are often crowded with pedestrians, bicycles, and horse-drawn carriages. Though Mackinac Island's best-known attractions include its shopping district – several blocks of false-fronted Victorian buildings that house cafés, gift shops, and inns – historic Fort Mackinac, and the stately Grand Hotel, about half of the island remains undeveloped and wooded. An eight-mile paved road allows cyclists to circumnavigate the island, taking in beautiful views of the Straits and the Mackinac Bridge and visiting quiet beaches along the way. In addition, 50 marked trails and paths offer hikers and horseback riders access to the natural wonders of the island's interior.

Getting There

The two main access points to Mackinac Island are Mackinaw City in the Lower Peninsula (280 miles from Detroit) and St. Ignace in the Upper Peninsula (seven miles from Mackinaw City). Three commercial ferry services run to the island: **Arnold Transit** (☎ 906-847-3351), which has catamarans that make the crossing in 10-15 minutes as well as other boats that provide a more leisurely ride; and **Shepler's (☎** 616-436-5023**)** or **Star Line (☎** 906-643-7635**)**, each of which offers a 20-minute hydroplane ride. All three ferry companies operate out of both Mackinaw City and St. Ignace, and they have standardized rates with an extra charge for bicycles and overnight parking. The ferries generally run every half-hour between 8 AM and 7 PM during the peak summer season and less frequently during the off-season. Call for current schedules and rate information.

The state park, which takes up over 80% of the island, is open year-round, as are several hotels. The peak tourist season occurs between mid-June and mid-September, though most ferries provide service from early May to late October. Aside from offering an escape from the crowds, spring brings wildflowers, while fall provides beautiful color. Only a few hearty souls visit Mackinac Island during the winter, though the island's roads and trails offer good cross-country skiing. Arnold Transit continues operating on a limited schedule through late December, but in the dead of winter the only way to reach the island is by plane or by snowmobile when the ice is solid enough. There are 600 year-round residents.

Mackinac Island is also accessible by air, boasting an airport with a 3,500-foot, paved, lighted runway. **Great Lakes Air (☎** 906-643-7165**)** offers regular service to the island from St. Ignace. Private planes can also land here for a small fee, and ample tie-down space is available. Call the airport at **☎** 906-847-3231. **Northwest Airlines (☎** 800-225-2525**)** makes scheduled flights to Pellston Airport, about 12 miles south of Mackinaw City, from both Detroit and Chicago. From there, you can take a land taxi to the ferry docks **(Wolverine Stages, ☎** 616-539-8635**)** or an air taxi (through **Great Lakes Air)** to the island's airport. Call for current schedules and rate information.

Private boats are welcome at Mackinac Island's popular state-owned marina **(☎** 906-847-3561**)**. Many of the 100 slips are available on a first-come, first-served basis, and are full during much of the summer season. Docking rates are based on the size of the vessel. When the marina is full, boaters are allowed to anchor in the harbor for free. Keep in mind that the Chicago-Mackinac and Port Huron-Mackinac sailboat races are held during the second and third weekends of July each year. It is best not to bring private craft to the island during this time, as the marina will be overflowing.

History

Hundreds of years ago, Mackinac Island was a place of great spiritual significance to the Native Americans of the Great Lakes region. The Chippewa Indians buried their dead on the island and told stories about its origins and landforms. It served as a base for French traders and missionaries in the late 1600s and early 1700s, then was transferred to British rule. The British built **Fort Mackinac** – which still towers 150 feet above the harbor, with white stone walls surrounding a large parade ground – in 1780 to defend their interests in the area. Today, you can tour several of the fort's buildings and watch as authentically costumed guides act out various military duties from that era (admission to the fort and several other historic attractions costs $6.50 for adults and $4 for children ages 6-12). Americans finally gained control of the island following the Revolutionary War, though it fell into British hands again for two years during the War of 1812.

Mackinac Island became the center for the region's fur trade during the early 1800s. The former offices and warehouse of John Ja-

Mackinac Island's famous Grand Hotel (Balthazar Koras).

cob Astor's American Fur Company are now a museum on Market Street. As the fur trade declined, the island became a fishing base between 1840 and 1880. In 1875, Mackinac Island became the second location in the United States (after Yellowstone) to be named a national park. Twenty years later, administration of the island was taken over by the state of Michigan. Eventually it was transformed into a premier summer vacation spot for wealthy travelers who arrived from all over the country by train or aboard luxury steamboats. A coalition of railroad tycoons led by Cornelius Vanderbilt constructed the Grand Hotel in 1886. The hotel's 800-foot-long, white-pillared porch was a centerpiece in the movie *Somewhere in Time*. Today, all except paying guests must pay an admission fee to come in, look around, and visit the hotel's shops, restaurants, swimming pool, and clay tennis courts. A number of other turn-of-the-century Victorian homes and buildings are still in use on the island as private residences or bed-and-breakfasts.

Flora & Fauna

Outside of the bustling marina and downtown, Mackinac Island offers many undeveloped areas to explore. In the transition zone between the conifers of the north and the hardwoods of the south, the island includes a healthy variety of both, as well as some 400 species of wildflowers. Particularly appealing are the blueberries and wild orchids that can be found in bog areas, the trillium blanketing forest floors, and the wild strawberries dotting meadows. Though the island does not support much large wildlife, it is home to many squirrels, raccoons, chipmunks, and rabbits. Birds inhabiting the island year-round include the purple finch, black-capped chickadee, and red-breasted nuthatch, while summer visitors include sea gulls, yellow warblers, and swallows. Mackinac's numerous rocks and caves also attract a large number of bats, which may seem like an eerie presence in evening skies but definitely help to keep the mosquito population in check.

Mackinac Island State Park

HUNTER PUBLISHING

2,000 FEET

Lake Huron

1. Tranquil Bluff Trail
2. Porter Hank's Trail
3. Swamp Trail
4. British Landing
   Nature Trail
5. Croghan Water Trail
6. Lydia Trail &
   Straits Trail
7. Norton Trail
8. Louisignon Trail
9. Coffee Trail
10. Allouez Trail
11. Trillium Trail
12. Medicine Man Trail
13. Firebreak Trail
14. Burl Trail
15. Lost Bear Trail
16. Cliffview Trail
17. Beechwood Trail
18. Morning Snack Trail
19. Juniper Trail
20. Scott's Trail
21. Soldier's Garden Trail
22. Murray Trail
23. North Blodgett Trail
24. South Blodgett Trail
25. Wildflower Nature
    Trail
26. North Bicycle Trail
27. Quarry Trail
28. Rock Trail
29. Winnebago Trail
30. Manitou Trail
31. South Bicycle Trail

Adventures

On Foot

Mackinac Island offers many natural wonders and scenic vistas that can be accessed on foot via its 100 miles of roads and paths. Over 50 different marked trails – ranging from easy strolls along paved paths to moderately strenuous hikes up wooded hillsides – lead to a wide variety of interesting sites. The island's best-known natural feature is **Arch Rock**, a spectacular limestone formation rising 150 feet above the water and spanning 50 feet from end to end. Another rock worth seeing is **Sugar Loaf**, a 75-foot-tall limestone tower that rises improbably in the middle of the forest. The island also features **Skull Cave**, which was once used as an Indian burial ground, and **Devil's Kitchen**, a smaller cave along the western shore. **Fort Holmes**, at the island's highest point, is an excellent picnic area offering enchanting views of the harbor and surrounding waters. As an added bonus, walking through the hilly, forested center of the island usually provides a break from the bicycle and carriage traffic that dominates the main roads. The island also features two public golf courses and several tennis courts.

Arch Rock, one of several spectacular rock formations in Mackinac Island State Park (Travel Michigan).

On Wheels

Bicycling & Mountain Biking

 Since automobiles are prohibited, most of the wheels on Mackinac Island belong to the 2,500 bicycles that generally spend the summer there. You can bring your own bikes across on the ferry for a small fee, or there are a number of places to rent them on the island. Near the Shepler dock on the west end of town, try **Iroquois Bike Rental (☎ 906-847-3321)**, **Island Bicycle Livery (☎ 906-847-3372)**, or **Ryba's Bikes (☎ 906-847-6261)**. Near the Arnold Line dock in the center of town, try **Lake View Bikes (☎ 906-847-3351)**. The most popular bike route is the eight-mile relatively flat paved road along the island's perimeter, which offers outstanding views as well as access to many other trails. Daring mountain bikers will enjoy the **Manitou Trail**, a half-mile single-track full of roots, rocks, and sharp turns that runs along the edge of a 50-foot cliff. The Manitou Trail ends at Arch Rock, but knobbies can continue their heart-pounding adventure along the ironically named **Tranquil Bluff Trail** for another three miles.

Horse-Drawn Carriages

Horse-drawn carts and carriages are major modes of transportation on the island. About 600 horses spend the summer on Mackinac Island, working in various capacities hauling tourists, luggage, mail, and garbage. Guided carriage tours can provide a good introduction to the island and its many attractions. **Arrowhead Carriages (☎ 906-847-6112)**, **Carriage Tours (☎ 906-847-6152)**, and **Gough (☎ 906-847-3391)** can arrange a private, customized tour for groups of four to six people. Carriage Tours also offers group tours to some of the island's highlights on 16- or 35-passenger carriages, while **Jack's Riding Stable (☎ 906-847-3391)** rents carriages that you can drive yourself. There are also carriage taxi services that will take up to 12 passengers wherever they want to go on the island. The taxis operate 24 hours per day, and can be flagged down on the street or dispatched to certain locations (**☎ 847-3323** for a pickup). It is best to avoid the taxi services if you are on a tight schedule, however, since they often alter routes to pick up and drop off other passengers along the way.

Jack's and two other stables, **Cindy's** (☎ 906-847-3572) and **Chambers'** (☎ 906-847-6231), rent saddle horses on an hourly basis. Saddle horses are not allowed on Main Street, Lake Shore Drive, or in front of the Grand Hotel, but riders can mosey through the woods or past many of the Victorian homes. A guide usually accompanies each small group of riders on rented horses.

In-Line Skating

In recent years, Mackinac Island has seen a tremendous influx of in-line skaters. Long outlawed because it can spook the island's horses, skating is now one of the most popular activities along its outer stretches (it is still forbidden in the downtown area). Many skaters flock to M-185, an 8.3-mile stretch of road that features many rest benches and unparalleled scenic views. In fact, this route is so popular that mid-day skates can degenerate into aggravating tests of maneuvering skill; better to hit the road in the morning or early evening. Skate rentals are available on the island.

On Water

The waters surrounding Mackinac Island offer nearly unlimited recreational opportunities, from swimming, sunbathing, stone-skipping, and freighter-watching along the beach to fishing and scuba diving in the Straits of Mackinac. Although shallow water and consistent boat traffic make fishing from the island's shore inadvisable, anglers can hook abundant king and coho salmon, as well as brown and lake trout, in the Straits. Two charter boat companies operate on the island, **Mackinac Island Charters** (☎ 906-847-6505) and **Professional Marine Services** (☎ 906-847-6580).

Scuba Diving

The **Straits Bottomland Preserve** contains several accessible shipwrecks that are popular with scuba divers, including the *Cedarville*, a 588-foot boat sitting in 35 feet of water. Call the **Straits Scuba Center** at ☎ 906-643-7009.

Camping & Accommodations

No camping is allowed on Mackinac Island, but there are several campgrounds nearby on the mainland. **Wilderness State Park** (☎ 616-436-5381), 12 miles west of Mackinaw City, offers 250 modern sites along a white sand beach. **Cheboygan State Park** (☎ 616-627-2811), three miles south of Cheboygan, has 75 wooded sites a short walk from Lake Huron. **Straits State Park** (☎ 906-643-8620), two miles from St. Ignace in the UP, offers 322 modern sites with a great view of the Mackinac Bridge.

Even without camping, there are many choices for accommodations on Mackinac Island. A wide variety of inns, bed-and-breakfasts, and tourist homes are available, in addition to the Grand Hotel. Franchise hotels are prohibited, so all lodgings are family owned and operated. In keeping with the historic atmosphere of the island, most are also quite old. Prices range from $50 per night for a basic cottage during the off-season to $500 per night for a peak-period suite at the Grand Hotel. But the Grand Hotel does provide luxury for the price, including immaculately decorated rooms, a heated pool, clay tennis courts, attractive gardens, and eight restaurants and lounges. Guests are expected to don formal attire after 6 PM (coat and tie for men, dress or nice pantsuit for women).

There are more than 40 dining options on the island, ranging from burger joints and sandwich shops to elegant steak and seafood restaurants. Most eateries are clustered on and around Main Street in the downtown area. Many of the more casual places will package picnics, and Zac's Deli will even loan you a backpack to take your lunch on the road. Some of the more popular restaurants include: the **Pub Oyster Bar and Grill**, an 1890s-style saloon with a large menu; **Jesse's Chuck Wagon**, an inexpensive, 1950s-style diner; the **Village Inn**, a favorite local watering hole that offers family dining; the **Harbor View Dining Room** at the Chippewa Hotel, a popular breakfast spot with a great view; the **Carriage House** at the Iroquois Hotel, known for its delicious lunch and dinner specials served on a terrace overlooking the Straits; and the **Mustang Lounge**, which has the distinction of being the only island restaurant open all year. While recovering from a hearty meal, you may enjoy strolling through the numerous gift shops in town, or standing outside the window of one of the dozen fudge shops to watch the bakers at work. The main shopping district is on Main and Market Streets between Fort Street and French Lane.

■ *Tips For A Greater Adventure* ■

Even though the **sailboat race weeks** are not the best time to bring a private boat to Mackinac Island, it is an exciting time to visit, particularly if you can time your trip to coincide with the arrival of the lead boats from Chicago or Port Huron. You can watch the captains of winning vessels being thrown in the harbor by their jubilant crews, and you can join in the major celebration that takes place after the sailors set foot on dry land. Just be sure to make reservations for overnight accommodations well in advance. Races are held the second and third weekends in July. Contact the **Port Huron Convention & Visitors Bureau**, ☎ 800-852-4242.

> *Mackinac Connection: An Insider's Guide*, by longtime summer resident Amy McVeigh, describes all the island's sights, shops, restaurants, and accommodations in detail, and even includes tips on how to avoid immediate identification as a "fudgie" (the locals' name for tourists).

■ Ottawa National Forest

E6248 US Highway 2
Ironwood, MI 49938
☎ 906-932-1330

Covering 954,000 acres of the western Upper Peninsula, Ottawa is Michigan's largest National Forest. It has something for every taste, including picturesque waterfalls, deep rock gorges, rugged hills, and placid inland lakes. Nearly 200 miles of hiking trails offer everything from easy strolls to vigorous multi-day backpacking trips. In addition, Ottawa features over 500 lakes and 1,500 miles of rivers and streams to attract anglers, canoeists, and kay-

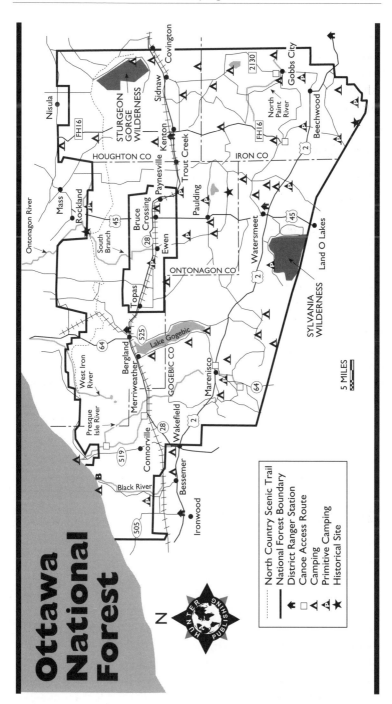

Ottawa National Forest

N

5 MILES

- - - North Country Scenic Trail
— National Forest Boundary
← District Ranger Station
□ Canoe Access Route
▲ Camping
▲ Primitive Camping
★ Historical Site

akers. And with more than 200 inches of snowfall each year, the forest provides innumerable opportunities for snowmobilers, skiers, and snowshoers. Ottawa has 27 developed campgrounds – most of which are along the shores of fishable lakes and rivers – and three designated wilderness areas.

Getting There

Ottawa is in the extreme western Upper Peninsula, occupying parts of Ontonagon, Gogebic, Houghton, and Iron Counties. It stretches from the Wisconsin border in the south to Porcupine Mountains State Park in the north. The two main points of access are US-2 and M-28, which traverse the UP from east to west.

History

Native Americans occupied the western UP region from prehistoric times. The copper they mined in the hills was traded across North America. Europeans arrived and joined in these early mining efforts in the 1700s. Around the turn of the century, the Europeans changed the landscape by logging many of the original pines, hemlocks, sugar maples, and yellow birches, making room for other species. Ottawa became a National Forest in 1931.

Flora & Fauna

The topography of Ottawa National Forest was formed with the retreat of glaciers from an ice age 10,000 years ago. The glaciers created rolling hills topped with exposed rock, and dotted the lowlands with lakes and swamps. Today, forested areas contain pine, maple, fir, spruce, and birch trees, while a wide variety of wildflowers occupy meadows and open areas. Fauna in the region includes black bears, white-tailed deer, moose, and wolves, as well as a number of smaller animals. Ottawa is also known as a haven for birdwatchers. More than 240 species have been identified, including bald eagles, broad-winged hawks, peregrine falcons, turkey vultures, green-backed herons, tundra swans, sandhill cranes, common loons, sandpipers, woodpeckers, ruffled grouse, and several types of owls.

Adventures

On Foot

Ottawa's nearly 200 miles of hiking trails provide access to dozens of waterfalls, scenic overlooks, fishing holes, and beaches. Ranging from easy strolls along paved paths to bushwacking treks through rugged wilderness, Ottawa has something to offer hikers of all interests and abilities. A 118-mile stretch of the **North Country National Scenic Trail** runs the width of the National Forest, leading through some of the most challenging (and rewarding) terrain in the entire trail system. The Ottawa section crosses multiple streams, climbs to the top of high ridges, follows the edge of towering cliffs, passes through heavy brush, and provides views of many waterfalls. For a complete description of the trail, see the *Hiking/Backpacking* section, page 281. The nine-mile **Gogebic Ridge Trail** is a popular spur that meets up with the North Country Trail at M-64, north of Bergland. Beginning at a trailhead on Forest Road 250, one mile north of M-28, it follows the shore of Weary Lake, climbs over Cookout Mountain, and provides an overlook of Lake Gogebic along the way.

Boasting dozens of named waterfalls on a variety of rivers and streams, Ottawa is sometimes referred to as "waterfall country." Many of the falls are accessible via relatively short – although often steep – trails from the National Forest's roads and campgrounds. For example, from a trailhead off Forest Road 2270, on the east side of the Sturgeon River Gorge Wilderness, you can hike a trail that winds down into the gorge and along the river to 40-foot **Sturgeon Falls**. Alternatively, follow the signs to Silver Mountain and climb the stairs up to the top for a stunning view of the whole area. Another popular trail runs from a parking area on Bond Falls Road, east of M-45 from Paulding, to the base of **Bond Falls** on the Middle Branch of the Ontonagon River (be on the lookout for poison ivy along the early portions of the trail). Further upstream, **Mex-I-Min-E Falls** can be accessed from the Burned Dam Campground. Beginning on CR-523 north of US-2, trails run along both sides of the Presque Isle River to a long stretch of tumbling rapids known as **Yondota Falls**. Some of the best waterfall viewing is in the Black River Harbor Recreation Area, in the northwestern end of Ottawa. A network of trails, complete with stairways and observation platforms, provides awesome views of a series of waterfalls running through the steep gorge.

Ottawa's **Sylvania Wilderness Area** – about four miles southwest of Watersmeet on CR-535, near the Wisconsin border – contains 30 miles of hiking trails that offer scenic views of numerous clear lakes and many opportunities for swimming. A permit is required for camping at the area's rustic campgrounds. ☎ 906-885-5275 or stop in the Watersmeet Visitor Center. This visitor center is also the starting point for one of Ottawa's five interpretive trails, which range from one to 2½ miles in length. The others are at the Bob Lake, Lake Ottawa, Lake Ste. Kathryn, and Norway Lake Campgrounds.

On Wheels

Mountain Biking

Ottawa features a mountain bike trail system that is considered one of the best in the state. The 27-mile **Ehlco Mountain Bike Complex** – southwest of Silver City, including a section of Porcupine Mountains Wilderness State Park – follows overgrown logging roads and features a bridgeless crossing of a branch of the Iron River. The **Pomeroy/Henry Lake Complex** – near Marenisco along the Wisconsin border – skirts the edge of over a dozen lakes.

The **State Line Rail Trail** runs along the Michigan-Wisconsin border for more than 100 miles, making it Michigan's longest rail-trail. It is one of the state's more demanding rail-trails, but the scenic component of the trip more than compensates. The pathway goes through beautiful hardwood forests and over more than 50 bridges, many of them straddling untamed wilderness rivers. In addition, the State Line Trail runs through prime bald eagle habitat. The region's beauty, coupled with the length of the trail, make it a natural for overnight trips. The northern end of the trail lies just south of Wakefield on Korpela Road, while the southern trailhead can be picked up at the Brule River south of Crystal Falls, near US-141. Two smaller rail-trails, the **Waters-meet/Land O' Lakes Trail** (nine miles) and the **Little Falls Trail** (6½ miles) can be accessed midway along the trail.

There are many other trails open to knobbies in Ottawa, but bikes are banned in designated wilderness areas, such as Sturgeon River Gorge and Sylvania. ☎ 906-575-3441 for maps and further information.

On Water

 With hundreds of different lakes and rivers, Ottawa offers endless opportunities for water recreation. Parts of six river systems that run through the National Forest have been classified as National Wild and Scenic Rivers: the Black, Ontonagon, Paint, Presque Isle, Sturgeon, and Yellow Dog.

Canoeing & Kayaking

Ottawa's topography provides two very different environments for canoeing and kayaking. South of M-28, the landscape is fairly flat, offering peaceful paddles on small inland lakes or wide, meandering rivers. But in the hilly country north of M-28, the rivers tend to drop over rock ledges and waterfalls as they rush headlong to meet Lake Superior. These northern rivers are also subject to extreme fluctuations in water level; what was running dangerously high in early spring might slow to a mere trickle in late summer. As a result, paddlers wishing to attempt the rivers in the northern half of the National Forest must plan carefully. The basic facts of a few of the most popular rivers are included here, but see *On Water, Canoeing/Kayaking* under *Adventures Region-Wide* (page 286) for further information.

Black River

The Black River, in Ottawa's northwestern corner, is one of the state's most challenging for experienced whitewater canoeists and kayakers. The eight-mile stretch between the put-in at CR-513 and the intersection of US-2 features Class I-II rapids. You must take out at the US-2 Bridge to avoid Neepikon and Gabro Falls – both impassable by canoe. The next access is at Blackjack

Ski Area, and for the next 9½ miles slow-moving water alternates with light rapids, making it suitable for paddlers with basic skills. But below The Narrows are several miles of Class II-III rapids, featuring large boulders and several significant drops, that should be attempted by only the most accomplished whitewater canoeists and kayakers.

Brule River

The mild-mannered Brule River forms the border between Michigan and Wisconsin in the southeastern corner of Ottawa National Forest. It features several stretches of Class I rapids interspersed with easier paddling, and just three stretches of Class II water that should not trouble experienced canoeists and kayakers. Paddlers can put in at the US Forest Service Campground just across the Wisconsin border off M-73 (Wisconsin-55), about two miles from the river's source at Brule Lake. Nearly 40 miles later, the Brule intersects with the Paint River above the Brule Island Dam.

Ontonagon River

The Ontonagon River system, in the northeastern section of Ottawa, offers a wide variety of possibilities for canoe and kayak adventures. Made up of the mainstream, the South Branch, the East Branch, and the Middle Branch, the Ontonagon system features many stretches of Class I-III rapids, excellent fishing, and abundant camping possibilities. The relatively challenging South Branch, accessible from the M-28 Bridge in Ewen, alternates slow-moving water with Class I-II rapids on its way to Victoria Basin, some 26 miles downstream. The remote East Branch features nearly continuous Class II-III rapids in the 7½-mile stretch between USFS-208 and US-45, and is only recommended for experienced whitewater paddlers. The Middle Branch is best accessed from the public site at the US-45 Bridge in Watersmeet. It offers a fairly easy paddle until the portage around Mex-I-Min-E Falls, nine miles downstream at the Burned Dam Campground. The remaining 11 miles of river before Bond Falls Dam include several moderately difficult Class I-II rapids.

Paint River

The North and South Branches of the Paint River run through the southeastern area of Ottawa, then meet up at the Paint River

Forks Campground and run another 38 miles to Little Bull Dam. The North and South Branches are accessed off USFS-16, nine and 4½ miles north of US-2, respectively. Each provides a relatively mellow ride to the campground. Beyond that point the mainstream requires portages around Upper and Lower Hemlock Rapids and the Crystal Falls Dam before reaching the final take-out at Little Bull Dam.

Presque Isle River

The Presque Isle River offers experienced whitewater paddlers some of the most challenging terrain in the Midwest. Beginning at the M-28 bridge access, the river gradually increases in speed and intensity over 17½ miles until it becomes a continuous

stretch of Class II-IV rapids. The last few miles of the river are within scenic Porcupine Mountains State Park, and there is a good take-out at South Boundary Road. Just below, the river plummets over a series of picturesque waterfalls before it meets Lake Superior.

Sylvania Wilderness Area

The Sylvania Wilderness, near Watersmeet in the south-central portion of Ottawa, contains 36 pristine lakes that are connected by portage trails, most under a half-mile long. The area also offers excellent and varied fishing, though special rules apply (catch and release, using artificial lures only).

Fishing

Nearly all of the National Forest campgrounds offer fishing opportunities, and most provide boat access. Ottawa's inland lakes, which dot the landscape in the southern half of the forest, range in size from the 4,260-acre **Lac Vieux Desert** on the Wisconsin border to tiny 12-acre ponds. The lakes primarily hold smallmouth bass, bluegill, walleye, and northern pike, though a few hold trout and muskies. In several recent years, the state record northern pike has been taken from **Bond Falls Flowage**.

Opportunities abound in the area's many rivers and streams to catch brook, rainbow, and brown trout. In fact, the Middle Branch of the Ontonagon between Agate Falls and Bond Falls is known as one of the most productive trout streams in the UP. Some of the larger rivers also hold walleye, while the fall brings salmon runs to the mouth of the Presque Isle, the Ontonagon East Branch, and the Black River. Chinook and hybrid salmon have been introduced into the mainstream Ontonagon in recent years.

On Snow

 Ottawa lies in the heart of the UP's "Big Snow Country," an area that features relatively mild winter temperatures and more than 200 inches of annual snowfall. There are several premier downhill skiing facilities nearby (including Big Powderhorn, Blackjack, Brule, Indianhead, and Porcupine Mountains), as well as North America's only ski-flying hill at Copper

Peak. Ottawa also offers more than 174 miles of groomed cross-country ski trails, plus abundant ungroomed areas for snowshoeing and backcountry skiing. There are also over 1,000 miles of groomed snowmobile trails on both National Forest and private land.

Camping

Scattered throughout Ottawa National Forest are 27 developed campgrounds, ranging in size from three to 40 sites. All of the campgrounds are accessible by road and open to both tents and RVs, and all provide picnic tables, fire grates, and toilet facilities. In addition, nearly all of the campgrounds are near lakes or rivers and offer fishing and boat access. Fees range from $5 to $8 per night in most locations, but there is no fee for camping at the Burned Dam, Robbins Pond, Matchwood Tower, Paint River Forks, or Block House Campgrounds. Reservations are accepted for some of the sites in the Norway Lake, Perch Lake, Black River Harbor, and Lake Ste. Kathryn Campgrounds (☎ 800-280-CAMP), and all other sites are available on a first-come, first-served basis. With a few exceptions, Ottawa campgrounds are only open from mid-May through mid-September.

Campgrounds in the **Bessemer Ranger District**, in the western half of the National Forest, include: **Black River Harbor**, 40 sites, 15 miles north of Bessemer on CR-513; **Bobcat Lake**, 12 sites, three miles southeast of Marenisco on FR-8500; **Henry Lake**, 11 sites, 10 miles southwest of Marenisco on FR-8100; **Matchwood Tower**, five sites, four miles southwest of Bergland on Matchwood Tower Road; **Moosehead Lake**, 13 sites, 16 miles southeast of Marenisco on FR-8500; **Pomeroy Lake**, 13 sites, 15 miles southeast of Marenisco on FR-6828; and **Langford Lake**, 11 sites, 20 miles southeast of Marenisco on CR-531.

Campgrounds in the **Iron River Ranger District**, in the southeast corner of the park, include: **Block House**, three sites, 10 miles east of Gibbs City on FR-2180; **Golden Lake**, 22 sites, 14 miles northwest of Iron River on H-16; **Lake Ottawa**, 32 sites, seven miles west of Iron River on Lake Ottawa Road; and **Paint River Forks**, four sites, one mile west of Gibbs City on CR-657.

In the **Kenton Ranger District**, in the east-central section of the National Forest, campgrounds include: **Lake Ste. Kathryn**, 25 sites, eight miles south of Sidnaw on Sidnaw Road; **Lower Dam**, seven sites, seven miles southeast of Kenton on FR-3500; **Norway Lake**, 28 sites, eight miles south of Sidnaw on FR-2400; **Perch Lake**, 20 sites, 11 miles south of Sidnaw on Winslow Lake Road; **Sparrow Rapids**, six sites, four miles northwest of Kenton on FR-1100; **Sturgeon River**, nine sites, five miles north of Sidnaw on FR-2200; and **Tepee Lake**, 17 sites, seven miles south of Kenton on FR-3630.

Campgrounds in the **Ontonagon Ranger District**, in the northeast corner of the National Forest, include: **Bob Lake**, 17 sites, 18 miles southeast of Greenland on FR-1960; and **Courtney Lake**, 21 sites, eight miles east of Greenland on FR-1960.

The **Watersmeet Ranger District**, in the central area of the National Forest, includes the following campgrounds: **Burned Dam**, six sites, seven miles northeast of Watersmeet on FR-4500; **Imp Lake**, 22 sites, six miles southeast of Watersmeet on FR-3978; **Marion Lake**, 39 sites, five miles east of Watersmeet on FR-3980; **Paulding Pond**, four sites, eight miles north of Watersmeet on US-45; **Robbins Pond**, three sites, nine miles northwest of Watersmeet on FR-5230; **Sylvania-Clark Lake**, 35 sites, eight miles southwest of Watersmeet on FR-6360; and **Taylor Lake**, 10 sites, eight miles east of Watersmeet on FR-3960. There is also a developed campground intended for groups of up to 100 people at **Marion Lake**, five miles east of Watersmeet. It features a picnic area, beach, and playing field. For reservations, ☎ 906-358-4551.

Low-impact backcountry camping is allowed in Ottawa, although a current map is required since 40% of the National Forest area consists of private land. Fires are permitted in the backcountry, but cookstoves are recommended. There are excellent opportunities for dispersed camping in the McCormick and Sturgeon River Gorge Wilderness Areas as well. Camping in the Sylvania Wilderness Area, however, is in designated sites by permit only. Obtain a permit for camping at the visitor center in Watersmeet, or ☎ 906-885-5275.

To Find Out More

The **forest supervisor's office** can be reached at E6248 US-Highway 2, Ironwood, MI 49938, ☎ 906-932-1330.

■ Pictured Rocks National Lakeshore

PO Box 40
Munising, MI 49862
☎ 906-387-3700 or 906-387-2607

Along the shore of Lake Superior near Munising, the relentless pounding of waves has carved colorful sandstone into intricate designs – arches, caves, spires, and imposing 200-foot cliffs. These unique features gave Pictured Rocks its name. But the 71,000-acre park also offers white sand beaches, huge sand dunes, dense hardwood forests, marshy areas, inland lakes, and waterfalls. Pictured Rocks has 80 miles of maintained hiking trails, including the 43-mile Lakeshore Trail, which follows the Lake Superior shoreline for the length of the park. Sea kayakers explore the imposing shoreline via kayak, while a privately run, narrated boat tour offers yet another way to view the impressive formations.

Getting There

Pictured Rocks National Lakeshore is in the northeastern Upper Peninsula, on the shore of Lake Superior between Munising and Grand Marais. The Lakeshore Zone at the heart of the park is 40 miles long and only three miles wide, but the park also includes an Inland Buffer Zone that combines public and private lands. The west visitor center, at the junction of M-28 and H-58 in Munising, is open year-round, as is the park headquarters on Sand Point Road. There is also a summer-only visitor center at the east end of the park, on H-58 near the junction of M-77 in Grand Marais. Both the Munising and Grand Marais entrances to Pictured Rocks are accessible from M-28, one of the main east-west drives across the UP.

Though H-58 runs the length of the park's southern boundary, only the western third is paved. The remainder can be treacherous – narrow and winding through deep woods, it often becomes extremely muddy and rutted. If the weather has been at all wet, a four-wheel-drive vehicle is recommended.

History

Ojibwa Indians hunted and fished the Pictured Rocks region for many generations, calling it "the land of thunder and the gods." Though French explorers and trappers visited in the 17th and 18th centuries, large-scale settlement did not occur until the logging boom of the 19th century. Many of today's trails in Pictured Rocks follow the old roads used by loggers to gain access to the white pine forests. The region earned designation as the country's first National Lakeshore in 1966.

Flora & Fauna

The best-known features of Pictured Rocks National Lakeshore are the rocks themselves. These colorful sandstone formations range from sheer cliffs towering 50 to 200 feet above the lake to delicate castle-like structures carved by the endless caress of wind and waves. Over the years, these monuments have acquired such colorful names as Miners Castle, Chapel Rock, and Indianhead. The rocks stretch 15 miles down the Lake Superior shore from Munising before giving way to **Twelvemile Beach**, a picturesque expanse of white sand and pebbles rimmed by woods and punctuated by streams. Finally, continuing east, you reach the **Grand Sable Banks and Dunes**, four square miles of gravel and sand deposited by receding glaciers 10,000 years ago and shifted constantly by winds off Lake Superior.

Fauna in the park includes black bears, white-tailed deer, beavers, and numerous small mammals and birds. There is some evidence that a pack of timber wolves frequents the area as well. In late spring and early summer, however, the most commonly encountered creatures are black flies and mosquitoes, so insect repellent

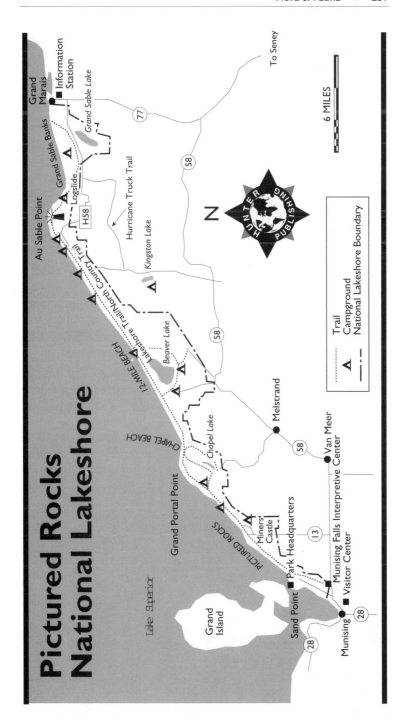

is a must. Since weather can be unpredictable, warm clothing and rain gear are recommended as protection against the sudden storms that sometimes whip up on the lake.

Adventures

On Foot

Exploring on foot is an excellent way to experience the many facets of Pictured Rocks. The main route through the park is the 43-mile **Lakeshore Trail**, which is part of the North Country National Scenic Trail system. The variety it offers makes it a great choice for a week-long backpacking trip. Beginning from the park headquarters, the Lakeshore Trail follows the top of the cliffs overlooking Lake Superior for 15 miles, then traces the edge of Twelvemile Beach to Au Sable Point, then clambers around the backside of the Grand Sable Dunes and past Grand Sable Lake. Hikers will find 13 rustic backcountry campgrounds and seven group sites spaced every two to five miles along the way. Only two of the campgrounds have pit toilets, and water must be obtained from Lake Superior or inland streams and fil-

A peaceful sunset along Lake Superior in Pictured Rocks National Lakeshore (Deborah Hausler).

tered or boiled before use. Campfires are not allowed, so cook-stoves are necessary equipment. Backpackers must obtain a camping permit from park headquarters before departing ($15 for a group of up to six for as many nights as needed), and advance reservations for backcountry campsites are strongly suggested between Memorial Day and Labor Day. A shuttle bus service is available from mid-June to late-September to return through-hikers to their point of origin ($10 per person). For schedule information and reservations, contact the **Alger County Public Transportation Department** at ☎ 800-562-7814.

Pictured Rocks also offers a number of interesting day-hikes or short backpacking trips. Several major trails begin in the Chapel Basin area, toward the west end of the park. Take H-58 east from Munising just past the tiny town of Melstrand, then go five miles north on unpaved Chapel Road. This trailhead accesses the **Mosquito Falls Trail**, which passes two waterfalls and skirts a beaver pond before meeting the Lakeshore Trail at Mosquito Beach, as well as the **Chapel Rock Trail**, which passes Chapel Falls and overlooks Chapel Lake on its way to some of the park's most impressive rock formations along the shore. When coupled with the section of the Lakeshore Trail that traverses Grand Portal Point, these trails form a spectacular seven-mile loop that gives you a taste of the best Pictured Rocks has to offer.

Though not overly strenuous, most trails at Pictured Rocks are hilly, and can often be muddy, rocky, or rooted. Sturdy, water-resistant hiking boots are a must.

On the way into or out of the Pictured Rocks area, don't miss two of the park's most beautiful and accessible waterfalls. **Munising Falls**, a five-minute walk down a paved path from the west visitor center, plummets 50 feet from the top of a rocky overhang and splashes onto a ledge below. You can walk around behind the falls for a better view. Just inside the Grand Marais park entrance is **Sable Falls**, which can be reached via an easy, quarter-mile dirt path through the woods. Steps follow Sable Creek as it tumbles through a narrow gorge and over rocky terraces on its way to Lake Superior.

On Water

Sea Kayaking

 Pictured Rocks offers some of the most spectacular sea kayaking in all the Great Lakes. Although the entire 40-mile shoreline can be explored, most kayakers flock to the great colored cliffs that dominate its west end. Paddlers can wind through and around the amazing pillars, arches, and caves that Superior's icy waves and fierce winds have carved into the cliffs, marveling all the while at the manner in which sunlight and shadow transform the character and hue of rock and water. But kayakers setting out for the 200-foot cliffs of the park's west end should not do so casually; those towering walls are extremely hazardous in bad weather and there's a real danger of being slammed against the rock face. Add to that the fact that there are few pull-out options in the area.

 Given the dangers, it is important for kayakers to obtain a reliable and current weather forecast before setting out. The park's headquarters can provide you with this information.

Sea kayakers interested in exploring Pictured Rocks National Lakeshore can put in at any number of sites. Prime spots on the west end include the Anna River, before it empties into Munising Bay; various access points in Munising Bay proper; and Sand Point. Further east, Miner's Beach, the Hurricane River Campground, and Grand Marais have emerged as popular launching points. Kayakers looking to camp overnight will find that most of the park's campgrounds are accessible from shore (posted signs along Twelvemile Beach direct you to sites further inland; as with the rest of the park, beach camping is not permitted).

Boating

Another popular way to see the highlights of Pictured Rocks is by boat. A private company operates a three-hour narrated tour of the shoreline from early June to mid-October. The boats depart from the Munising docks five times per day between July 1 and

August 31, and two times per day in spring and fall (weather permitting). Prices are $20 for adults and $7 for children ages 6 to 12, and advance reservations are recommended. Though the boats are large enough to accommodate about 200 passengers, they still pass quite close to the shoreline in many areas. Some of the most impressive sights include Chapel Rock – a craggy, stand-alone sandstone spire several stories tall that is anchored to the cliff behind it by a tenuous bridge of roots from the lone pine tree clinging to its top – and Rainbow Cave – a deep overhang in

Sea kayakers maneuvering along Pictured Rocks (Stan Chladex).

which light bouncing off the teal-green waters of Lake Superior illuminates the multi-colored layers of rock and seeping minerals. Contact the **Alger County Chamber of Commerce**, PO Box 405, Munising, MI 49862, or ☎ 906-387-2379 to make reservations. Private boats can also explore the shoreline. Public launch ramps are available in Munising and Grand Marais. Keep in mind that conditions on Lake Superior can change quickly and may become too rough for small craft.

Fishing

The inland lakes and streams in Pictured Rocks National Lakeshore offer excellent opportunities for anglers to catch northern pike and panfish, and Munising Bay is known for its ice fishing and its spring runs of steelhead, trout, and salmon. Though most streams in the park are too shallow for boats, canoes and motorboats under 10 horsepower are allowed on Beaver Lake and Grand Sable Lake. A Michigan fishing license is required. Pick one up at any tackle shop or store that sells outdoor equipment.

Scuba Diving

Another marine attraction in the area is the **Alger Underwater Preserve**, which extends from Au Train (west of Munising) to Au Sable Point, near the eastern end of Pictured Rocks. The preserve is a haven for scuba divers, containing large, colorful rocks and a dozen shipwrecks. Contact the Alger County Chamber of Commerce for a listing of charter services, and see the scuba diving coverage below under *Adventures Region-Wide, On Water* (page 298) for additional information on the preserve.

On Snow

Boasting an average annual snowfall of over 200 inches, the Pictured Rocks area also offers prime cross-country skiing and snowshoeing. The park maintains 15 miles of groomed trails, and there are many off-trail areas. Park rangers warn against tackling the Lakeshore Trail in winter, however, because it is prone to high winds and dangerous snowdrifts. Several park roads are left unplowed for the enjoyment of snowmobilers.

Camping & Accommodations

Pictured Rocks National Lakeshore has three campgrounds, totaling 67 sites, that are accessible by car: **Beaver Lake**, near the center of the park; and **Twelvemile Beach** and **Hurricane River**, toward the east end of the park. Each of these campgrounds is available on a first-come, first-served basis and provides pit toilets, drinking water, picnic tables, and grills. They are closed from December through April each year, and open sites tend to be difficult to find during July and August. Beaver Lake, consisting of eight sites at the end of a dirt road, is very small but offers access to prime fishing areas. Twelvemile Beach has 37 secluded campsites in a white birch forest on a sandy bluff overlooking Lake Superior. It also provides easy access to the beach, which is ideal for walking and rockhounding but usually a bit cold for swimming. The 22-site Hurricane River Campground is just a 1½-mile hike from the Au Sable Light Station, a well-preserved 1874 structure that is listed on the National Registry of Historic Places. Both Twelvemile Beach and

Hurricane River are accessed from unpaved H-58. There are also a number of other campgrounds nearby, in Hiawatha National Forest, Lake Superior State Forest, and several local parks. The closest accommodations and supplies are found in Munising or Grand Marais.

To Find Out More

Pictured Rocks National Lakeshore, PO Box 40, Munising, MI 49862, ☎ 906-387-3700.

■ Porcupine Mountains Wilderness State Park

412 South Boundary Road
Ontonagon, MI 49953
☎ 906-885-5275
Fax 906-885-5798

At 92 square miles, Porcupine Mountains is the largest state park in the nation and one of the few remaining large wilderness tracts in the Midwest. Named for the jagged granite peaks that jut out from amidst the surrounding old-growth forest, "the Porkies" have a great deal to offer the adventurous traveler. Ninety miles of hiking trails, which lead along steep cliffs and wild rivers to waterfalls, secluded lakes, and scenic vistas, make this a premier location for backpacking. You can also enjoy swimming, fishing, rockhounding, or sunset-viewing along the park's 25 miles of white sand beaches on Lake Superior, as well as excellent camping and skiing facilities further inland.

Getting There

Porcupine Mountains Wilderness State Park is on the shore of Lake Superior in the western Upper Peninsula, west of the Keweenaw Peninsula and just 25 miles from the Wisconsin border. It is accessible by car from M-2 and M-28 (the two main east-west routes across the UP) via M-64, which meets up with M-107 in

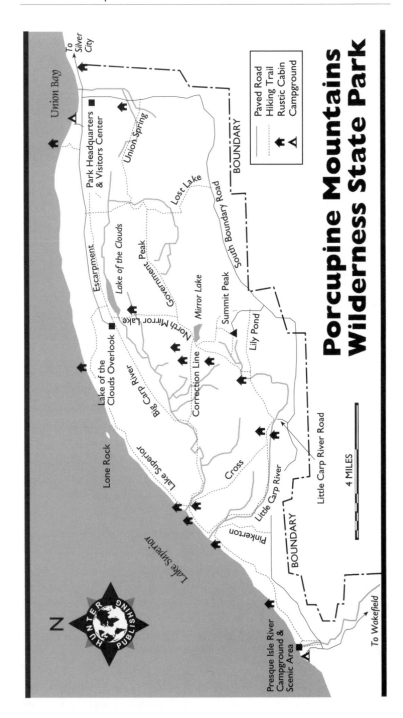

Porcupine Mountains Wilderness State Park

Legend:
- Paved Road
- Hiking Trail
- ♠ Rustic Cabin
- ▲ Campground

4 MILES

Silver City. All of these roads are paved two-lane highways, though M-107 is not plowed after the end of November. The park visitor center, near the junction of M-107 and South Boundary Road, has a gift shop, maps and displays, a multimedia interpretive program, and a ranger on duty to answer questions. Though the park is open year-round, the visitor center is open only from mid-May to mid-October. The Porcupine Mountains are 580 miles from Detroit, 380 miles from Chicago, and only 100 miles from Duluth.

Near the mouth of the Little Carp River, Porcupine Mountains State Park.

History

The series of 1,900-foot peaks that make up the Porcupine Mountains – some of which include rocks that are 3½ billion years old – were carved by retreating glaciers during the Ice Age. Native Americans were the first human visitors to the area, coming in search of game and veins of copper exposed in the rock formations. Though the Porkies saw some of the earliest mining and logging activity in the Midwest, much of the region remained untouched. In fact, today it boasts the largest stand of old-growth northern hardwood forest in the United States. Plans to designate the area as a national park were scuttled with the onset of World War II. Instead, it was established as a state park in 1945 by the Michigan legislature.

Flora & Fauna

The view overlooking the Porcupine Mountains' **Lake of the Clouds** in peak autumn colors is one of the best-known images of

Michigan, gracing the pages of numerous coffee-table books and wilderness calendars. Situated in a long valley filled with a brilliant potpourri of maples, birches, aspens, hemlocks, pines, spruces, and balsams, Lake of the Clouds gets its name from the wisps of steam frequently seen rising from its surface. Colors in the park can begin to change as early as the end of August, though the peak viewing time is usually late September. The locals refer to spring as "the other color season" due to the wide variety of wildflowers that appear along roads and trails and in forest clearings. Unfortunately, spring is also the season for voracious black flies in Upper Michigan, so insect repellent and head nets are recommended. The fauna of the Porkies includes black bears, white-tailed deer, coyotes, beavers, and numerous species of small mammals, as well as bald eagles and nearly 200 other species of birds.

Adventures

On Foot

Porcupine Mountains Wilderness State Park features 90 miles of marked hiking trails, ranging from easy half-hour strolls to rugged multi-day hikes. Though many of the park's longer trails involve slogging up steep grades and crossing cold streams, hikers are rewarded with spectacular views of Lake Superior, as well as numerous opportunities to enjoy the quiet splendor of sheltered inland lakes or the raucous tumble of waterfalls. Many loop options are available for day-hikes beginning from the major trailheads at the Lake of the Clouds overlook and the Summit Observation tower, or from several other points along M-107 or South Boundary Road.

Perhaps the best way to experience the Porkies is by donning a backpack and setting out on a several-day trip. Backpackers must obtain a permit ($6 per night for a party of four or less) at the park headquarters before entering the park's interior. Several backpacker campsites are available along the trail on a first-come, first-served basis. These sites feature tent pads, campfire rings, and pit toilets. At-large camping is also allowed, but not within a quarter-mile of cabins, scenic areas, or roads. The usual rules for minimum-impact camping apply: pack out all garbage, bury human waste, and build fires only in designated areas.

To avoid encounters with the dozens of black bears that call the park home, backpackers are required to hang their food and any scented personal items from a tree at least 100 feet from their campsite.

One of the most scenic trails in the state park is the **Escarpment Trail**, a four-mile route that begins at the Lake of the Clouds overlook. Skirting sheer cliffs and climbing over Cloud and Cuyahoga peaks, it provides outstanding views of the lake and valley. Another popular route is the **Lake Superior Trail**, which follows the rocky shore of the largest of the Great Lakes for 16 rugged and scenic miles, passing through virgin stands of hemlock. Though well-marked, this trail is not easy – it can be extremely muddy and is often obstructed by trees blown down in the high winds off Lake Superior. Its endpoints can be accessed from the west end of South Boundary Road or from the Lake of the Clouds overlook, and it intersects with several other main trails. The nine-mile **Big Carp River Trail** leads west along the escarpment from the Lake of the Clouds overlook to a number of prime observation points, then descends into the Big Carp River Valley. The trail follows the river past an old mine site to where it tumbles over 25-foot Shining Cloud Falls. Further south, the **Little Carp River Trail** (11 miles) follows the Little Carp up to where it empties into Lake Superior, passing through beautiful, rugged woodlands along the way. Highlights of the 7½-mile **Government Peak Trail** include the Carp River, Trap Falls, and majestic stands of hardwoods.

On Wheels

Cycling

Mountain biking is not permitted on the backcountry trails of the Porkies, but the park is still a highly attractive destination for bicyclists. South Boundary Road and M-107 both provide gorgeous views of the park's myriad charms,

*Cyclists looking over the Porkies' famous
Lake of the Clouds (Raymond J. Malace).*

from Lake of the Clouds to the Presque Isle River. Large Union
Bay Campground is a good launch point for rides.

On Water

Fishing

 The park's inland lakes offer excellent walleye, bass, and
perch fishing. Streams that empty into Lake Superior also
have lake trout and salmon, while splake, brook trout,
and rainbow trout can be found in **Mirror Lake** and **Lily Pond**.
Lake of the Clouds holds trophy-sized smallmouth bass. A
Michigan fishing license is required (from any tackle shop or store
that sells outdoor equipment) and state catch limits apply.

On Snow

Downhill Skiing

Thanks to a unique combination of weather and terrain,
the western UP offers the finest skiing in the Midwest.
The Porcupine Mountains receive over 200 inches of an-

nual snowfall, sometimes beginning as early as October, but temperatures remain relatively moderate due to the proximity of Lake Superior. The park also features some of the highest elevations in the Midwest, including Summit Peak at 1,958 feet. Best of all, skiers at the Porcupine Mountains Ski Area are treated to heavily wooded runs and breathtaking views of the ever-changing ice patterns on Lake Superior.

The **Porcupine Mountains Ski Area** features 15 groomed downhill ski runs – three novice, seven intermediate, and five expert – covering 11 miles of slope, with a vertical drop of 640 feet. The longest run is over 5,400 feet in length. With a triple chair, a double chair, and a T-bar, the ski area boasts a lift capacity of 3,600 skiers per hour. In addition, the Porcupine Mountains Ski Area is a real bargain. It offers ski conditions that are superior to those found at most Lower Michigan resorts, but it is considerably less expensive. An adult one-day lift ticket costs $20 during the week and $25 on a weekend or holiday – about half the rate charged by the premier Lower Peninsula ski areas. Lift tickets for juniors (ages 13-17) and seniors (65 and older) are $15 weekdays and $20 weekends, while children under 12 ski free. Equipment rentals range from $13 to $18, and snowboards, snowshoes, and snowmobiles are available for rent in addition to skis.

The **Porcupine Mountains Ski Chalet** offers a cozy warming area with several large fireplaces and picture windows overlooking the slopes. It also contains a ski shop, cafeteria, and first-aid office, as well as equipment rental and repair facilities. For information on skiing the Porkies, contact **Big Snow Country**, PO Box 706, Ironwood, MI 49938, or call the park headquarters. For 24-hour snow reports, ☎ 800-BSC-7000, and for the ski shop/rental information, ☎ 906-885-5612.

Cross-Country Skiing

The Porcupine Mountains Ski Area also features 26 miles of double-track cross-country ski trails through peaceful, wooded areas. There are two novice trails, 1½ and three miles long, plus the intermediate **River Trail** (seven miles) and expert **Union Spring Trail** (12 miles). The longer trails access two warming shelters and three rustic ski-in cabins that can be reserved in advance. The cost for a full-day cross-country ski pass is $6 during the week and $8 on weekends and holidays for adults, or $3/$5 for juniors and seniors. The price includes a one-ride lift ticket that carries skiers from the chalet to the heart of the Nordic trail system.

Camping & Accommodations

The park has a modern campground at Union Bay, near its eastern end, with 95 sites, flush toilets, showers, electricity, and RV-dumping facilities. It is situated in a grassy area and provides an excellent view of Lake Superior. There is also an 88-site, semi-modern campground (no electricity) on Lake Superior at the mouth of Presque Isle River, near the western end of the park. From here, don't miss the chance to day-hike a mile upstream to where the river drops 125 feet through a gorge and over three picturesque waterfalls. The park also offers four developed but rustic camping areas, accessible by car on unpaved roads. These sites are ideal for tenters who enjoy seclusion and don't mind pit toilets, though they tend to be a bit muddy in spring. All the campgrounds are closed from December 1 through April 30.

Sixteen rustic hike-in cabins are spaced between one and four miles apart on the trail. These cabins – which are in constant use throughout summer and fall – must be reserved well in advance by contacting the park headquarters. Each clean, roomy, and well-kept cabin has between two and eight bunks with mattresses, as well as a wood heating stove, a table and benches, cooking and eating utensils, and a saw and axe. In addition, rowboats are furnished at the Mirror Lake, Lily Pond, and Lake of the Clouds cabins. Campers must provide their own bedding and personal items, and a small cookstove is also a good idea. You are encouraged to record your thoughts in a logbook housed in each cabin, and many do – ranging from wilderness experiences to philosophical musings, inspirational messages to abstract poetry, and from weather reports to wildlife sightings. Going back several seasons, the logbooks make for fascinating reading on rainy days. The cabins cost $35-$45 per night and rent from 3 PM to 3 PM, so anglers have plenty of time to catch their breakfast.

There are also a number of more luxurious options nearby, including the **Best Western Porcupine Mountain Lodge** near Silver City, which offers weary travelers a heated indoor pool overlooking Lake Superior. ☎ 906-885-5311. Rental cabins on the lake are available through **Superior Shores Resort**, ☎ 800-344-5355, and **Lambert's Chalet Cottages**, ☎ 906-884-4230. Contact the **Ontonagon County Chamber of Commerce**, PO Box 266, Ontonagon, MI 49953, ☎ 906-884-4735 for a complete listing.

For a detailed description of the park and its trail system, see Jim DuFresne's *Porcupine Mountain Wilderness* (1993) or *The Porcupine Mountains Companion* (1996), by park rangers Michael Rafferty and Robert Sprague.

To Find Out More

Porcupine Mountains Wilderness State Park, 412 South Boundary Rd., Ontonagon, MI 49953, ☎ 906-885-5275.

■ Tahquamenon Falls State Park

Paradise, MI 49768
☎ 906-492-3415

The showpiece of Tahquamenon Falls State Park, in the northeast corner of the Upper Peninsula, is Michigan's largest waterfall and the second-largest waterfall east of the Mississippi (after Niagara Falls). At 200 feet wide and 50 feet tall, **Upper Tahquamenon Falls** resembles a mini-Niagara in its horseshoe shape and thunderous flow of 50,000 gallons per second. The most immediate difference, aside from the scale, is that the water rushing over Tahquamenon Falls acquires a deep red color from the tannin of hemlock trees upstream. Four miles later the river reaches **Lower Tahquamenon Falls**, where it divides in two around a large, mid-

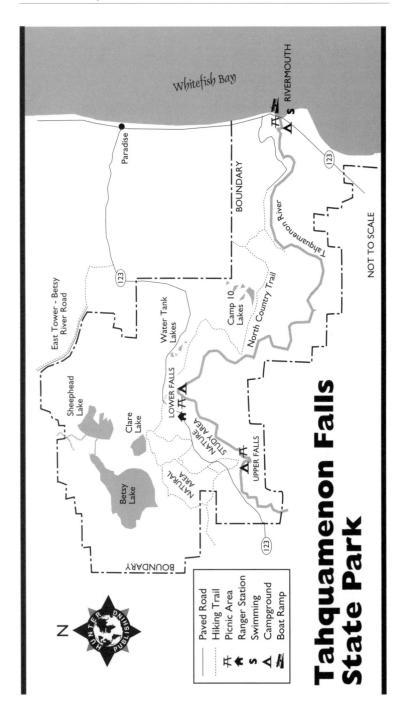

Tahquamenon Falls State Park

Mighty Tahquamenon, America's second-largest waterfall east of the Mississippi (Travel Michigan).

stream island and tumbles another 23 feet over boulders and down rock ledges.

Thanks to the appeal and accessibility of its waterfalls, Tahquamenon Falls State Park attracts over half a million visitors annually. Most either pass through in a day or spend a night at one of the park's three modern campgrounds. But as Michigan's second-largest state park, with over 35,000 acres, Tahquamenon also offers more adventurous travelers 25 miles of hiking trails and 14 miles of scenic river suitable for canoeing and fishing.

Getting There

Tahquamenon Falls State Park is on Lake Superior's Whitefish Bay. From I-75 on the UP side of the Mackinac Bridge, take M-123 north to the small town of Paradise near Whitefish Point. The Lower Falls are 10 miles west of Paradise on M-123, and the Upper Falls are four miles further along the same road. The Rivermouth area, which includes a campground and boat launch, is five miles south of Paradise on M-123.

History

The Chippewa Indians used the Tahquamenon River area as a hunting and fishing ground for many generations. They originated the name Tahquamenon, which may have meant "marsh of the blueberries" or simply "good land or place." The river was later mentioned in Longfellow's famous poem *Song of Hiawatha*. During the lumber era, an estimated one billion board feet of white pine were harvested in the area. It was added to the state park system in 1947.

Flora & Fauna

The natural setting in Tahquamenon Falls State Park ranges from rocky riverbeds to dense hardwood forests to picturesque bog lakes. The park boasts majestic stands of beech, hemlock, pine, and spruce trees, among others. In the spring the wildflowers bloom, while the fall provides a spectacular color display, as well as wild cranberries. The park also houses a number of unusual plant species, including the insect-eating pitcher plant. Park fauna includes black bears, moose, white-tailed deer, an occasional wolf, beavers, and a number of small mammals and birds.

Adventures

On Foot

Part of the reason that Tahquamenon Falls State Park is so popular with tourists is the accessibility of its main attractions. You can view the Upper Falls by walking a quarter-mile paved path from the parking lot through a wooded area. Another paved path then leads 200 yards in either direction along the river. At the end of the upstream path, you can descend stairs to a viewing platform that is so close to the top of the falls that it is often enveloped in mist. The downstream path offers a number of prime river-level views of the falls, then continues on for four miles (unpaved but well-maintained) to the Lower Falls. Likewise, you can reach the Lower Falls area on a 100-yard paved path from the parking lot. Just downstream from the falls, a concessionaire rents rowboats that provide access to the island in the middle of the river. Easy trails along the island's shoreline offer ideal vantage points for viewing the falls.

In addition to waterfall paths, Tahquamenon Falls State Park has 25 miles of maintained hiking trails. Some of these make up part of the North Country National Scenic Trail system, which will run continuously from Maine to North Dakota when completed. The 15-mile **River Trail**, which parallels the Tahquamenon River through much of the park, is excellent for backpacking. A popular

The River Trail provides hikers with stunning views of Tahquamenon Falls (Michigan Bell).

two-day trip begins at the campgrounds near the Lower Falls, runs through forests and past marshy inland lakes, then follows the Tahquamenon River to its mouth at Whitefish Bay. Though the trail is clearly marked, it is somewhat hilly and rooted, so sturdy hiking boots are recommended. Backcountry camping is allowed along the trail, with a permit from the visitor center. There are also several loop possibilities for day-hikes originating from the Upper Falls parking area, ranging in length from four to 13 miles. As a whole, this trail system is known as the **Natural Area Pathway**. The eight-mile **Wilderness Loop** passes Wolf Lake and the remains of an old logging camp. The five-mile **Clark Lake Loop**, which follows an old Indian trail, passes Betsy and Clark Lakes.

On Water

The **Tahquamenon River** provides many opportunities for water recreation, both above and below the falls. The scenic 14-mile stretch of river below the Lower Falls is very popular with canoers and fisherman. Access to the river is

278 ■ Tahquamenon Falls State Park

available at the park's boat-launch facility in the picnic area just across M-123 from the Rivermouth Campground. This launch also provides motorboats with access to Whitefish Bay.

 Like all of Lake Superior, the waters of Whitefish Bay are cold and can be treacherous, so extreme caution is advised.

Another way to explore the Tahquamenon on water is provided by two private riverboat-tour companies that operate above the falls. **Toonerville Trolley and Boat Trips** depart from Soo Junction – on CR-381 about two miles north of M-28 – once a day from June 15 to October 6. This combination narrow-gauge railroad ride and narrated riverboat cruise follows the river all the way to the Upper Falls viewing area. The 6½-hour round-trip costs $17 for adults and $7 for children ages 6 to 15. ☎ 906-876-2311 in summer or 906-293-3806 in winter for information. A shorter combination trip is available through the **Tom Sawyer River Boat & Paul Bunyan Timber Train Company**. Tours depart from Slater's Landing – 10 miles north on North Hulbert Road from M-28 – from Memorial Day to October 10, with two trips daily in July and August. The 4½-hour round-trip costs $14 for adults, $12 for seniors, and $7 for children ages 5 to 15. ☎ 800-732-2331 in tour season, or 906-632-3727 from November to April.

On Snow

 Since the vast majority of tourists visit in summer, winter in the Tahquamenon area can be a very peaceful experience. The Upper Falls are framed by ever-changing, blue-tinged ice sculptures during this season. The park also offers six miles of groomed cross-country ski trails and 16 miles of snowmobile trails. The Natural Area Pathway hiking trails provide another 13 miles of routes for Nordic enthusiasts.

Camping & Accommodations

 Though Tahquamenon Falls State Park has three developed campgrounds with a total of 319 sites, its popularity means that open sites are usually in short supply during the summer months, so reservations are recommended. Both the **Rivers Bend** and **Overlook Campgrounds**, with a combined 183 sites, are situated in wooded areas above the Tahquamenon River near the Lower Falls. Some sites in Rivers Bend offer a view of the river, but the sites in Overlook generally provide more privacy. Both campgrounds are completely modern, with flush toilets, showers, and electricity. The **Rivermouth Campground**, as its name suggests, lies along a bend in the Tahquamenon River near the mouth at Whitefish Bay. It has a modern section with 76 sites, as well as a rustic tent section with 60 sites. The state park and all three campgrounds are open year-round, although the modern restrooms are closed between October 15 and May 15. Contact the park headquarters for further information, or call the state park hotline at ☎ 800-44-PARKS for reservations.

Two smaller campgrounds are in nearby **Lake Superior State Forest**, six and 10 miles north of Paradise off of Vermillion Road. ☎ 906-293-5131. For those wanting more luxurious accommodations, there are two chain motels in Newberry (**Comfort Inn**, ☎ 906-293-3218, and **Days Inn**, ☎ 906-293-4000), and several motels and rental cottages in Paradise. Contact the **Paradise Chamber of Commerce**, PO Box 82, Paradise, MI 49768, ☎ 906-492-3219, for a listing.

If you need a break from dehydrated trail food, the newly opened **Tahquamenon Falls Brewery and Pub** – in an oak lodge near the Upper Falls – serves sandwiches and microbrewed beer in a cozy atmosphere. Another well-known local eatery is the **Fish House** in Paradise, which serves delicious, fresh-caught Lake Superior trout and whitefish on paper plates.

To Find Out More

Contact park headquarters at ☎ 906-492-3415.

▪ Adventures Region-Wide

On Foot

Backpacking & Hiking

Some of the best trails for hiking and backpacking in Michigan's Upper Peninsula can be found within such prime attractions as Isle Royale National Park, Porcupine Mountains Wilderness State Park, and Pictured Rocks National Lakeshore (see the descriptions of these areas above). But the UP has numerous other options for scenic travel on foot, many of which also provide opportunities for camping, fishing, swimming, or canoeing.

Canada Lakes Pathway

This system of maintained hiking/skiing trails, in Lake Superior State Forest southeast of Newberry, is arranged in six interconnected loops ranging from one to eight miles. It covers gently rolling terrain and passes several small lakes. The main trailhead is on CR-403, 1½ miles south of M-28.

Craig Lake State Park

To get to this remote 7,000-acre park, you drive five miles north from M-28 near Nestoria on muddy, rutted Craig Lake Road. The park's 10 miles of hiking trails connect a series of pristine lakes and make the trip worthwhile. The main trail is a seven-mile loop around Craig Lake, which offers excellent fishing and access to a rustic campground.

Estivant Pines Nature Sanctuary

This 377-acre sanctuary, just south of Copper Harbor on the Keweenaw Peninsula, protects a grove of 400-year-old pine trees, including one – the Leaning Giant – that measures 23 feet in circumference. A loop trail also leads past some of the sanctuary's 13 species of orchids, 23 species of ferns, and 85 species of birds.

Fox River Pathway

This little-known trail connects two of the UP's major attractions. Beginning five miles north of Seney National Wildlife Refuge on Fox River Road, it runs northwest 27 miles and ends four miles from the boundary of Pictured Rocks National Lakeshore. The moderately difficult trail climbs gentle hills through jack pine and red pine forests, skirts wetlands, and meanders along the scenic Fox River Valley. There are four small campgrounds along the way: **Seney Township, Fox River, Stanley Lake** (look for wild blueberries near the Stanley Lake Dam), and **Kingston Lake**. In addition, the US Forest Service has placed a number of interpretive markers along the trail that detail the history of the area.

North Country National Scenic Trail

When completed, this trail will extend about 4,000 miles, from Maine to North Dakota. The longest section of the trail, at 875 miles, will be in Michigan. By connecting established trails with newly constructed trails, Michigan's section will run north from the Ohio border in the Lower Peninsula, cross the Mackinac Bridge to the Upper Peninsula, and continue west into Wisconsin. Two major sections of trail have been completed in the UP. The eastern half runs from St. Ignace to Munising, while the western half runs from the Sturgeon River Gorge to Ironwood. Tahquamenon Falls State Park, Porcupine Mountains Wilderness State Park, and Pictured Rocks National Lakeshore all contain sections of the North Country Trail.

The first section of trail in the eastern UP runs 65 miles over sand dunes, through woods, and across rivers from St. Ignace to Tahquamenon. The St. Ignace trailhead is seven miles northwest of the city on Castle Rock Road, near the intersection of CR-3105. While of moderate difficulty, the trail can be tricky to follow in some parts. A major section was rerouted during the 1980s because hikers were disturbing the habitat of the rare hart's tongue fern, which was once believed to grow only in New York State. Many camping areas lie along the trail in Hiawatha National Forest. This section ends on the shore of Lake Superior, at the Rivermouth campground in Tahquamenon Falls State Park.

Another noteworthy part of the North Country Trail in the eastern UP runs 27 miles from Tahquamenon to Pictured Rocks National Lakeshore. From Tahquamenon's Natural Area Pathway, it proceeds west into Lake Superior State Forest, passing Pike Lake and the Two-Hearted River (made famous by Hemingway's fish stories). It then follows the Lake Superior shoreline through Muskallonge Lake State Park, which offers excellent fishing as well as a 179-site modern campground with flush toilets and showers. The trail continues on to the boundary of Pictured Rocks National Lakeshore near Grand Marais.

From the west, the North Country Trail enters the UP near Ironwood. It proceeds north along the Black River, which offers hikers views of several waterfalls, to Black River Harbor on Lake Superior. After about 12 miles, this section of trail meets up with the South Boundary Road of Porcupine Mountains Wilderness State Park. The Trap Falls part of the trail picks up on the east side of the state park and extends 30 miles to Norwich Road, nine miles northeast of Bergland. This section traverses rugged, hilly terrain and requires numerous stream crossings. Along the way, however, you are treated to scenic overlooks as well as side trails that lead to waterfalls. There are no established campgrounds along here, and hikers are advised to take precautions to protect their food from bears.

The final completed segment of the western UP half of the North Country Trail picks up near Victoria Dam, about 15 miles southeast of Ontonagon. After crossing many streams in the first few miles, it reaches **Bob Lake Campground** around the halfway point of its 35-mile length. After ascending to the **Silver Mountain Lookout Tower**, which provides a stunning view of the area's hills and lakes, the trail reaches the scenic **Sturgeon River Gorge**, which is among the largest and deepest in the Midwest at 400 feet. A side trail traverses the edge of the steep, rocky slopes overlooking the river. Two campgrounds are nearby in Ottawa National Forest and Big Lake State Forest.

Sylvania Wilderness Area
Around the turn of the century, the Sylvania Wilderness was a private hunting and fishing club, and its clear, glacial lakes are still popular with fishermen and canoeists today. The 21,000-acre area – about four miles southwest of Watersmeet on CR-535, near the Wisconsin border – also contains 30 miles of hiking trails that offer scenic views of the lakes and many opportunities for swimming. The **Clark Lake Trail** traces the shoreline of the lake past six rustic campgrounds. Each campground consists of three

tent sites with fire rings, and a community pit toilet. Drinking water is also available at some locations. Obtain a permit for camping at the visitor center in Watersmeet, or ☎ 906-885-5275. Campsites cost $5 per site nightly, but the $4 vehicle entry fee is waved with an overnight stay.

On Wheels

The number of established bicycling tours and mountain biking trails in the UP pales when compared with those that can be found "under the bridge," in Michigan's Lower Peninsula. But while the variety of established trails and routes might not be as great, the Upper Peninsula is a much-loved sanctuary for independent and enterprising cyclists who welcome the opportunity to create their own itinerary. Bicyclists enjoy seemingly endless roadways and blissfully light traffic, while adventurous mountain bikers can plunge into the region's extensive network of old logging roads and fire trails. Of course, both groups are also rewarded with some of the most spectacular scenery in the northern United States, from wild rivers and waterfalls to flowering meadows and majestic forestlands.

Mountain Biking

Among Michigan mountain bikers, the Upper Peninsula is known as the domain of adventure cyclists. Literally thousands of miles of old logging roads and two-tracks await intrepid bikers with a taste for exploration and remote wilderness. These trails are abundant in both national forests (see the sections on Hiawatha and Ottawa National Forests) and state forests (Copper Country State Forest, Escanaba River State Forest, and Lake Superior State Forest).

Take note: the old logging trails of the peninsula are not ornamented with directional arrows or mileage markers, and good luck finding a reliable map. Topographic maps should be consulted with a skeptical and discerning eye, too; many of them do not provide a complete picture of trail networks. Given such realities, veterans of the UP trails

> *counsel their fellow peddlers to pack
> accordingly (in other words, don't forget your
> compass and survival essentials for
> unplanned overnighters).*

The Upper Peninsula also includes a sprinkling of trails specifically designated for mountain bikers left cold by the vagaries of
backcountry riding. Several of these are rail-trails, pathways created from abandoned railroad corridors and are popular with
snowmobilers in the winter (the trails are also open to equestrians and ORV operators). Top rail-trails in the UP include:

Bergland-Sidnaw Rail Trail

This 43-mile jaunt through wooded sections of Houghton and
Ontonagon Counties is highlighted by its passage over a couple of
major bridges. It is a mix of forestland and pasture for much of its
length, but also includes a couple of high ridgeline stretches. The
lack of parking at the trailhead leads many users to start from Bergland Township Park, on Lake Gogebic.

Bill Nichols Rail Trail

This teeth-rattler is a favorite of veteran UP bikers. Studded with
the remains of old railroad ties and stretches of loose gravel, the
Nichols Trail serves warning early and often about its ornery temperament. The 41-mile trail also rewards visitors with peaceful
lakes and attractive woodlands. The trailheads are at Adventure
Mountain, outside of Mass City, and on Canal Drive, west of
downtown Houghton.

Felch Grade Rail Trail

The 40-mile Felch Grade Trail runs alongside M-69 for much of
its length, passing through wetlands, woodlands, and a couple of
small towns on its way. The surface is rough until its final few
miles (when the trail hops on another abandoned railbed), but it
does not have the spill factor that many other trails do, making it
attractive for relatively inexperienced riders. The trail starts in the
Dickinson County community of Felch, off Old Dump Road.

Hancock-Calumet Rail Trail

This 14-mile trail, also known as the Jack Stevens Trail, is high up in the northern portion of the Keweenaw Peninsula. It roughly parallels US-41, providing a scenic, undemanding pathway through forest and wetland areas. Riders hitting the trail from Hancock can pick it up at the Portage Lake Lift Bridge, while those from Calumet can find the trailhead at the town's old railroad depot.

For more information on this and other UP rail-trails, contact the Michigan chapter of the **Rails-to-Trails Conservancy** at ☎ 517-393-6022.

A couple of other prime mountain biking destinations can also be found on UP islands. **Grand Island** offers superb riding for gritty bikers (see the section on Hiawatha National Forest, page 218), but the oft-overlooked **Drummond Island** is another worthwhile option. The island is home to a steadily expanding mountain biking network that offers stretches appropriate for everyone from beginners to scab-encrusted veterans. The former generally stick to the island's gravel roads and easier trails, while the latter can ride technically challenging single-tracks deep into the forests.

Finally, a rugged 200-mile network of forest roads and single-track trails known as the **Mines and Pines Trail System** has materialized in the last few years. For information on this system, which extends through the western UP and portions of eastern Wisconsin, contact the **Iron County Development Authority** at ☎ 715-561-2922.

Cycling

One of the state's top cycling destinations is the **Seney National Wildlife Refuge**, a 95,000-acre area that is home to more than 200 bird species, including trumpeter swans, loons, ospreys, owls, bald eagles, sandhill cranes, and a huge variety of songbirds and waterfowl. In addition, the refuge has black bear, white-tailed deer, coyote, river otter, beaver, grouse (ruffed, spruce, and sharp-tailed), and other wildlife. The refuge includes nearly 50 miles of trails and roadways suitable for regular bicycle use (though many explore the refuge's gravel double-track trails on mountain bikes). The entrance roads to Seney National Wildlife Refuge are on M-77 south of Seney.

In addition, several of the beautiful lakes here serve as the centerpiece of pleasing roadway loops. Routes around and along **Indian Lake, Portage Lake**, and **Gogebic Lake** blend water and woods in most pleasing fashion. The Indian Lake Loop, for instance, starts in Manistique and works its way north and west to the lakeshore via forest-garnished county roads (M-94 to CR-440); from there, county roads (441, 442, M-149) go down the lake's beach-heavy southern portions to US-2, which in turn heads up along the shores of mighty Lake Michigan and back to Manistique.

For the most part, however, cyclists traveling through the Upper Peninsula establish their own routes and agendas, which are virtually limitless. They range from multi-day treks through the Keweenaw Peninsula to one-day excursions along remote highways (M-28 from Marquette to Munising and M-35 from Menominee to Escanaba are favorites) to tours of Drummond Island. Excursions into Wisconsin (via any number of roads) or Canada (via the Sault Ste. Marie International Bridge) can be easily accomplished as well.

On Water

Canoeing & Kayaking

See the whitewater chart on page 27. Michigan's Upper Peninsula offers some of the best paddling experiences in the Midwest, ranging from quiet floats through pristine wilderness to demanding passages through rushing rapids. Many inland lakes are connected by portages, while the shorelines of the three Great Lakes surrounding the UP also beckon to be explored. See the sections on Isle Royale National Park (page 229), Pictured Rocks National Lakeshore (page 262), and Hiawatha National Forest's Grand Island Recreation Area (page 218).

Black River (Class II-III)
Located in Gogebic County in the extreme western UP, the Black River is one of the state's most challenging for experienced whitewater canoeists and kayakers. You can put in from the bridge at

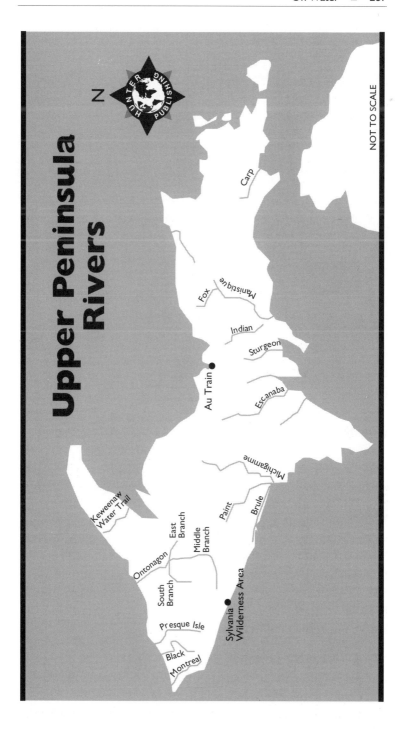

CR-513, where the river is relatively slow and between 15 and 30 feet wide with tag alders along the banks. The eight-mile stretch leading to the intersection of US-2 includes numerous Class I and two sections of Class II rapids. Paddlers must take out at the US-2 Bridge to avoid Neepikon and Gabro Falls – both impassable by canoe – and either portage (on a trail that can be difficult to follow) or shuttle two miles downriver to the covered bridge at the entrance to Blackjack Ski Area. From here, the river widens to 40-80 feet and meanders 9½ miles through hardwood forests to Narrows Roadside Park. Long stretches of slow-moving water alternate with light rapids in this section, making it suitable for paddlers with basic skills.

It is important for beginners to take out at The Narrows, just before an island splits the river in two, since below this point are four miles of continuous Class II-III rapids.

This route features large boulders and several four-foot drops, and passes between steep banks that make scouting difficult. It is suitable for only the most daring whitewater canoeists and kayakers. The last take-out before the river drops over six major – and essentially unrunnable – waterfalls on its way to Lake Superior is an unnamed two-track road on the left about a half-mile below Chippewa Falls. Folks who do not take out prior to Algonquin Falls, the first of those six waterfalls, face a long day of difficult portages. Black River National Forest Campground lies at the rivermouth, just off CR-513. Like many western UP rivers, the Black varies considerably in its water level with the seasons. May is generally considered the best time to go; the river can be dangerously high and extremely cold in April, while in the late summer and fall its flow may decline to a trickle.

Brule River (Class I-II)

The mild-mannered Brule River forms the border between Michigan and Wisconsin in the southwestern UP. It features several stretches of Class I rapids interspersed with easier paddling, and just three stretches of Class II water that should not trouble experienced canoeists and kayakers. The water level generally remains high enough for canoeing throughout the summer months, and good campsites are easy to come by on the public land lining both sides of the river. Paddlers can put in at the US Forest Service campground just across the Wisconsin border off M-73 (Wisconsin-55), about two miles from the river's source at Brule Lake. In its early stages, the Brule is about 30-50 feet wide and about two feet deep, so you may experience bumping and scraping at low water. About 13 miles downstream, after the M-189 Bridge, it becomes considerably deeper and faster. It also takes on a dark red hue after it meets up with the Iron River. The Brule continues past several possible take-out sites – including Pentoga Bridge (25 miles from M-73), Carney Dam Public Access Site, and the US-2 bridge (38½ miles from M-73) – before it intersects with the Paint River above the Brule Island Dam. Most paddlers will wish to take out at the public access site one mile below Washburn Bridge or at the dam. Below this point, the Brule joins the big waters of the Menominee River and continues on into Green Bay.

Escanaba River (Class I-II)

The Escanaba River cuts through the central UP between Marquette and Escanaba. You can put in on the East Branch at Gwinn Community Park (off M-35), which meets up with the Middle Branch a short time later. At this point, the river tends to be between one and six feet deep, and from 60 to 80 feet wide. It passes through remote, hilly terrain covered with hardwood forests, and plenty of campsites are available along the way in the Escanaba State Forest. You'll encounter a short stretch of rapids shortly after departing from Gwinn, and another just before reaching the West Branch, 13 miles downstream. At this point, the Middle Branch widens to 100 feet or more and becomes shallower. During times of low water, paddlers may wish to take out at the Escanaba River State Forest Campground six miles later. If the water level is high enough, the next eight miles on the river can be rewarding, as it passes between banks that rise in picturesque rock ledges before opening into Boney Falls Basin. Paddlers may then take out at the public access site or portage around the Boney Falls Dam two miles down.

Fox River (Class I)

Legend has it that the Fox River, in the north-central UP, was the true inspiration for Ernest Hemingway's famous fish story *Big Two-Hearted River*. Locals claim that the author used the more poetic name of a neighboring river in order to conceal the identity of his favorite trout stream. With moderate flow over a sandy bottom – and no rapids to speak of – the Fox is perfect for canoeists with basic skills. Water levels do not fluctuate much throughout the summer, but fallen trees present frequent challenges. In addition, the area is notorious for its mosquitoes, which makes finding high, dry campsites a priority. Beginning at the Wagner Dam public access (16 miles north of Seney, off CR-460), the Fox is 25-35 feet wide and one to four feet deep. It meanders through mixed lowland forests for nine miles to the Fox River State Forest Campground, then continues another seven miles to the M-28 Bridge in Seney. Below Seney, the river widens to 40-60 feet and passes through pristine wilderness for 14 miles until it joins the Manistique River. A good take-out is at the roadside park just upstream of the M-77 Bridge near Germfask. Contact **Northland Outfitters** (☎ 906-586-9801) for information on kayak and canoe rentals on the Fox.

Keweenaw Water Trail

Unveiled in September 1996, this 47-mile trail system follows the Portage Waterway through the heart of the Keweenaw Peninsula, from Keweenaw Bay on the sandy southeast side to McClain State Park on the rugged north coast. It is Michigan's first operational segment in a planned Lake Superior Water Trail network that might someday circumnavigate the lake (a lengthy route already exists in Minnesota, and additional Michigan routes are planned for Marquette and Munising). All types of small boats are welcome, but the trail is especially well-suited to sea kayaks. The first eight miles from the bay to Chassell passes through interesting marshes. The trail then enters Portage Lake, with more motorboat traffic, and continues on for 11 miles to the twin cities of Houghton and Hancock. The final 10 miles consist of the formal shipping channel into Lake Superior. An 18-mile spur heads through the Torch Bay Channel from Houghton into Torch Lake and Lake Linden. Every three to five miles along the way, there are

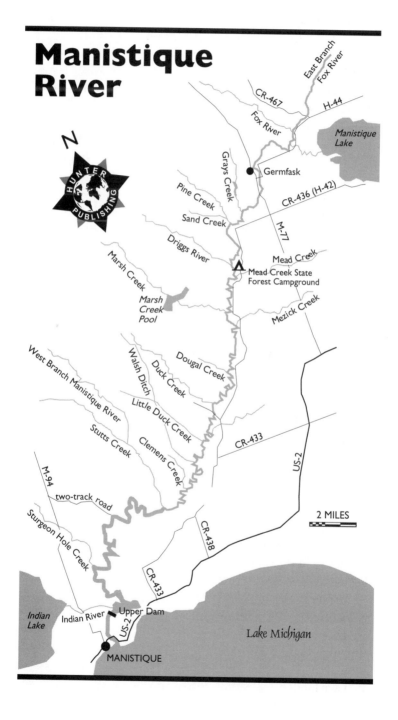

Manistique River

East Branch Fox River

CR-467

H-44

Fox River

Manistique Lake

Grays Creek

Germfask

CR-436 (H-42)

Pine Creek

Sand Creek

M-77

Driggs River

Mead Creek

Mead Creek State Forest Campground

Marsh Creek

Marsh Creek Pool

Mezick Creek

Dougal Creek

Walsh Ditch

Duck Creek

West Branch Manistique River

Little Duck Creek

CR-433

US-2

Stutts Creek

Clemens Creek

M-94

two-track road

Sturgeon Hole Creek

CR-438

CR-433

Indian Lake

Indian River

Upper Dam

US-2

Lake Michigan

MANISTIQUE

2 MILES

N

HUNTER PUBLISHING

boat launches, scenic stops, or places to restock supplies. Contact the **Keweenaw Tourism Council** at ☎ 888-MI-NORTH.

Manistique River (Class I)

Mellow and accessible with plentiful opportunities for camping, the Manistique River is popular with canoeists and kayakers of all abilities. It begins at the west end of Manistique Lake and runs wide and sandy through Seney National Wildlife Refuge to the city of Manistique, on the shore of Lake Michigan. You can put in at the public access site two miles east of Germfask on Ten Curves Road. Shortly afterward the river joins the Fox, then passes through the wildlife refuge for 10 miles, where there are ample opportunities to spot waterfowl and other animals – including trumpeter swans, bald eagles, deer, otter, beaver, and black bears. Camping is prohibited within the refuge, but 16 miles from the put-in is **Mead Creek State Forest Campground**. The river then widens to 90-120 feet and meanders past **Merwin Creek Campground** (45 miles from the put-in) and through a series of interesting backwaters until it finally reaches the city. A small community park on the north side of town provides a good take-out point. Canoe and kayak rentals for use on the Manistique are available through **Northland Outfitters** (☎ 906-586-9801).

Montreal River (Class I-III)

The Montreal River forms the boundary between Michigan and Wisconsin in the northwest corner of the UP. Although subject to seasonal fluctuations in water level, the last 16½ miles of the river provide some of the most spectacular scenery in the state and are very popular among whitewater enthusiasts. Put in on the East Fork at the US-2 Bridge west of Ironwood, where the river tends to be shallow, rocky, and swift. A few miles upstream from International Falls (also known as Peterson Falls), the river's east and west branches join, and the stream enters into several miles of continuous Class I rapids. The current slows and the bottom becomes sandy as the Montreal reaches the Saxon Falls Flowage. Paddlers must take out at the first of two hydroelectric dams and shuttle or portage one mile downstream, past the second dam, where access to the river is through power company property. Below the Saxon Falls Dam, the Montreal cuts 3½ miles through a scenic gorge characterized by sheer 100-foot cliffs and low hills covered with pine and hemlock forests. The nearly continuous rapids range from Class I to III and include numerous rock gardens, drops, chutes, and high standing waves (the rapids are reputed to hit Class IV levels during high water release periods). Because of the inaccessibility of the terrain, the lower Montreal is not recommended for those lacking whitewater experience; experienced paddlers will find it a challenging ride. Take out at the bridge at Lake Superior Road (CR-505), as another dam blocks the path to Lake Superior.

Ontonagon River (Class I-III)

At the base of the Keewenaw Peninsula in Ottawa National Forest is the Ontonagon River system. Made up of the mainstream, the South Branch, the East Branch, and the Middle Branch, the Ontonagon system features many stretches of Class I-III rapids, excellent fishing, and abundant camping possibilities. A trip on the **mainstream** generally begins at Military Bridge on US-45 and ends at the public access near the marina in Ontonagon. During the 24-mile stretch in between, the river tends to be quite wide (125-200 feet) and slow, passing through a deep, wooded valley. There are two brief stretches of rapids eight and 11 miles from the put-in that may cause problems for beginners, however – particularly in high water. The more challenging **South Branch** is entered at the public access site at the M-28 Bridge in Ewen, where the river is 40-60 feet wide and rather slow. Class I-II rapids begin about 12 miles downstream and alternate with slow water for the next 10 miles. The South Branch widens and slows after it intersects with the West Branch, but then it encounters some tricky rapids for about 1½ miles – with a four-foot drop and several standing waves big enough to swamp an open canoe, especially in high water – before it empties into Victoria Basin. The remote **East Branch** features 7½ miles of nearly continuous Class II-III rapids between USFS-208 and US-45, and is recommended only for experienced whitewater paddlers. The **Middle Branch** is best accessed from the public site at the US-45 Bridge in Watersmeet, where the river is clear and 15-25 feet wide. It runs through low, wooded hills with a few easy drops and chutes until it reaches

Mex-I-Min-E Falls, nine miles downstream. There is a 300-foot portage trail on the right at the **Burned Dam Forest Service Campground**. The remaining 11 miles of river before Bond Falls Dam include several moderately difficult Class I-II rapids. Canoe and kayak rentals for the Ontonogan are available through **Sylvania Outfitters** (☎ 906-358-4766).

Paint River (Class I-III)

The North and South Branches of the Paint River run through Ottawa National Forest in the southwestern UP, then meet up as they leave Ottawa and run another 38 miles to Little Bull Dam. The North and South Branches can be accessed off of USFS-16, nine and 4½ miles north of US-2, respectively, and provide a mellow ride to the **Paint River Forks Campground**. The combined river is 40-75 feet wide at this point and alternates between deep, slow water and shallow, fast-moving water. It flows through mixed forests and alder thickets that offer abundant opportunities to view wildlife, especially deer and bald eagles. About 13 miles downstream you will encounter Upper Hemlock Rapids, which should be attempted only by experienced whitewater paddlers and only during moderate to low water levels; others can make an easy portage on the left. The even more difficult Lower Hemlock Rapids come a quarter-mile later. Afterward, the river widens and flows 16 miles to a portage around Crystal Falls Dam, then eight more miles through remote country to the take-out at Little Bull Dam, which also offers camping. Paddlers continuing down the river to the Brule will have to portage Horse Race Rapids.

Presque Isle River (Class III-IV)

This offers experienced whitewater paddlers some of the most challenging terrain in the Midwest. Indeed, *Canoe* magazine has hailed it as one of 10 North American rivers that "define the outer edge of contemporary whitewater paddling." Ideal water levels are found in May and early June, and paddlers should set aside at least two days to make the trip. Beginning at the M-28 Bridge access, the river gradually increases in speed and intensity over 17½ miles until it becomes a continuous stretch of Class II rapids with several Class IV chutes. The first half of the river includes many stretches of rock ledges, chutes, and backrollers that require scouting, as well as 15-foot Nimikon Falls, which must be portaged. The second half of the Presque Isle is even more difficult. You will find several miles of continuous whitewater below Steiger's Bridge. This leads into Triple Drop, a flurry of small falls and chutes, and the notorious Presque Isle Gorge, a one-mile stretch of Class III-IV chaos (Class V in the spring). To avoid this stretch – and all but the most advanced whitewater experts should do so – make a difficult portage around this section on the left prior to Triple Drop; you can rejoin the river below Nakomis Falls. From there through Lepisto Falls, expect flurries of Class II rapids and Class III-IV drops (portage Lepisto Falls on the left). The last few miles of the river are within scenic Porcupine Mountains State Park, and there is a good take-out at South Boundary Road. Just below, the river plummets over a series of picturesque waterfalls before it meets Lake Superior. A map of this river can be found on page 253.

Sylvania Wilderness Area

The 21,000-acre Sylvania Wilderness, near Watersmeet in the southwestern UP, contains 36 pristine lakes that are connected by portage trails. Once a private hunting and fishing club, its clear, glacial lakes are still popular with fishermen, canoeists, and swimmers today. Many of the lakes feature rustic campgrounds with tent sites, fire rings, and a community pit toilet. Visitors must obtain a permit for camping at the visitor center in Watersmeet. ☎ 906-885-5275 for more information. Campsites cost $5 per site nightly, and the $4 vehicle entry fee is waved with an overnight stay.

Fishing

Even before Ernest Hemingway penned his classic story *Big Two-Hearted River* – a nostalgic tale of the joys of trout fishing in the region – Michigan's Upper Peninsula was widely regarded as an angler's paradise. In addition to its 1,700 miles of shoreline on three Great Lakes, the UP features 4,300 inland lakes and 12,000 miles of rivers and streams that support a wide variety of fish species. An angler could spend a lifetime plying the UP's waters and never fish the same spot twice.

Anglers try their luck in one of Michigan's trout streams.

Inland Lakes

The numerous lakes dotting the landscape across the UP offer up northern pike, walleye, yellow perch, bluegills, lake trout, rock bass, largemouth bass, smallmouth bass, muskellunge, sturgeon, splake, and a number of other species. **Lake Gogebic** – the largest in the UP, with a surface area over 20 square miles – is known for its walleye, and also features bass and perch. There is good access at Lake Gogebic State Park (off M-64 on the west shore), which has 165 campsites and a nice boat launch. **Brevoort Lake**, which features a spawning reef, is another excellent spot for walleye. **Craig Lake**, in the state park of the same name, has been called the best muskie lake in Michigan, and also holds walleye and smallmouth bass. **Portage Lake** is known for its large northern pike, as is **Bond Falls Flowage** (which is also good for walleye). Some other popular fishing lakes include **Big Manistique Lake** (walleye, yellow perch, northern pike, rock bass), **Chicago Lake** (bluegills, northern pike), **Camp 7 Lake** (managed for splake), **Grand Sable Lake** (lake trout, smallmouth bass, rock bass, northern pike, splake), **Indian Lake** (walleye, northern pike, muskie, sturgeon, smallmouth bass, bluegill, perch), **Lac Vieux Desert** (walleye, muskie, northern pike), **Lake Independence** (walleye, northern pike, perch), **Lyman Lake** (largemouth bass, bluegill), and **Victoria Dam Flowage** (walleye, bass, perch, northern pike).

Rivers and Streams

The waters flowing across the UP to the Great Lakes support a number of fish species, particularly brook, brown, and rainbow trout. The river mouths also see runs of chinook and coho salmon, while their ponds and reservoirs hold walleye, northern pike, largemouth bass, smallmouth bass, and several other species. The stretch of the **Ontonagon River** between Bond Falls and Agate Falls is known as some of the best rainbow trout fishing around, while the remainder of the river system is good for brook and brown trout, walleye, and smallmouth bass. Many UP rivers have earned a good reputation for brook trout, including the **Ogontz, Whitefish, Iron, Otter, Fishdam, Fence**, and **Fox**. The **Carp River** produced the state record pink salmon, and also holds brown trout, brook trout, and steelhead. Some other popular fishing rivers include the **Anna River** (coho salmon), **Black River** (brook and brown trout, chinook salmon, coho salmon), **Brule River** (brook and brown trout, walleye, smallmouth bass, northern pike), **Big Huron River** (steelhead), **Cedar River** (smallmouth bass, walleye), **Chocolay River** (brook and brown trout, steelhead, coho salmon), **Escanaba River** (brook and brown trout), **Ford River** (brook trout, smallmouth bass), **Firesteel River** (steelhead, rainbow, brook, and brown trout), **Menominee River** (smallmouth bass, sturgeon, walleye, northern pike, brown trout, steelhead, chinook salmon), **Michigamme River** (walleye, smallmouth bass, northern pike, yellow perch), **Net River** (smallmouth bass), **Paint River** (brook trout, brown trout, smallmouth bass), **Presque Isle River** (brook trout, steelhead, whitefish, coho and chinook salmon), **Sturgeon River** (walleye, smallmouth bass, brook and brown trout), **Two-Hearted River** (brook trout, rainbow trout, whitefish), and **Yellow Dog River** (brown trout). The **St. Mary's River**, which connects Lakes Superior and Huron, contains a wide variety of species, including chinook, pink, and Atlantic salmon, muskie, northern pike, walleye, yellow perch, smallmouth bass, lake herring, and whitefish.

Great Lakes

The many bays and inlets along the UP shoreline offer anglers excellent opportunities to pursue lake trout, steelhead, walleye, northern pike, whitefish, perch, bass, and coho and chinook salmon. Some of the top lake trout fishing can be found in Lake Superior along the eastern Keweenaw Peninsula, in **Keweenaw, L'Anse**, and **Huron Bays**. These waters also feature steelhead, salmon, perch, bass, and northern pike. The shore of **Union Bay**, near Ontonagon, is a good spot to catch lake trout and salmon in the spring and fall. Anglers can enjoy good fishing for chinook salmon off **Fairport** on the Garden Peninsula in Lake Michigan. **Little Bay de Noc** offers walleye in its upper region, north of Gladstone, and northern pike near Rapid River and Kipling. Northern pike are also available in **Big Bay de Noc** – in Ogontz Bay and Martin Bay, and near **Fayette State Park**. Ice fishing is popular on shallow **Munuscong Bay**, in the **St. Mary's River**, as well as on **Munising Bay**.

Scuba Diving

All of the Great Lakes have a sense of myth and dark mystery about them. For more than 300 years, vessels have roamed those waters, their holds filled with everything from furs to copper to automobiles. But thousands of those ships never completed their voyages, falling victim instead to rocky shoals or storm-swept seas, and Great Lakes' shorelines still bear mute reminders of the perils associated with those journeys in the form of worn widows' walks and lonesome lighthouses.

But while all of the Great Lakes have their tales of tragedy and heartbreak, none can match the mystique that surrounds the icy, unpredictable waters of Lake Superior. Notorious for its cold water and its fierce and sudden storms, Superior has taken down 350 ships over the years. The most famous of these is undoubtedly the *Edmund Fitzgerald*, the massive freighter that was immortalized in Gordon Lightfoot's haunting song, *Wreck of the Edmund Fitzgerald*.

Some of those vessels rank among the most coveted dive sites in all the Great Lakes. Indeed, Lake Superior's proud but calamity-pocked maritime legacy has made it one of America's premier scuba diving attractions. But the lake's popularity with the scuba diving community is due not only to the variety, historical value, and mythic flavor of the shipwrecks it houses, but also to the quality of sport diving it offers. For one thing, the sheer number of divable shipwrecks along the Upper Peninsula's northern coastline dilutes traffic. Moreover, Superior's bone-chilling water – noted for its clarity – has helped preserve many vessels in pristine condition.

All of these factors contributed to Michigan's decision to create four bottomland preserves off the northern coast of its Upper Peninsula in 1980 as part of its preserve system. These four preserves – Keweenaw Underwater Preserve, Marquette Underwater Preserve, Alger Underwater Preserve, and Whitefish Point Underwater Preserve – protect many of Superior's most important wreck sites.

Keweenaw Underwater Preserve

The westernmost of the UP preserves, Keweenaw offers a variety of dive sites within its 103 square miles. The preserve follows the shoreline of the Keweenaw Peninsula for about 65 miles, beginning near its western base and concluding at Bete Grise Bay on the peninsula's eastern side. About a dozen significant wrecks can be found within its boundaries, many of them in less than 50 feet of water. The shallow location of these ships makes the preserve a good one for less experienced divers, but also means that the vessels absorb more punishment from winter ice and pounding waves. In fact, some of the ships within the preserve have been ground into rubble by Superior's harsh hand.

The most significant of the wrecks in the Keweenaw area is the *Mesquite*, a US Coast Guard cutter that ran aground off Keystone Bay on December 4, 1989. Subsequent storms pulverized the vessel, and the decision was eventually made to sink the ship in the preserve area. It currently lies at a depth of 100 feet on its main decks (120 feet along its keel). The most popular dive site in the entire Keweenaw area, the 180-foot *Mesquite* remains in excellent condition, with a good deal of its deck equipment still on hand. Exploration of the vessel's interior, however, should only be undertaken by advanced divers with appropriate equipment.

Other noteworthy shipwrecks within Keweenaw's boundaries include the **Tioga**, a 285-foot freighter that met its end on Sawtooth Reef in 1919; the **City of St. Joseph**, a 254-foot steel barge that was lost during a 1942 gale; and the **Traveller**, a 200-foot side-wheeler that was crippled by fire in 1865. All three of these ships lie in less than 40 feet of water. Advanced divers can head to the wreck of the **Langham**, a freighter that caught fire during a 1910 storm and sank in Bete Grise Bay in about 105 feet of water. Other notable wrecks include the **James Pickands** (a 232-foot wood steamer) and the **William C. Moreland** (a 580-foot steel steamer).

Area dive shops providing services in the Keweenaw Preserve include **Narcosis Corner Divers/Easy Diver Charters** (474 Third St., Calumet, MI 49913, ☎ 906-337-3156, www.filias.com/narcosis) and **Grand Island Charters** (1204 Commercial St., Munising, MI 49862, ☎ 906-387-4477). For information on the preserve, contact the **Keweenaw Tourism Council** (PO Box 336, Houghton, MI 49931, ☎ 906-482-2388).

Marquette Underwater Preserve

This preserve is divided into two distinct geographic sections – the **Marquette Unit** and the **Huron Islands Unit**. The most notable of the wrecks contained within the Marquette Unit is probably the **Charles J. Kershaw**, a vessel that sank back in 1895. The *Kershaw*, a 223-foot wooden steamer, struck a reef after its boiler exploded in a storm. It sank in 35 feet of water. Ill-fated salvage efforts and the passage of time have scattered the ship's remains along the lake floor, but small artifacts can still be found in the area. The wreckage is near Chocolay Reef, at the mouth of Chocolay River. Other big attractions in the Marquette Unit include the **George Sherman**, a schooner that was lost in an 1887 storm, and the **D. Leuty**, a 179-foot steamer that ran aground near the Marquette lighthouse during a 1911 whiteout. Relatively little remains of these vessels, but their location (each sits in less than 30 feet of water) make the sites attractive to less experienced divers. The most popular dive site in the Huron Islands Unit is the **Southwest**, a 137-foot steamer that ran aground in 1898. Portions of the hull remain intact, and artifacts can still be spotted in the area. The depth at which the ship sits (90-110 feet) makes it more suitable for experienced divers than beginners. Other vessels within the Huron Islands Unit include the *Arctic*, a 237-foot sidewheeler that wrecked on the west side of Huron Island in 1860, and the *George Nestor*, a schooner that was destroyed in 1909 when a storm forced her on the rocks near the Huron Island lighthouse.

In addition to the above-mentioned vessels, the Marquette Preserve also has other interesting options for divers. Shore diving is a popular pastime because of the large number of artifacts that can be found along the shoreline. These artifacts are all that remain of countless unnamed schooners that were lost out on the lake. Unusual geologic formations can be found within the preserve as well, especially in the northwestern part of the Marquette Unit. Both the Gold Mine Pinnacle and the Black Rocks site are home to gamefish, though, so watch for tangled fishing line.

Finally, the preserve's proximity to Marquette, the largest town in the UP, provide sport divers with nightlife too.

Diver services are available through **Diver Down Scuba Shop**, 717 N. Third St., Marquette, MI 49855, ☎ 906-225-1699. Information on the preserve can be obtained by contacting the **Marquette Country CVB**, 2552 W. US-41, Suite 300, Marquette, MI 49855, ☎ 906-228-7749 or 800-554-4321 (www.visit-usa.com/mi/marquette).

Alger Underwater Preserve

The most popular of the UP underwater preserves, Alger offers an abundance of exciting exploration options for sport divers of all ability levels. Unlike most other preserves, Alger boasts natural features that are more than a mere afterthought to divers. The spectacular **Pictured Rocks National Lakeshore**, which serves as the preserve's shoreline border for a time, is an amazing underwater playground. The sandstone cliffs of Pictured Rocks feature beautiful underwater caverns that can be explored on calm days (rough seas will smash divers up against the cliff face). These shallow caves are most extensive near Miner's Castle and on the northwest side of Grand Island, and can be explored by divers of varying skill levels. Underwater photography opportunities in the area are excellent.

Ultimately, though, the preserve's shipwrecks remain the principle magnet. Alger's wrecks are many and scattered, and most of them are marked with buoys. Most importantly, several major wrecks within the preserve are in remarkably good shape, making penetration possible at several sites. All of these factors, combined with the region's good visibility, make Alger a center of Great Lakes scuba diving.

One of the best-known of Alger's wrecks is a nameless schooner that sank in Murray Bay, a protected bay near Grand Island. Sheltered from Superior's wrath by the bay, the 145-foot ship, commonly known as the **Murray Bay Wreck**, remains in very good condition. Its cargo hold can be easily penetrated, and most of the deck is intact. The vessel, which sits in about 30 feet of water, is also home to large schools of rock bass and other fish. Another hugely popular wreck is that of the **Smith-Moore**, a steamer that sank in 1889 after a collision with another steamer. The vessel lies on the lake bottom in an upright position, its deck largely intact, in about 95 feet of water. Penetration of the boat, which attracts schools of gamefish as well as divers, is possible. But whereas the Murray Bay Wreck can be enjoyed by divers of varying levels of expertise, exploration of the *Smith-Moore*, which lies in the east channel between Grand Island and the mainland, should only be undertaken by experienced divers.

Another immensely popular site for divers is the **Steven M. Selvick**, a 71-foot tugboat that was sunk in the preserve in 1996 after its retirement from active service. The interior of the *Selvick* is easily accessible, providing divers of varying ability levels with the chance to explore its pilothouse, engine room, and crew quarters. It sits in about 60 feet of water, but the water in the area is so clear that the vessel's upper parts can be seen from the surface. The **Kiowa** is an attractive site for basic and intermediate divers. A 251-foot steel steamer that fell prey to bad weather in 1929, the *Kiowa* sits on a reef south of Au Sable Point. The wreck, which is in multiple pieces, lies in about 35 feet of water.

Other wrecks in the Alger Preserve are less well-preserved than its marquee attractions, but will still be of interest. These include the **Manhattan**, a 250-foot steamer that sank in 1903, and the **Herman H. Hettler**, a 210-foot steamer that sank in 1926. The vessels themselves are a fading memory, destroyed by fire, wind, water, and the passage of time. But pieces of hull and various tools and equipment remain to mark their final resting places. The *Manhattan* and the *Hettler* can be explored together, since they lie near one another on the east side of Grand Island.

Finally, the Alger Preserve features a couple of good shore access sites. Perhaps the best of these can be found at the US Forest Service dock on Grand Island Drive, off M-28 about one mile west of Munising. Attractions in this shoreline area include the wreck of a small boat, schools of fish, and shallow caverns.

Businesses providing diver services in Alger Underwater Preserve include **Grand Island Charters** (1204 Commercial St., Munising, MI 49862, ☎ 906-387-4477) and **Fun Time Dive Charters** (3120 Branwood Drive, Wisconsin Rapids, WI 54494, ☎ 715-424-0181 or 800-582-7817). For information on the preserve, contact the **Munising Visitors Bureau**, 422 E. Munising Ave., PO Box 405, Munising, MI 49862, ☎ 906-387-2138.

Whitefish Point Underwater Preserve

Over the years the Whitefish Bay area of Lake Superior became known as the "Graveyard of the Great Lakes" because of the terrors that it inflicted on passing ships. Indeed, this dangerously capricious stretch of Superior cast dozens of unlucky vessels down in to its depths over the years. Today, some of those shipwrecks rank as among the most highly prized in the entire underwater preserve system. A number of the known wrecks lie at deep – and cold – depths, and inclement weather can pop up at any time (including July and August, when most divers visit the preserve), making boat selection a factor of considerable importance. If your boat can't hack rough weather – and maybe even if it can – make arrangements with one of the area's charter operators. Divers who do decide to use their own boats can launch from Bay Mills, Brimley State Park, Tahquamenon Bay, Little Lake Harbor, and Whitefish Point. Caution should also be exercised in dive site selection. Exploration of many of the wrecks should be attempted only by advanced divers with good gear. Whitefish is not the place for beginners.

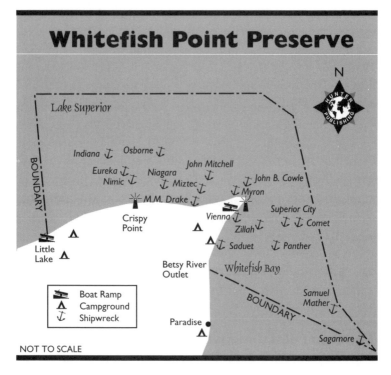

Of the many ships contained within the preserve's 376 square miles, several stand out as particularly noteworthy attractions. The *John Mitchell*, a 420-foot freighter that sank after a collision with another freighter in 1911, lies about three miles north-northwest of Whitefish Point in 140-150 feet of water. The depth at which the ship sits makes it an exceedingly cold dive with limited visibility; visits should be attempted only by advanced divers. East of the *John Mitchell* lies another huge vessel that is out of range to all but the top echelon of divers. The *John B. Cowle*, a 420-foot steel steamer that was lost in 1909 after a collision with another steamer, sits at a forbidding depth of 220 feet. Some penetration diving is possible on the *Cowle,* but any such ventures should be undertaken with extreme caution.

One of the more popular dive sites in Whitefish Point Underwater Preserve is the *Indiana*, a wooden steamer that foundered off Crisp Point in 1858. Propelled by one of the world's first steam engines, the loss of the *Indiana* received significant attention, and in 1979 – nearly 150 years after the ship sank – the engine was salvaged and put on display at the Smithsonian Institution. Limited penetration diving is possible on the *Indiana*, which sits in about 115 feet of water. Other popular wrecks in the preserve include the *Niagara*, a 205-foot schooner that capsized in 1887; the *Myron*, a wooden steamer that was lost in an ice storm in 1919; and the *Panther*, a 249-foot wooden steamer that sank as a result of a fogbank collision with another steamer in 1916. The *Myron* lies at a depth of 45-55 feet, making it suitable for intermediate divers, while the *Niagara* lies at more than 100 feet.

Divers visiting the Whitefish Bay area should also make sure that they leave sufficient time to visit the **Great Lakes Shipwreck Museum**, a fascinating collection of maritime memorabilia and historical documents out on the tip of Whitefish Point. For more information, contact the **Great Lakes Shipwreck Historical Society** at 111 Ashmun, Sault St. Marie, MI 49783, ☎ 906-635-1742.

Outfits offering charters in Whitefish Point Underwater Preserve include **Lake Superior Dive Tours** (90 Chartwell Dr., Sault Ste. Marie, Ontario, Canada P6A 6A2, ☎ 705-946-3929) and **Superior Scuba** (120 Ann St. West, Sault Ste. Marie, Michigan, ☎ 906-632-1332). For information on the preserve itself, contact the **Paradise Area Tourism Council** at PO Box 64, Paradise, MI 49768, ☎ 906-492-3927.

DeTour Passage

This area, which encompasses both the DeTour Passage and the waters surrounding Drummond Island, has more than its share of interesting dive sites. The most popular destinations in the area include the *John B. Merrill*, which was discovered south of Drummond Island in 1992, a full 99 years after it sank in a storm. The ship lies in 60-70 feet of water and can be explored by intermediate divers. Other significant dive sites include the *J.C. Ford*, a steamer that sank off Little Trout Island after a 1924 explosion; and the *General*, a tugboat that was lost off Frying Pan Island in 1930. Both of these vessels lie in less than 20 feet of water, making them ideal for beginning divers. For information on sport diving in the DeTour Passage and Drummond Island areas, contact the **Drummond Island Tourism Association**, PO Box 200, Drummond Island, MI 49726, ☎ 906-493-5245.

Sailing & Boating

Lake Superior

At 400 miles long, 160 miles wide, and an average of 500 feet deep, Superior is the largest lake in the world. Its 32,000 square miles of surface area approximates the size of New England, excepting Maine. With its icy waters and legendary storms, it has acquired the greatest mystique of all the Great Lakes. More than 350 known shipwrecks dot its bottom, the most familiar being the freighter *Edmund Fitzgerald*, which went down off of Whitefish Point in 1975. Many boaters might tend to dismiss Lake Superior out of hand, fearing that the risks of plying its historically unforgiving waters outweigh the benefits. But with advance planning and careful attention to weather reports, even smaller craft can enjoy the serenity offered by its remarkably varied shorelines, remote islands, and quaint lakeside villages.

Despite its harsh reputation, Lake Superior is often quite tame in the summertime. In fact, boaters can expect moderate winds and waves of two feet or less 60-70% of the time. Of course, heavy fogs and severe storms are always a possibility, so it is important to take precautions. Summer water temperatures in mid-lake hover around 46°, but by mid- to late-summer it has usually warmed up enough along protected shorelines for hearty souls to take a refreshing dip.

The **northern shore** of Lake Superior – which extends over 325 miles between Sault Ste. Marie and Thunder Bay in Ontario, Canada – is mostly wild and lined with rugged cliffs. Although there are only two port towns along the way, boats can take refuge in natural harbors formed by sheltering islands every five to 25 miles. The key to safe and enjoyable travel along the north coast is to be completely self-sufficient, with extra provisions in case of bad weather or mechanical difficulty.

Significantly closer to the Canadian shore than any other, but still part of Michigan, is **Isle Royale National Park** – a wilderness archipelago consisting of one large and over 200 small islands. It offers numerous secluded anchorages in natural harbors, as well as docks that provide access to a variety of campgrounds and hiking trails. Fuel and supplies are available at **Rock Harbor**, on the southeastern side of the island. See the section on Isle Royale (page 222) for further information.

Another popular cruising ground is **Apostle Islands National Lakeshore**, which extends 20 miles from the Wisconsin shore in the southwest end of Lake Superior. The lakeshore consists of 21 rugged islands characterized by sandstone formations, sandy beaches, and wooded wilderness. The area provides excellent sheltered cruising grounds but has few natural harbors, so many boaters start from one of several marina bases along the mainland and explore via day trips. Providing testament to its rocky character – and the need to carry good navigational charts of the area – the Apostle Islands have more lighthouses per square mile than any other location in the Great Lakes.

Natural harbors are relatively scarce along Superior's **south shore**, but 16 different ports are available in Michigan waters alone. About 20 miles east of the Wisconsin border is the Black River Harbor, a natural setting with hiking trails nearby. Continuing east, the next recreational harbor is in the small, friendly town of Ontonagon. Nearby, watch for the striking line where the dark red current of the Ontonagon River meets the cool green waters of Lake Superior.

Boaters next encounter the 60-mile long **Keweenaw Peninsula** – the heart of Michigan's Copper Country – which features dramatic, rocky outcrops along its northwest side and rolling, forested hills along its southeast. Smaller craft may elect to cross through the peninsula on the **Keweenaw Waterway**, which provides access to the marina at Houghton-Hancock. But there are also several harbors scattered around the scenic coast of the peninsula – at Eagle Harbor, Copper Harbor, and Bete Grise Bay. Keweenaw Bay, at the other end of the Waterway, can be rough but features a harbor at Baraga.

Boaters continuing east will pass a coastline ranging from mountains to high sand dunes to flat beaches. There is a small harbor at Big Bay, followed by one at the UP's version of a booming metropolis – Marquette. The next harbor to the east, at Munising, is sheltered by the heavily wooded hills and sandstone cliffs of Grand Island (see the section on Hiawatha National Forest (page 218), of which Grand Island is a part, for information on recreational activities). The stretch of coastline between Munising and Grand Marais comprises **Pictured Rocks National Lakeshore**, which offers some of the most sensational scenery in all of the Great Lakes. Colorful sandstone cliffs, caves, arches, and spires – topped with fringes of trees and punctuated by occasional waterfalls – continue for 15 miles. To best capture the distinctive colors of the rocks on film, make a westbound boat journey early in the morning, or an eastbound journey late in the afternoon. Eventually the rocks give way to aptly named Twelvemile Beach, followed by the impressive Grand Sable Dunes, before reaching Grand Marais.

The next harbor to the east, at Little Lake, is wild and scenic but quite shallow. Then boaters must make their way out to **Whitefish Point**, where Lake Superior narrows significantly and tends to become rough. Whitefish Point is the last recreational harbor before Sault Ste. Marie, which marks the eastern end of Lake Superior.

Lake Michigan

Lake Michigan borders the southern UP between Menominee, on Green Bay, and St. Ignace, on the Straits of Mackinac. There is a full-service marina in the pleasant town of **Menominee**, a few miles from the mouth of the Menominee River, which forms the border between Michigan and Wisconsin. Traveling northeast along the coast, which tends to be low and wooded with some nice sandy beaches, boaters enter **Little Bay de Noc**. There are two harbors in the bay, at Escanaba and Gladstone, both of which are within city parks. From there, you can continue around **Peninsula Point** – known for its dangerous shoals – to Big Bay de Noc. Here the shoreline scenery changes to feature limestone bluffs. Snail Shell Harbor is at the old iron-smelting town of Fayette on the east side of the bay. Continuing southeast, you will pass Poverty Island and again be exposed to the open waters of Lake Michigan. It is 37 miles along the northern shore to the full-service recreational harbor in **Manistique**, 45 more miles to **Naubinway**, and then 80 miles along largely uninhabited sand beaches to **St. Ignace**. Many boaters instead choose to cross the top of Lake Michigan on a more scenic and protected southerly route, past Beaver Island.

Lake Huron

Lake Huron laps the shores of the southeastern UP for a relatively short distance, between the Mackinac Bridge and Drummond Island. Still, this coastline features some of the most popular boating attractions in all of the Great Lakes. Just across the way from St. Ignace in the westernmost part of the lake is **Mackinac Island** – with its picturesque harbor beneath the shadow of historic Fort Mackinac, its quaint Victorian village crowded with pedestrians, bicycles, and horse-drawn carriages (no automobiles are allowed), and its many wooded trails leading to unique rock formations and unmatched views of the Straits. Slips in the busy marina are limited, particularly during the last two weekends in July, when they are occupied by sailboats competing in the annual races from Chicago or Port Huron to Mackinac. The island is well worth a visit, and private boats are allowed to anchor in the protected harbor. See the section on Mackinac Island (page 237).

Just northeast of Mackinac, the 36 **Les Cheneaux Islands** create a maze of scenic channels and bays along the northern shore of Lake Huron. There is a recreational harbor in the mainland town of Hessel, three miles from the west entrance to the area, as well as restaurants, shops, and a casino. Each year in early August, Hessel plays host to an **antique boat show**. ☎ 906-484-3935 for further information.

Continuing east, just beyond the entrance to the St. Mary's River is **Drummond Island**, which is part of the Manitoulin chain that separates the main body of Lake Huron from the North Channel. It was named after British commander Sir Gordon Drummond, who built a fort there in the early 1800s despite the fact that the island had already become American territory. The 136-square-mile island features many quiet inlets and several transient boat harbors.

The Soo

Connecting Lake Superior to Lake Huron is the St. Mary's River, an island-strewn passage that ranges in size from narrow channels to wide bays and lakes. It is bordered on its northern end by two cities known as Sault Ste. Marie – one in Michigan and one in Ontario, Canada. The Sault area (or Soo, as it is pronounced and sometimes spelled) is home to the world's longest and busiest locks, which were constructed in 1855 to help ships pass around the rapids of the St. Mary's River. Before this time, an Ojibwa canoe portage trail was the only way to take a boat upstream, since the river dropped 21 feet in the course of a mile. Today, however, the locks enable massive freighters to transport grain and ore from the Midwest to ports all over the world.

Private boats are allowed to pass through the locks along with the freighters. Alternatively, there is a public viewing area along the shore in Sault Ste. Marie, Michigan, where you can watch as pilots guide 1,000-foot freighters through the gates with just inches to spare. **Soo Locks Boat Tours** (☎ 800-432-6301) offers a two-hour narrated excursion through the locks, as well as longer, sunset dinner cruises that also include part of the North Channel.

There is a recreational harbor on the southern end of the St. Mary's River at **DeTour**, across from Drummond Island, and another on the northern end in **Sault Ste. Marie**, Michigan. The shortest distance up the river is via the shipping channel, at 63 miles, but it is also the least scenic. Instead, many boaters decide to cruise through Potagannissing Bay and around picturesque St. Joseph Island.

Inland Lakes

There are thousands of inland lakes in the UP suitable for boating, as well as nearly 350 public boat access sites. Three of the largest lakes – **Indian Lake, Muskallonge Lake**, and **Lake Gogebic** – feature state parks along their shorelines. Other UP lakes popular for boating include **Brevort, Manistique**, and **Au Train**.

On Snow

Cross-Country Skiing

With abundant snowfall and public land, it is little wonder that cross-country ski trails abound in Michigan's Upper Peninsula – ranging from quiet treks through snow-shrouded forests to heart-pounding adventures on challenging hills to mellow glides along the edges of towns. A wide variety of trails are available in the UP's national and state forests, state and city parks, and ski resorts. All designated trails have signs indicating the direction of travel and the level of ability required, from novice to expert, and some provide rest shelters along the way or warming huts at the trailhead. Most of the trails are well-groomed, but some harken back to an earlier time when skis provided people with transportation through deep powder. Some of the premier cross-country trails can be found within major regional attractions, such as Hiawatha and Ottawa National Forests, Porcupine Mountains and Tahquamenon Falls State Parks, and Pictured Rocks National Lakeshore (see the sections on these areas). Descriptions of some other popular trails follow:

Keweenaw Peninsula

The snowy Keweenaw features a variety of groomed trails for Nordic enthusiasts, as well as backcountry skiing opportunities along shorelines, on unplowed roads, and through ghost towns. One popular loop trail runs through a stand of magnificent virgin pines at **Estivant Pines Nature Sanctuary** near Copper Harbor. No motorized vehicles are allowed in the 377-acre sanctuary, enhancing the sense of solitude. Also near Copper Harbor, **Lake Fanny Hooe Resort** offers four trails totaling 25 miles of groomed and tracked snow, along with a warming shelter. **Swedetown Trails** near Calumet is an 11-mile system divided into three loops, with just over a mile lighted for night skiing. Beginning at the Houghton Country Arena, the **Maasto Hiihto Trail** runs for 11 miles through a forested area. There are also two novice trails totaling six miles in **McLain State Park** along the Lake Superior shore, and three trails for different ability levels totaling 45 miles in **Copper Country State Forest**.

Big Snow Country

The extreme western UP offers excellent cross-country skiing opportunities, with 200 inches of annual snowfall and winter temperatures averaging 20°. In fact, Big Snow Country features some 175 miles of groomed and tracked trails, ranging in skill level from novice to expert. Several area ski resorts have extensive cross-country ski trail networks, including **Brule**, which maintains a 14-mile trail system with an Adirondack shelter at the halfway point (☎ 800-DO-BRULE). Some of the finest Nordic skiing in the state can be found at **Porcupine Mountains State Park** (☎ 906-885-5275). The 26-mile trail system features outstanding scenery and leads to three rustic cabins that are available for rent. In addition, the price of a trail pass includes a one-ride lift ticket into the heart of the Nordic area. There are also eight groomed and tracked trails totaling 20 miles near **Watersmeet**, some of which are lighted. The Watersmeet cross-country ski area also features a warming hut, equipment rentals, and lessons. In the Wakefield area, **Johnson Nordic Trails** maintains 10 trails totaling 19 miles for all ability levels, with instruction, rentals, and a warming hut available. In Iron River, the **George Young Recreation Complex** offers 10 trails that wind around lakes and through varying terrain for a total of 15 miles. Finally, the Ironwood area offers 22 miles of trails in the scenic **Black River and Black River Harbor trail systems**.

Central UP

In addition to the many cross-country trails in Hiawatha National Forest and Pictured Rocks National Lakeshore, the central UP offers a number of shorter trails. The **Blueberry Ridge Pathway** near Ishpeming (trailhead at the junction of CR-480 and CR-553) maintains six trails totaling 12 miles for skiers of all ability levels. There are also three scenic trails ranging from one to 10 miles in length at **Seney National Wildlife Refuge** near Germfask, where motorized vehicles are prohibited. The **Escanaba River State Forest** features four trails totaling nine miles, while the **Lake Mary Plains Pathway** east of Crystal Falls (trailhead off M-69 at the State Forest Campground) provides three novice trails totaling 12 miles that pass by Glidden Lake.

Eastern UP

The eastern UP presents Nordic enthusiasts with a number of options in addition to the trails in Hiawatha National Forest and Tahquamenon Falls State Park. The **Algonquin Trail** near Sault Ste. Marie, for example, is a nine-mile system through a heavily wooded area, with one loop lighted for night skiing. The **DeTour Pathway** (trailhead five miles west of DeTour on M-134) runs four miles through the woods to St. Vitals Point, where skiers are treated to a great view of Lake Huron. In the Manistique area, the

The Upper Peninsula

Ashford Lake Pathway (trailhead 16 miles north of Manistique off M-94) offers three trails totaling 18 miles, while the **Indian Lake Trail** (trailhead three miles west of Manistique off M-149) has three trails totaling nine miles. There are also three trails totaling 14 miles near **Curtis**, which cater to skiers of all ability levels. **Lake Superior State Forest** features five trails totaling 40 miles, some of which are lighted for night skiing.

Downhill Skiing & Snowboarding

Some of the finest downhill skiing and snowboarding is in Michigan's Upper Peninsula, the extreme western portion of which is known as "Big Snow Country." During the winter, this region's proximity to Lake Superior keeps temperatures moderate but also deposits over 200 inches of snow annually (that's more than 16 feet!). There are five premier ski areas in the region – Big Powderhorn, Blackjack, Brule, Indianhead, and Porcupine Mountains – and another just across the border in Wisconsin – Whitecap. Though they don't see too many visitors from the Lower Peninsula in January and February, when the Traverse City-area resorts have nearly as much snow and require half the drive time, they are quite popular with those who want to extend their ski season well into March and April. In fact, the Big Snow Country resorts boast an average 149-day ski season, compared to 91 days for northern LP ski areas and 127 days in the Rocky Mountains. The western UP ski areas also charge less for lift tickets than LP resorts. Adult weekend/holiday rates average $27 at the major western UP locations, and an Adventure Card is available that offers a one-day ticket to each of five resorts for $75. For general information about Big Snow Country, call the **Western UP Visitors Bureau** at ☎ 800-272-7000. For lodging referrals in the area, ☎ 906-932-4850.

Big Powderhorn Mountain

Located on Powderhorn Road two miles north of US-2, between Ironwood and Bessemer, Big Powderhorn bills itself as a family resort. It offers 24 trails – nine novice, nine intermediate, and six expert – with some nearly a mile long, and a 600-foot vertical drop. Its 250 acres of skiable terrain are served by nine double chairs with total lift capacity of over 10,800 skiers per hour. Like most other UP resorts, Big Powderhorn is open 9 AM to 4 PM daily, and snowboards are welcome on all hills. There are three cozy restaurants and lounges offering après-ski food and spirits, as well as a fully equipped ski shop with rentals. A variety of lodging is available, ranging from $58 to $221 per night. Weekend/holiday lift tickets cost $27 for adults, $21 juniors (ages 13-17), and $16 for children (7-12). Kids under 6 stay and ski free at Big Powderhorn, and the resort's Kinderschool provides babysitting services and ski lessons for 2- to 7-year-olds. Weekday lift ticket rates drop by $4, and a variety of discounts are available for mid-week and multi-day packages. ☎ 906-932-4838 for skiing information, or 800-222-3131 for reservations.

Blackjack Ski Resort

Located off Blackjack Road, two miles north of US-2, this resort harkens back to the UP's logging past. It offers 20 trails – 20% novice, 40% intermediate, and 40% expert – a longest run of 5,300 feet, and a 465-foot vertical drop. These hills are served by four double lifts and two rope tows, giving Blackjack an uphill capacity of 4,800 skiers per hour. Snowboarders will find a half-pipe and snowboard park for their enjoyment, while skiers can entertain themselves on a terrain trail complete with tunnel and jumps. Blackjack also features a dual giant-slalom race course on weekends. Rather than stopping for lunch, you can select a group picnic site on the mountain and have campfire and picnic supplies delivered. Après-ski activities center around the **Loggers Saloon**, which offers live music on weekends. Lodging is available in trailside condominiums – all of which feature a full kitchen, cable TV, sauna, and fireplace – ranging from $45 per night for a studio during the week to $400 per night for a three-bedroom during the holidays. ☎ 800-848-1125 for reservations. Weekend/holiday adult lift tickets are $22, and juniors (ages 9-15) are $17. The rates drop by $5 on during the week. Children 8 and under are free, and the Kindercamp provides supervised indoor and outdoor play and ski lessons. ☎ 800-848-1125, or visit the Blackjack Web site at http://www.skiblackjack.com.

Indianhead Mountain Resort

Indianhead, near Wakefield, boasts one of the highest vertical drops in the area at 638 feet. It offers 22 trails – 20% novice, 40% intermediate, and 40% expert – served by three double chairs, one triple, and one quad. For snowboarders, it also features the largest terrain park in Michigan – with a 75-foot half pipe, gap jumps, and table tops – which was designed by the same person who will build the facilities for the 1998 Winter Olympics. Après-ski activities at Indianhead include snow tubing, dog sledding, and bonfires. Weekend/holiday adult lift tickets cost $33, juniors (ages 13-17) are $26, and children (ages 7-12) are $20. The prices drop $3-$5 during the week, and package discounts are available. The resort provides a kinderschool for children ages 2-8, and lessons and equipment rentals are available for other guests as well. Accommodations at Indianhead range from $65 per night during the week in the lodge complex to $541 on a weekend for a six-bedroom chalet. ☎ 800-3INDIAN for further information or reservations, visit the Web site at http://www.indianheadmtn.com, or send e-mail inquiries to bestsnow@aol.com.

Porcupine Mountains

The Porcupine Mountains Ski Area, within the State Park of the same name, has 15 groomed downhill ski runs – three novice, seven intermediate, and five expert – covering 11 miles of slope, and a vertical drop of 640 feet. The longest run is over 5,400 feet. With a triple chair, a double chair, and a T-bar, the ski area boasts a lift capacity of 3,600 skiers per hour. An adult, one-day lift ticket costs $25 on a weekend or holiday, while juniors (ages 13-17) and seniors (65 and older) pay $20, and children under 12 ski free. The Porcupine Mountains Ski Chalet offers a cozy warming area with several large fireplaces and picture windows overlooking the slopes. It also contains a ski shop, cafeteria, and first-aid office, as well as equipment rental and repair facilities. Snowboards, snowshoes, and snowmobiles are available for rent in addition to skis. For information on skiing the Porkies, call the park headquarters at ☎ 906-885-5275. For 24-hour snow reports, ☎ 800-BSC-7000, and for the ski shop/rental information, ☎ 906-885-5612.

Ski Brule

Located near Iron River on Brule Mountain Road, Brule offers 14 runs – three novice, eight intermediate, and three difficult – served by four chairlifts, and a 500-foot vertical drop. In addition to a 15-acre snowboard arena and half-pipe, the resort features a terrain trail for skiers with a tunnel and an assortment of bumps and berms. Weekend/holiday lift ticket prices are $27 for adults and $21 juniors (ages 10-17), while children 9 or under ski free. Weekday skiers enjoy a savings of $4-$6, and special discounts are available. Guests can enjoy an après-ski excursion by horse-drawn sleigh to the Homestead Lodge – an authentic log cabin heated by potbelly stoves and decorated with antique farm implements – for an all-you-can-eat barbecue on weekends. Accommodations in Brule Village include chalets and condominiums ranging from $36 to $56 per person per night. ☎ 800-DO-BRULE, or visit the Web site at http://www.skibrule.com.

Whitecap Mountains

Not really in Michigan, but usually included in descriptions of Big Snow Country, Whitecap is Wisconsin's largest ski resort. It is just across the border in Montreal, off H-77 on CR-E, in the ancient Penokee mountain range. The ski area offers 35 runs on three different mountains – including 12 novice, nine intermediate, and 14 expert runs – served by six chairlifts with a total capacity over 8,000 skiers per hour. Skiers can warm up at the **Wine Hut**, conveniently located on the slopes in an authentic log cabin. Weekend/holiday lift ticket rates are $29 for adults, $23 for juniors (ages 12-17), and $18 for children (ages 6-11). Weekday savings range from $3-$5, and a variety of package deals are available. The resort offers Kinderschule for children 3-10, as well as equipment rentals, lessons, and a pro shop. Lodging options range from lavish trailside chalets to budget motel rooms starting at $39 per night double occupancy. ☎ 800-933-SNOW for information or reservations.

Norway Mountain

Norway Mountain is close to Big Snow Country, on Brier Mountain Road near Norway in the southwestern UP. It features 18 runs served by two chairs, and a 400-foot vertical drop. It is also a full-service ski area, offering instruction, equipment rentals, and snowboarding. ☎ 906-563-9700.

Pine Mountain

Pine Mountain is another full-service ski area in the southwestern UP, near Iron Mountain along the Wisconsin border. It offers 15 runs served by three lifts and a 500-foot vertical drop. ☎ 800-321-6298.

Marquette Mountain

The largest ski area outside of Big Snow Country, Marquette Mountain is near Marquette in the north-central UP. It features 18 runs served by three chairs – the longest run an impressive 8,300 feet – and a 600-foot vertical drop. It also offers instruction and rentals, and there is plentiful lodging nearby. ☎ 906-225-1155.

Luge

Lucy Hill Naturbahn Luge Track

Michigan is home to two of only three luge tracks in the country. The Lucy Hill Naturbahn in Negaunee, just west of Marquette, is part of Northern Michigan University's US Olympic Education Center. The half-mile ice track, which features 29 curves, is open to amateurs wanting to experience the thrill of twisting and turning down a narrow pipe at high speed. Instruction is provided on the lower portion of the track, and luges and safety equipment are available for rent. ☎ 906-475-LUGE.

Dogsledding

Every winter, Michigan's UP comes alive with an image reminiscent of one of Jack London's Yukon tales: dog sled teams, racing across the snow in a blur of flashing legs, lolling tongues, and shining eyes. The practice of raising – and in some instances racing – sled dogs never wholly disappeared from Michigan's northern realms, but it has unquestionably benefited in recent years from a resurgence of interest in both dog sled racing and guided dog sledding trips. Indeed, the UP's plentiful snow, myriad pathways, and spectacular outdoor expanses make the region ideal for

Dogsled races are among the most popular events in the UP (Travel Michigan).

all manner of dog sledding, from fiercely contested races to wilderness cruises.

Of course, some of these trails are also utilized by snowmobilers, who buzz around in prodigious numbers every winter. (Trail use disputes have sparked some feuding between the two camps in recent years, but lines of communication seem to have improved.) But mushers can still find long stretches of isolated trail in the peninsula's sprawling forests and meadows. **Lake Superior State Forest** and **Hiawatha National Forest** are among the most popular areas for dogsledding in the UP (see the section on Hiawatha National Forest, page 217, for more info on dogsledding).

Wilderness dogsledding adventures are available through several outfitters. Excursions vary considerably in length, from a couple of hours to several days. Contact **Caribou Creek** (☎ 906-439-5747), **Triple Creek Kennels** (☎ 906-249-3470), **Keweenaw Adventure Tours** (☎ 906-289-4303), **Side Treks** (☎ 906-228-8735), **Wolfsong Outfitters** (☎ 906-658-3356), or **Buckstop Bed and Breakfast** (☎ 906-446-3360).

Snowmobiling

Snowmobiling is more than just recreation during the long winters in Michigan's Upper Peninsula – it's transportation. With average annual snowfalls ranging from 50 to 200 inches, there is generally plenty of white stuff for sleds between Thanksgiving and mid-April. As a result, the opportunities for riders are limitless: the region boasts 2,500 miles of interconnecting snowmobile trails that crisscross the entire region. An ambitious rider

More than 2,500 miles of snowmobile trails wind through the Upper Peninsula (Travel Michigan).

could easily travel from the Mackinac Bridge to the Wisconsin border, or from Lake Superior to Lake Michigan, all on groomed and marked trails. It is even possible to snowmobile from the Lower Peninsula to the Upper by making advance arrangements to trailer across the Mackinac Bridge for a fee of $1 per machine (☎ 906-643-7600). When ice conditions are right, sleds can make the trip across frozen waters to Grand Island, Drummond Island, and Mackinac Island. In addition, many roads in major regional attractions are open to snowmobiles, providing new perspectives on such familiar sights as the Lake of the Clouds overlook in Porcupine Mountains State Park.

Most snowmobile trails in the UP pass through communities that offer cold or tired riders access to restaurants, lodging, and gas stations. Many trails also lead to such spectacular winter scenery as ice caverns along the Great Lakes shorelines, ice sculptures created by frozen waterfalls, and vistas of snow-covered forests and hills. Established trails are usually groomed to 12 feet wide and posted with signs directing riders to the nearest sources of gas and food. The Department of Natural Resources has instituted a UP-wide system of trail numbering in which even numbers indicate east-west trails, and odd numbers signify north-south trails. Also under this system, trails bearing single-digit numbers are long, mainline trails, while double-digit numbers identify connecting trails and triple-digit numbers mark feeder trails. It is important to note that anyone riding a snowmobile on UP trails is required to obtain a State of Michigan snowmobile permit, which costs $10 annually. Get one from the **Michigan Department of Natural Resources**, ☎ 517-373-4175. Some of the more popular areas for snowmobiling include:

Big Snow Country

This area of the extreme western UP – which received 300 inches of snow during the winter of 1995-96 – features over 450 miles of groomed and marked snowmobile trails. At 102 miles, the **State Line Trail** is the longest rail-trail in Michigan. It roughly parallels US-2 along the Wisconsin border from Wakefield (trailhead on Korpela Road) through Marenisco, Watersmeet, and Iron River to Mastedon Township Park. Another rail-trail popular with snowmobilers is the 43-mile **Bergland-Sidnaw Trail**, which roughly follows M-28 from the shores of Lake Gogebic eastward. Along the way, riders cross several high bridges over rivers, including one that provides a view of Agate Falls on the Middle Branch of the Ontonagon. Some of the other lengthy trails in Big Snow Country include the **Ironwood Trail** (42 miles), **Bessemer Area Trails** (53 miles), **Bergland-Porcupine Mountains Trail** (50 miles), and **Lac Vieux Trail** (50 miles; trailhead southwest of L'Anse on US-41).

Keweenaw Peninsula

Thanks to the lake effect off of Superior, rarely a winter day goes by without snowfall in the scenic Keweenaw. The peninsula features 250 miles of snowmobile trails that connect to greater UP systems. A special treat for riders in the area is crossing the Portage Lift Bridge between the twin cities of Houghton and Hancock. The upper level supports highway traffic, while the lower level is reserved for two-way snowmobile traffic. The 40-mile **Bill Nicholls Trail** begins on Canal Drive west of downtown Houghton, climbs to provide a nice view of the Portage Lake Ship Canal, and then crosses several bridges before ending at Adventure Mountain. The 13-mile **Hancock-Calumet Trail** begins at the old depot in Calumet and passes relics of the mining era on its way to Poorvoo Park in Hancock, just across the canal from the Bill Nicholls trailhead in Houghton. At Copper Harbor on the tip of the peninsula, the **Brockway Mountain Trail** climbs 10 miles to provide a scenic view out over the village, a lighthouse, and Lake Superior.

Central UP

Snowmobiling opportunities abound in the central UP, from Grand Island and Pictured Rocks National Lakeshore in the north to Escanaba and Manistique in the south. The 33-mile **Haywire Trail** (trailhead south of Shingleton on M-94, near Pictured Rocks) meanders through heavily wooded Hiawatha National Forest and Lake Superior State Forest, crossing 14 small bridges on its way to Manistique on Lake Michigan. The 45-mile **Felch Grade Trail** follows M-69 across the south-central UP toward Escanaba, passing a store and tavern at its halfway point in LaBranche. Other popular trails in the area include **Big Bay-L'Anse Trail** (45 miles), **Negaunee Area Trails** (40 miles), **Little Lake-Northland Trail** (40 miles), and **North Menominee County Trails** (61 miles; trailhead at Wilson on US-41).

Eastern UP

Snowmobiling is particularly popular in the eastern UP during the dead of winter, when the lakes freeze over to provide riders with easy access to numerous islands, including the Les Cheneaux chain and Mackinac Island. One of the best areas for sleds is **Drummond Island**, which features 100 miles of trails through forests and along the coastline. The ferry to the island operates hourly throughout the winter and can handle both snowmobiles and trailers. But a more adventurous way to make the trip is via the **International Ice Bridge**, a route across the frozen lake that is lined with Christmas trees from mid-January to late March or early April each year. It is 11 miles to neighboring St. Joseph Island or 18 miles to Thessalon on the Canadian mainland, which gives access to Ontario's vast trail system. Snowmobiles crossing the border must check in with customs and purchase a Canadian Trail Permit ($14 US per day, $40 per week, or $115 annually). Some of the longer trails on the eastern UP mainland include the **Charcoal Grade Trail** (22 miles; trailhead one mile north of

Newberry on M-123), **Pine Stump Trail** (30 miles; trailhead 19 miles north of Newberry on Deer Park Road), **Paradise Area Trails** (45 miles), **Raco-Hulbert-Trout Lake Trail** (39 miles), and **Soo-Raco Trail** (20 miles; trailhead one mile east of Sault Ste. Marie at Sherman Park).

▪ Where To Sleep

In addition to the chain hotels that can be found in its larger towns, the UP nourishes many fine country inns, cottages, and B&Bs. Here's a brief rundown on a few of your options.

Price Guide	
$	up to $50 per night
$$	$50-$100
$$$	$100-$175
$$$$	more than $175

Western Upper Peninsula

Big Bay Point Lighthouse Bed and Breakfast (No. 3 Lighthouse Rd., Big Bay, MI 49808, ☎ 906-345-9957, $$-$$$). This privately owned, renovated lighthouse offers six comfortable rooms, stunning scenic views from the top of the lighthouse, and a mile of Lake Superior shoreline to explore.

Keweenaw Mountain Lodge (Copper Harbor, MI 49918, ☎ 906-289-4403, $-$$). Inexpensive accommodations in rustic cabins (stone fireplaces, hardwood floors) and motel units with cathedral ceilings. A mecca for active travelers, the lodge offers tennis courts, an 18-hole golf course, and hiking trails through hundreds of wooded acres. Good dining room, too.

Lambert's Chalet Cottages (287 Lakeshore Rd., Ontonagon, MI 49953, ☎ 906-884-4230, $-$$). This place is equipped with a private beach and nice cabins, several of which have fireplaces. Centrally located between the varied attractions of the Keweenaw Peninsula and Porcupine Mountains Wilderness State Park.

Superior Shores Resort (1823 M-64, Ontonagon, MI 49953, ☎ 800-344-5355, $-$$). This resort offers cozy cabins right alongside the scenic shores of Lake Superior. As with the Lambert offerings, these cabins are ideally situated between the Porkies and the Keweenaw.

Tiroler Hof Motel (150 Carp River Hill, Marquette, MI 49855, ☎ 906-226-7516, $$). This reasonably priced alternative has 41 rooms set on spacious, attractive grounds overlooking Lake Superior. It also maintains a small chapel and a dining room that specializes in Austrian cuisine.

Eastern Upper Peninsula

Celibath House (Route 1, Box 58-A, Blaney Park, MI 49836, ☎ 906-283-3409, $$). A warm and friendly B&B that includes seven bedrooms, a library, and a living room complete with fireplace.

Georgian House Lakefront Inn (1131 North State, St. Ignace, MI 49781, ☎ 906-643-8411, $$-$$$). This Best Western hotel has 85 rooms, including several lakefront units with balconies, and extensive indoor offerings (heated pool/recreation area) that make it a popular destination for families.

Helmer House Inn (CR-417, McMillan, MI 49853, ☎ 906-586-3204, $$). Five guest rooms filled with attractive antique furniture. This 19th-century inn also boasts a highly regarded dining room.

MacLeod House (Newberry, MI 49868, ☎ 906-293-3841, $$). This 1898 Victorian inn offers travelers a central locale from which to explore many area attractions, from the shores of Lake Superior to the peaceful woods of the Seney National Wildlife Refuge.

Ojibway Hotel (240 West Portage, Sault Ste. Marie, MI 49783, ☎ 906-632-4100, $$-$$$). This historic inn overlooking the Soo Locks has 71 rooms, a heated indoor pool, and a dining room that is open for all three meals.

Pinewood Lodge Bed and Breakfast (PO Box 176, Au Train, MI 49806, ☎ 906-892-8300, $$). This pine log B&B offers great views of Au Train Island and Lake Superior in a warm atmosphere.

Weavers Sunrise Cottages (Paradise, MI 49768, ☎ 906-492-3378, $-$$). Comfortable cottages for travelers exploring the Whitefish Point area.

■ Where To Eat

In many Upper Peninsula communities, eating options are dominated by mom-and-pop diners and pasty shops that specialize in providing hardy meat-and-potatoes fare. But the UP also supports a variety of other restaurants that provide delightful food in a pleasing atmosphere. Here's a sampling.

Price Guide
$ . . . . inexpensive
$$ . . . . moderately priced
$$$ . . . . expensive

Western Upper Peninsula

Armando's/Douglass Saloon (517 Sheldon Ave., Houghton, MI, ☎ 906-482-2003, $$). A perennial hang-out of Michigan Tech students, this restaurant features tasty breakfasts, a variety of buffets, and Sunday brunches, all in a classy setting (the building is listed on the National and State Historical Registers).

Caribou Lodge (Big Powderhorn Ski Resort, Powderhorn Rd., Bessemer, MI, ☎ 906-932-4714, $$$). This moderately expensive restaurant is a huge favorite of skiers, who flock to its tables to sample its wonderfully varied menu. The Caribou is closed during the summer. The Big Powderhorn Ski Resort lies two miles north of US-2 between Ironwood and Bessemer.

Mama Get's (US-2, Ironwood, MI, ☎ 906-932-1322, $$). This bustling dining spot features a cozy, rustic atmosphere – the restaurant is a warmly decorated log-frame structure – and a good variety of American fare, served in generous portions. Options range from Mexican food to beef- and chicken-oriented entrées.

The Mariner North (Copper Harbor, MI, ☎ 888-MA-NORTH, $$$). This spacious restaurant, which is part of a larger lodging complex, features a full menu, with seafood and prime rib buffets on some weekends.

Mike's (106 E. Cloverland Dr., Ironwood, MI, ☎ 906-932-0555, $$). A hot spot for breakfast, Mike's also offers crowd-pleasing fare (Italian sandwiches, pizza, steak) for lunch and dinner.

Shute's Bar (Calumet, MI, ☎ 906-337-1998, $). This is Michigan's oldest known tavern. Closed for many years, it recently reopened with many of its former charms – including antique fixtures and an impressive bar – still intact. A singularly atmospheric place in which to grab a burger and a beer.

Central Upper Peninsula

Brownstone Inn, Highway 28, Au Train, MI, ☎ 906-892-8332, $$). An excellent choice for dinner, this restaurant offers good food and a variety of draft beers for parched throats.

Crispigna's (1213 Ludington, Escanaba, MI, ☎ 906-786-8660, $$). One of the best Italian restaurants in the UP, Crispigna's is an established favorite.

The Dog Patch (25 E. Superior, Munising, MI, ☎ 906-387-9948, $$). A fabulously popular spot among winter snowmobilers, this restaurant hangs its hat on heaping breakfast dishes and great seafood buffets.

Hereford & Hops (624 Ludington St., Escanaba, MI, ☎ 906-789-1945, $$). This busy restaurant/microbrewery offers a half-dozen or more frosty home brews and a variety of steakhouse favorites (the cuts come from the restaurant's own butchershop). A popular Sunday offering is the formidable Grand Brewmeister Buffet.

Northwoods Supper Club (260 Northwoods Rd., Marquette, MI, ☎ 906-228-4343, $$). Affectionately known as "The Woods" by locals, this log-hewn restaurant has been family-owned and operated since 1934. Located 3½ miles west of Marquette on US-41 and SR-28.

The Stonehouse (Marquette, MI, ☎ 906-786-5003, $$). Prime rib is the specialty at this popular restaurant, which sits at the crossroads of US-2, US-41, and M-35.

Vierling Saloon and Sample Room (119 South Front, Marquette, MI, ☎ 906-228-3533, $$). Hard to beat the breakfasts at this friendly place, which is set in a painstakingly renovated 19th-century saloon.

Eastern Upper Peninsula

The Antler's (804 E. Portage Ave., Sault Ste. Marie, MI, ☎ 906-632-3571, $$). This atmospheric restaurant features a blizzard of outdoor paraphernalia and some of the best burgers on the peninsula.

Galley Restaurant and Lounge (241 N. State, St. Ignace, MI, ☎ 906-643-7960, $$). This restaurant, which looks out over Mackinac Island, serves a wide variety of dinners for every kind of taste.

Lake Superior Brewing Company at the Dunes Saloon (N14283 Lake Ave., Grand Marais, MI, ☎ 906-494-BEER, $$). This microbrewery draws folks in with a variety of home-made brews and a diverse menu. Decorated with photo and rock displays, the restaurant features time-lapse videos of the lake and provides guided brewery tours.

North Bay Inn (1192 N. State St., St. Ignace, MI, ☎ 906-643-8304, $$). Family-friendly restaurant, with an emphasis on char-broiled steaks and fresh whitefish.

The Northwood (Drummond Island, MI, ☎ 906-493-5282, $$). One of the island's primary gathering spots, this restaurant specializes in steak and whitefish dinners.

Appendix

■ Hunting in Michigan

Hunting is a hugely popular activity throughout Michigan. This is due not only to the state's sizable community of sportsmen, but to its extensive public land holdings and private ownership of large tracts of prime hunting grounds. In recent years, Michigan hunters have benefited from generally healthy species numbers. Some gamebirds (grouse, woodcock, pheasant) have experienced a decline over the past few seasons, but many other species, including rabbit, squirrel, bear, and deer, have maintained healthy to excellent numbers during the 1990s. The state's deer season draws far more hunters than any other. The bowhunting season alone sees approximately 350,000 deer hunters each year, and the firearms season (muzzleloading and regular firearms) flushes more than twice that number out into Michigan's fields and woodlands in search of venison. Other species hunted in Michigan include elk, coyote, duck, goose, quail, wild turkey, bobcat, fox, and raccoon.

> Each year brings changes in hunting season dates for various species as well as other rule changes. Hunters are advised to familiarize themselves with the DNR's annual *Michigan Hunting and Trapping Guide* before heading out to their blinds. This guide includes regulations on everything from licenses to fur harvesting, as well as information on all facets of hunting, from baiting to clothing requirements to use of private and public lands.

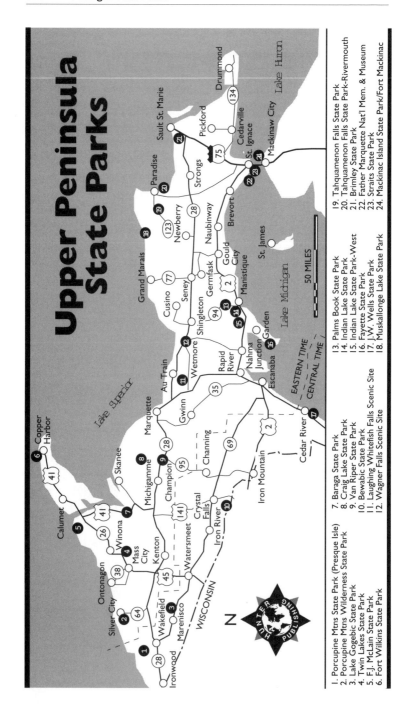

Upper Peninsula State Parks

1. Porcupine Mtns State Park (Presque Isle)
2. Porcupine Mtns Wilderness State Park
3. Lake Gogebic State Park
4. Twin Lakes State Park
5. F.J. McLain State Park
6. Fort Wilkins State Park

7. Baraga State Park
8. Craig Lake State Park
9. Van Riper State Park
10. Bewabic State Park
11. Laughing Whitefish Falls Scenic Site
12. Wagner Falls Scenic Site

13. Palms Book State Park
14. Indian Lake State Park
15. Indian Lake State Park-West
16. Fayette State Park
17. J.W. Wells State Park
18. Muskallonge Lake State Park

19. Tahquamenon Falls State Park
20. Tahquamenon Falls State Park-Rivermouth
21. Brimley State Park
22. Father Marquette Nat'l Mem. & Museum
23. Straits State Park
24. Mackinac Island State Park/Fort Mackinac

■ Michigan State Parks

For camping reservations at any of Michigan's state parks, ☎ 800-44-PARKS.

Upper Peninsula

1. Porcupine Mountains Wilderness S.P. (Presque Isle Unit). 88 sites, ☎ 906-885-5275.
2. Porcupine Mountains Wilderness S.P. – 95 sites, ☎ 906-885-5275.
3. Lake Gogebic S.P. – 125 sites, ☎ 906-842-3341.
4. Twin Lakes S.P. – 62 sites, ☎ 906-288-3321.
5. F.J. McLain S.P. – 103 sites, ☎ 906-482-0278.
6. Fort Wilkins S.P. – 165 sites, ☎ 906-289-4215.
7. Baraga S.P. – 119 sites, ☎ 906-353-6558.
8. Craig Lake S.P. – wilderness camping, ☎ 906-339-4461.
9. Van Riper S.P. – 189 sites, ☎ 906-339-4461.
10. Bewabic S.P. – 144 sites, ☎ 906-875-3324.
11. Laughing Whitefish Falls Scenic Site – no camping, ☎ 906-339-4461.
12. Wagner Falls Scenic Site – no camping, ☎ 906-341-2355.
13. Palms Book S.P. – no camping, ☎ 906-341-2355.
14. Indian Lake S.P. – 158 sites, ☎ 906-341-2355.
15. Indian Lake S.P. (West Unit). 144 sites, ☎ 906-341-2355.
16. Fayette S.P. – 80 sites, ☎ 906-644-2603.
17. J.W. Wells S.P. – 178 sites, ☎ 906-863-9747.
18. Muskallonge Lake S.P. – 179 sites, ☎ 906-658-3338.
19. Tahquamenon Falls S.P. – 183 sites, ☎ 906-492-3415.
20. Tahquamenon Falls S.P. (River Unit). 136 sites, ☎ 906-492-3415.
21. Brimley S.P. – 270 sites, ☎ 906-248-3422.

Appendix

22. Father Marquette National Memorial – no camp
    ing, ☎ 906-643-8620.

23. Straits S.P. – 322 sites, ☎ 906-643-8620.

24. Mackinac Island S.P. – no camping, ☎ 906-
    436-5563.

Northern Lower Peninsula

25. Wilderness S.P. – 250 sites, ☎ 616-436-5381.

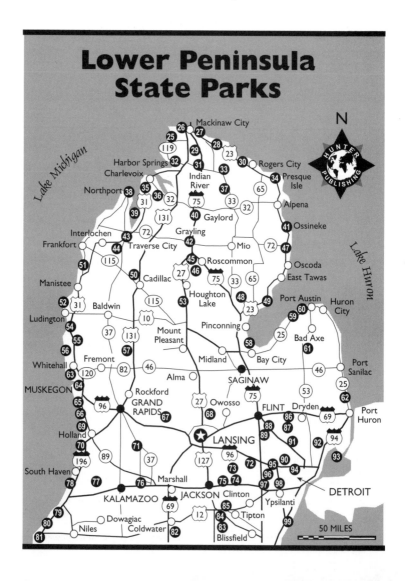

26. Colonial Michilimackinac S.P. – no camping, ☎ 616-436-5563.

27. Mill Creek S.P. – no camping, ☎ 616-436-5563.

28. Cheboygan S.P. – 78 sites, ☎ 616-627-2811.

29. Aloha S.P. – 300 sites, ☎ 616-625-2522.

30. P.H. Hoeft S.P. – 144 sites, ☎ 517-734-2543.

31. Burt Lake S.P. – 375 sites, ☎616-238-9392.

32. Petoskey S.P. – 190 sites, ☎ 616-347-2311.

33. Onaway S.P. – 101 sites, ☎ 517-733-8279.

34. Thompson's Harbor S.P. – no camping, ☎ 517-734-2543.

35. Fisherman's Island S.P. – 90 sites, ☎ 616-547-6641.

Appendix

25. Wilderness State Park
26. Colonial Michilimackinac State Park
27. Mill Creek State Park
28. Cheboygan State Park
29. Aloha State Park
30. P.H. Hoeft State Park
31. Burt Lake State Park
32. Petoskey State Park
33. Onaway State Park
34. Thompson's Harbor State Park
35. Fisherman's Island State Park
36. Young State Park
37. Clear Lake State Park
38. Leelanau State Park
39. Old Mission State Park
40. Otsego Lake State Park
41. Negwegon State Park
42. Hartwick Pines State Park
43. Traverse City State Park
44. Interlochen State Park
45. Higgins Lake State Park-North
46. Higgins Lake State Park-South
47. Harrisville State Park
48. Rifle River State Park
49. Tawas Point State Park
50. Wm. Mitchell State Park
51. Orchard Beach State Park
52. Ludington State Park
53. Wilson State Park
54. Charles Mears State Park
55. Hart-Montague Trail State Park
56. Silver Lake State Park
57. Newaygo State Park
58. Bay City State Park
59. Albert E. Sleeper
60. Port Crescent State Park
61. Sanilac Historic Site
62. Lakeport State Park

63. Duck Lake State Park
64. Muskegon State Park
65. P.J. Hoffmeister State Park
66. Grand Haven State Park
67. Ionia Recreation Area
68. Sleepy Hollow State Park
69. Holland State Park
70. Saugatuck Dunes State Park
71. Yankee Springs State Park
72. Brighton Recreation Area
73. Lakelands Trail State Park
74. Pinckney State Park
75. Waterloo Recreation Area
76. Fort Custer Recreation Area
77. Kal-Haven Trail Sesquicentennial State Park
78. Van Buren State Park
79. Grand Mere State Park
80. Warren Dunes State Park
81. Warren Woods Natural Area
82. Coldwater Lake State Park
83. Lake Hudson Rec. Area
84. Cambridge State Hist. Park
85. W.J. Hayes State Park
86. Metamora-Hadley Rec. Area
87. Ortonville Recreation Area
88. Holly Recreation Area
89. Seven Lakes State Park
90. Pontiac Lake Recreation Area
91. Bald Mtn. Recreation Area
92. W.C. Wetzel State Park
93. Algonac State Park
94. Dodge No. 4 State Park
95. Highland Recreation Area
96. Proud Lake Recreation Area
97. Island Lake Recreation Area
98. Maybury State Park
99. Sterling State Park

36. Young S.P. – 293 sites, ☎ 616-582-7523.

37. Clear Lake S.P. – 200 sites, ☎ 517-785-4388.

38. Leelanau S.P. – 50 sites, ☎ 616-922-5270.

39. Old Mission Point – formerly designated as future state park; now managed by township.

40. Otsego Lake S.P. – 203 sites, ☎ 517-732-5485.

41. Negwegon S.P. – no camping, ☎ 517-739-9730.

42. Hartwick Pines S.P. – 100 sites, ☎ 517-348-7068.

43. Traverse City S.P. – 343 sites, ☎ 616-922-5270.

44. Interlochen S.P. – 550 sites, ☎ 616-276-9511.

45. North Higgins Lake S.P. – 218 sites, ☎ 517-821-6125.

46. South Higgins Lake S.P. – 512 sites, ☎ 517-821-6374.

47. Harrisville S.P. – 229 sites, ☎ 517-724-5126.

48. Rifle River Recreation Area – 181 sites, ☎ 517-473-2258.

49. Tawas Point S.P. – 210 sites, ☎ 517-362-5041.

50. William Mitchell S.P. – 270 sites, ☎ 616-775-7911.

51. Orchard Beach S.P. – 175 sites, ☎ 616-723-7422.

52. Ludington S.P. – 388 sites, ☎ 616-843-8671.

53. Wilson S.P. – 160 sites, ☎ 517-539-3021.

54. Charles Mears S.P. – 179 sites, ☎ 616-869-2051.

Southern Lower Peninsula

55. Hart-Montague Trail S.P. – no camping, ☎ 616-873-3083.

56. Silver Lake S.P. – 249 sites, ☎ 616-873-3083.

57. Newaygo S.P. – 99 sites, ☎ 616-745-2888.

58. Bay City State Recreation Area – 264 sites, ☎ 517-684-3020.

59. Albert E. Sleeper S.P. – 280 sites, ☎ 517-856-4411.

60. Port Crescent S.P. – 181 sites, ☎ 517-738-8663.

61. Sanilac Historic Site – no camping, ☎ 517-373-0510.

62. Lakeport S.P. – 315 sites, ☎ 810-327-6224.

63. Duck Lake S.P. – no camping, ☎ 616-744-3480.

64. Muskegon S.P. – 377 sites, ☎ 616-744-3480.

65. P.J. Hoffmaster S.P. – 293 sites, ☎ 616-798-3711.

66. Grand Haven S.P. – 182 sites, ☎ 616-798-3711.

67. Ionia S.P. – 100 sites, ☎ 616-527-3750.

68. Sleepy Hollow S.P. – 181 sites, ☎ 517-651 – 6217.

69. Holland S.P. – 250 sites, ☎ 616-399-9390.

70. Saugatuck Dunes S.P. – no camping, ☎ 616-399-9390.

71. Yankee Springs Recreation Area – 325 sites, ☎ 616-795-9081.

72. Brighton Recreation Area – 222 sites, ☎ 810-229-6566.

73. Lakelands Trail S.P. – no camping, ☎ 734-426-4913.

74. Pinckney Recreation Area – 245 sites, ☎ 734-426-4913.

75. Waterloo Recreation Area – 434 sites, ☎ 734-475-8307.

76. Fort Custer Recreation Area – 219 sites, ☎ 616-731-4200.

77. Kal-Haven Trail S.P. – no camping, ☎ 616-637-4984.

78. Van Buren S.P. – 220 sites, ☎ 616-637-2788.

79. Grand Mere S.P. – no camping, ☎ 616-426-4013.

80. Warren Dunes S.P. – 182 sites, ☎ 616-426-4013.

81. Warren Woods Natural Area – no camping, ☎ 616-426-4013.

Appendix

82. Coldwater Lake S.P. – undeveloped.
83. Lake Hudson Recreation Area – 50 sites, ☎ 517-445-2265.
84. Cambridge State Historic Park – no camping, ☎ 517-467-7401.
85. W.J. Hayes S.P. – 200 sites, ☎ 517-467-7401.
86. Metamora-Hadley Recreation Area – 220 sites, ☎ 810-797-4439.
87. Ortonville Recreation Area – 25 sites, ☎ 810-627-3828.
88. Holly Recreation Area – 161 sites, ☎ 810-634-8811.
89. Seven Lakes S.P. – 78 sites, ☎ 810-634-7271.
90. Pontiac Lake Recreation Area – 176 sites, ☎ 810- 666-1020.
91. Bald Mountain Recreation Area – no camping, ☎ 810-693-6767.
92. W.C. Wetzel S.P. – no camping, ☎ 810-465-2160.
93. Algonac S.P. – 300 sites, ☎ 810-465-2160.
94. Dodge # 4 S.P. – no camping, ☎ 810-666-1020.
95. Highland Recreation Area – 30 sites, ☎ 810-685-2433.
96. Proud Lake Recreation Area – 130 sites, ☎ 810-685-2433.
97. Island Lake S.P. – no camping, ☎ 810-229-7067.
98. Maybury S.P. – no camping, ☎ 810-349-8390.
99. Sterling S.P. – 288 sites, ☎ 734-289-2715.

■ Major Festivals & Outdoor Events

Alma Highland Festival (Alma), ☎ 517-463-8979
Alpenfest (Gaylord), ☎517-732-6333 or 800-345-8621
Anchor Bay Triathlon (New Baltimore), ☎ 810-725-0291

Ann Arbor Art Fair (Ann Arbor), ☎ 734-995-7281 or 800-888-9487

Au Sable River International Canoe Marathon and Canoe Festival (Grayling), ☎ 517-348-2921 or 800-937-8837

Bass Festival (Crystal Falls), ☎ 888-TRY-IRON

Bavarian Festival (Frankenmuth), ☎ 800-FUN-FEST

Berrien County Youth Fair (Berrien Springs), ☎ 616-473-4251

Big Mac Scenic Bike Tour (Mackinac Island), ☎ 616-436-5664 or 800-666-0160

Blessing of the Bikes (Baldwin), ☎ 616-745-4331 or 800-245-3240

Blue Water Classic (Harbor Beach), ☎ 800-35-THUMB

Brockway Mountain Cross-Country Ski Challenge (Copper Harbor), ☎ 800-338-7982

Budweiser Pro-Am Fishing Tournament (Manistee), ☎ 616-398-FISH

Budweiser Walleye Tournament (Caseville), ☎ 517-856-3818 or 800-606-1347

Buick White Pine Stampede, Cross Country Ski Race (Bellaire), ☎ 616-533-8621 or 800-678-4111

Cereal Festival (Battle Creek), ☎ 800-534-7359

Cherry Blossom Festival (Traverse City), ☎ 616-947-2255

Classic Fishing Tournament (Baraga), ☎ 906-353-6958 or 800-323-8045

Co-Expo 250 Snowmobile Race (Mt. Pleasant), ☎ 517-433-2029

Color Cruise and Island Festival (Grand Ledge), ☎ 517-627-2383

Copper Island Classic Cross-Country Ski Race (Calumet), ☎ 906-337-0626 or 800-338-7982

Dogwood Pedal (Dowagiac), ☎ 616-782-5704

Dulcimer FunFest (Evart), ☎ 616-734-2181

Fahrrad Bike Tour (Frankenmuth)☎ 517-652-9162

Festival on Ice (Baraga), ☎ 906-524-7444

Firecracker 100 Bicycle Tour (Howell), ☎ 810-545-0511

Appendix

Fishfly Festival (New Baltimore), ☎ 810-725-5148

Five-Card Ski Showdown (Cedar), ☎ 800-968-0576

500 Miler Snowmobile Race (Grand Marais), ☎ 906-387-2138

Frog Island Music Festival (Ypsilanti), ☎ 734-761-1800

G-M Classic Sled Dog Race (Gwinn), ☎ 800-544-4321

Goose Festival (Fennville), ☎ 616-561-8555

Gran' Travers' VASA Cross-Country Ski Racing (Traverse City), ☎ 616-938-4400

Great Bear Chase (Calumet, cross-country skiing), ☎ 906-337-4520 or 800-338-7982

Great Lakes Sport-Kite Championships (Grand Haven), ☎ 616-846-7501

Grosse Ile Island Duathlon (Grosse Ile), ☎ 734-278-1350

Harborfest (South Haven), ☎ 616-637-5252

Hebda Cup (Wyandotte rowing regatta), ☎ 734-246-4505

Holland Tulip Time Festival (Holland), ☎ 616-396-4221 or 800-822-2770

I-500 Snowmobile Race (Sault St. Marie), ☎ 906-635-1500

Ice Fishing Derby (Iron Mountain), ☎ 906-774-2772

Ice Sculpture Spectacular (Plymouth), ☎ 734-453-1540

Iceman Cometh Mountain Bike Challenge (Kalkaska), ☎ 616-938-5882

Ididaride (Adrian), ☎ 734-971-2748

Intercontinental Cup Ski-Jumping Championship (Ishpeming), ☎ 800-544-4321

International Balloon Festival (Battle Creek), ☎ 800-397-2240

International Festival of Lights (Battle Creek), ☎ 800-397-2240

International Freedom Festival (Detroit), ☎ 313-923-7400

International Snowmobile World Series (Lewiston), ☎ 517-786-2293

Irish Festival (Clare), ☎ 517-386-2442

Kal-Haven Trail Blazer (Kalamazoo, South Haven), ☎ 616-657-3232

Keweenaw Ride-In Snowmobile Races (Copper Harbor), ☎ 906-289-4637 or 800-338-7982

King Salmon Spectacular (Manistee), ☎ 616-398-FISH

Kirtland's Warbler Festival (Roscommon), ☎ 517-275-5121

Lake Macatawa Triathlon (Holland), ☎ 616-396-2345

Leelanau Peninsula Wine Festival (Northport), ☎ 616-386-5806

Loppet Cross-Country Ski Race (Rothbury), ☎ 616-894-4444 or 800-879-9702

Mackinaw Mush Dog Sled Race (Mackinaw City), ☎ 616-436-5664 or 800-666-0169

Manchester Canoe Race (Manchester, on the Raisin River), ☎ 734-428-7722

Mark Mellon Memorial Triathlon (Gaylord), ☎ 517-732-6521

Michigan Brown Trout Festival (Alpena), ☎ 800-4-ALPENA

Michigan Cup Nordic Ski Marathon (Grayling), ☎ 517-348-9266

Michigan Festival (East Lansing), ☎ 800-935-FEST

Michigan Renaissance Festival (Holly), ☎ 800-601-4848

Michigan State Fair (Detroit), ☎ 313-369-8250

Michigan Tastefest (Detroit), ☎ 313-872-0188

Michigan Trail Marathon (Pinckney Recreation Area), ☎ 734-769-5016

Michigander Mountain Bike Ride (West Michigan), ☎ 517-393-6022

Midwest 300 Snowmobile Race (Cadillac), ☎ 616-775-9776 or 800-22-LAKES

Mighty Mac Scenic Bike Tour (St. Ignace), ☎ 906-643-6950 or 800-338-6660

Mogul Classic (Marquette), ☎ 800-944-SNOW

Montreaux-Detroit Jazz Festival (Detroit), ☎ 313-963-7622

Morel Mushroom Festival (Boyne City), ☎ 616-582-6222

Mountain Bike Challenge (Ithaca), ☎ 616-453-4245

National Canoe Championships (Niles), ☎ 616-683-3720

National Cherry Festival (Traverse City), ☎ 616-947-4230 or 800-968-3380

North American International Auto Show (Detroit), ☎ 800-624-2795

North American Snowmobile Festival (Cadillac), ☎ 616-775-9776 or 800-22-LAKES

Northern Michigan Tall Ship Parade (Traverse City), ☎ 616-941-0467

Paradise Tahquamenon Wilderness Canoe Race (Paradise), ☎ 906-492-3219

Perch Festival (Caseville fishing contest), ☎ 800-35-THUMB

Perchville USA (East Tawas, Tawas City), ☎ 800-55-TAWAS

Pine Mountain Music Festival (Upper Peninsula), ☎ 906-487-2844

Polar-Equator Trail Bike Tour (Gaylord area), ☎ 800-225-7568

Port Huron to Mackinac Island Yacht Race (Mackinac Island), ☎ 313-822-1853

Red Earth Loppet Cross-Country Race (Marquette), ☎ 906-228-7749 or 800-544-4321

Red Flannel Festival (Cedar Springs), ☎ 616-696-3260

Red Man Bass Fishing Tournament (Grand Haven), ☎ 309-828-4317 or 800-303-4096

Ride Around Torch Lake (Elk Rapids), ☎ 616-941-2553

Ride of Note Bicycle Tour (Corunna), ☎ 517-743-4822

River Roar (Bay City), ☎ 888-BAY-TOWN

Riverfest (Ontonagon), ☎ 906-884-4735

Sault Salmon Slam (Sault St. Marie), ☎ 800-MI-SAULT

Schu's International Triathlon (St. Joseph), ☎ 616-983-4670

Shanty Days (Caseville), ☎ 800-606-1347

Ship & Shore Festival (New Buffalo), ☎ 616-469-0410

Shiver on the River Walleye Fishing Contest (Saginaw), ☎ 517-776-9704 or 800-875-6397

Shoreline Circle Tours (Throughout Michigan), ☎ 888-MI-BIKES

Ski-A-Thon (Cedar), ☎ 616-228-1867 or 800-968-0576

Slush Cup, VASA Trail Mountain Bike Race (Traverse City), ☎ 616-938-5882

Snowfest (Cedarville-Hessel, Les Cheneux Islands), ☎ 906-484-3935

Snowmobile Poker Runs (St. Ignace), ☎ 517-366-5644 or 800-248-LAKE

Spring Bicycle Tour (Montague), ☎ 616-894-8052

Spring Carnival (Marquette), ☎ 800-944-SNOW

Spring Mountain Bike Race (Boyne Falls), ☎ 616-453-4245

Starker Mann Biathlon (Gaylord), ☎ 517-732-6333

Sturgeon Shivaree (Onaway, fishing and snowmobiling), ☎ 517-733-2933

Summer Arts Festival (Interlochen), ☎ 616-276-6230

Superior Snow Challenge Snowmobile Races (Copper Harbor), ☎ 800-858-4869

Tahquamenon Falls Nordic Invitational (Newberry), ☎ 906-293-3218 or 800-831-7292

Taste of Saugatuck (Saugatuck), ☎ 616-857-5615

Thumb's Up Bicycle Tour (Port Austin), ☎ 517-269-7136

Tip-Up Town USA (Houghton Lake), ☎ 517-366-5644 or 800-248-LAKE

Tott Tour of the Thumb (Bay City), ☎ 517-659-2155

Tour de UP (Marquette), ☎ 906-228-7997

Tri-State Regatta Festival (St. Joseph), ☎ 616-923-6739

Trillium Season (Mackinac Island biking tours), ☎ 906-847-3783 or 800-4-LILACS

Triple Trail Triathlon Challenge (Pinckney), ☎ 734-662-1000

Troutarama (Baldwin), ☎ 616-745-4331

Appendix

Underwater Treasure Hunt, Straits of Mackinac (St. Ignace), ☎ 906-643-8717 or 800-338-6660

UP Snowboard Championships (Marquette), ☎ 800-944-SNOW

Upper Peninsula 200 Sled Dog Race (Marquette), ☎ 906-226-6591 or 800-544-4321

VASA Cross-Country Ski Race (Traverse City), ☎ 616-938-4400

Vermontville Maple Syrup Festival (Vermontville), ☎ 517-726-0394

Victorian Christmas Sleighbell Parade and Old Christmas Weekend (Manistee), ☎ 800-288-2286

Victorian Festival (Grand Ledge), ☎ 517-627-2383

Walleye Fishing Tournament (East Jordan), ☎ 616-536-7351

Walleye Fishing Tournament (Port Austin), ☎ 517-738-5171 or 800-35-THUMB

Walleye Jamboree (Pickford), ☎ 906-632-3301

Wayfarer Regatta (Harbor Beach), ☎ 800-35-THUMB

White Lake Perch Festival (Montague-Whitehall), ☎ 616-893-4585 or 800-879-9702

Winter Carnival (Cheboygan, snowmobile racing), ☎ 800-968-3302

Winter Festival (Mackinac Island), ☎ 906-847-3853

Winter Funfest and Sled-Dog Enduro (St. Ignace), ☎ 906-643-8717 or 800-338-6660

Winter Wolf Festival (Grayling), ☎ 517-348-2921 or 800-937-8837

Winterfest (Baldwin), ☎ 616-745-4331 or 800-245-3240

Winterfest (Gaylord), ☎ 517-732-6333 or 800-345-8621

Winterfest Ice Fishing Contest (Roscommon), ☎ 517-275-8760

Woodward Dream Cruise (Metro Detroit), ☎ 248-540-4880

World Balloon Festival (Battle Creek), ☎ 616-962-0592

■ Outdoor & Conservation Organizations

Great Lakes Natural Resource Center
Michigan Office, National Wildlife Federation
506 E. Liberty, 2d Floor
Ann Arbor, MI 48104-2210
☎ 734-769-3351

Izaak Walton League - Michigan
55 Kenton SE
Grand Rapids, MI 49508-5011
☎ 616-455-3339

Lansing Oar & Paddle Club
PO Box 26254
Lansing, MI 48909
www.voyager.net/loapc

League of Michigan Bicyclists
PO Box 16201
Lansing, MI 48901
☎ 616-452-BIKE

Michigan Environmental Council
115 W. Allegan St., #10B
Lansing, MI 48933
☎ 517-487-9539

Michigan Hang Gliders
939 Boyd Ave.
Traverse City, MI 49684
☎ 616-922-2844

Michigan Mountain Biking Association
PO Box 29
Belmont, MI 49306
☎ 616-785-0120

Michigan Recreational Canoeing Association
PO Box 357
Baldwin, MI 49304

Appendix

Michigan Snowmobile Association
☎ 616-361-2285

Michigan Steelhead and Salmon Fishing Association
PO Box 213
Paw Paw, MI 49079
☎ 616-657-2518

Michigan Trail Riders Association
1650 Ormond Rd.
White Lake, MI 48384-2344
☎ 810-889-3624

Michigan Trailfinders Club
2680 Rockhill NE
Grand Rapids, MI 49505
☎ 616-242-6912

Michigan Underwater Preserve Council
560 N. State St.
St. Ignace, MI 49781-1429
☎ 800-338-6660

Michigan United Conservation Clubs (MUCC)
PO Box 30235
Lansing, MI 48909
☎ 517-371-1041

MUSH (Mid-Union Sled Haulers)
4480 Hendershot NW
Grand Rapids, MI 49544
☎ 616-784-2919

National Rails-to-Trails Conservancy - Michigan Chapter
913 W. Holmes, Suite 145
Lansing, MI 48909-0411
☎ 517-393-6022

Nature Conservancy - Michigan
2840 E. Grand River, Suite 5
E. Lansing, MI 48823
☎ 517-332-1741

North Country Trail Association
49 Monroe Center NW, Suite 200B
Grand Rapids, MI 49503
☎ 616-454-5506

Sierra Club
Mackinac Chapter
300 N. Washington Square, Suite 411
Lansing, MI 48933
☎ 517-484-2372
http://www.sierraclub.org/chapters/mi

Three Oaks Spokes Bicycle Club
110 N. Elm
Three Oaks, MI 49128
☎ 616-756-3361

Trout Unlimited - Michigan Council
106 Pheasant Run Dr.
Troy, MI 48098
☎ 248-828-0688

UP Sled Dog Association
PO Box 15
Marquette, MI 49855

West Michigan Coastal Kayakers Association
☎ 616-241-3163
http://www.iserv.net/~wmcka

■ Booklist

The shelves of Michigan bookstores often include volumes primarily devoted to one of the state's outdoor activities or geographic regions. Many of these works provide helpful, detailed information to adventurers pondering a trip into the wilds of the Great Lakes State. Here is a brief rundown.

Geographic Guides

Borealis: An Isle Royale Potpourri. Houghton, MI: Isle Royale Natural History Association, 1992.

Carney, Tom. *Natural Wonders of Michigan: A Guide to Parks, Preserves, and Wild Places.* Castine, ME: Country Roads Press, 1995.

DuFresne, Jim. *Isle Royale National Park.* Seattle, WA: Mountaineers, 1989.

DuFresne, Jim. *Michigan State Parks.* Seattle, WA: Mountaineers, 1989.

DuFresne, Jim. *Porcupine Mountains Wilderness State Park.* Lansing, MI: Thunder Bay Press, 1993.

Isle Royale: Moods, Magic & Mystique. Houghton, MI: Isle Royale Natural History Association, 1990.

McVeigh, Amy. *Mackinac Connection: An Insider's Guide.* Mackinac Island, MI: Mackinac Pub., 1989.

Penrose, Laurie. *A Guide to 199 Michigan Waterfalls.* Davison, MI: Friede Publications, 1987.

Rafferty, Michael, and Robert Sprague. *The Porcupine Mountains Companion.* 3d ed. White Pine, MI: Nequaket Natural History Associates, 1996.

Activity Guides

Abramowski, Dwain. *Mountain Biking Michigan: The Best Trails in Southern Michigan.* Holt, MI: Thunder Bay Press, 1997.

Allen, Pat, and Gerald L. DeRuiter. *Backpacking in Michigan.* 2d ed. Ann Arbor, MI: University of Michigan Press, 1989.

Burnett, Nicholas. *The Best Adventure Yet.* St. Ignace, MI: Upper Peninsula Diving Council, 1995.

Dennis, Jerry, and Craig Date. *Canoeing Michigan Rivers: A Comprehensive Guide to 45 Michigan Rivers.* Davison, MI: Friede Pub., 1986.

DuFresne, Jim. *Isle Royale National Park.* Seattle, WA: Mountaineers, 1989.

DuFresne, Jim. *Porcupine Mountains Wilderness State Park.* Lansing, MI: Thunder Bay Press, 1993.

Faitel, John. *Horseman's Guide to Michigan Trails.* Keego Harbor, MI: JF Press, 1996.

Gentry, Karen. *Cycling East Michigan: 30 of the Best Bike Routes in East Michigan.* Lansing, MI: Thunder Bay Press, 1995.

Gentry, Karen. *Cycling Michigan: 25 of the Best Bike Routes in West Michigan.* Lansing, MI: Thunder Bay Press, 1993.

Hansen, Dennis R. *Trail Atlas of Michigan.* 2d ed. Okemos, MI: Hansen Publishing, 1997.

Harrington, Steve. *Divers Guide to Michigan.* Mason, MI: Maritime Press, 1990.

Huggler, Tom. *Fish Michigan Series.* Davison, MI: Friede Publications, 1991 – .

Johnson, Kathy. *Diving and Snorkeling Guide to the Great Lakes: Lakes Superior, Michigan, Huron, Erie, and Ontario.* Houston, TX: Pisces Books, 1991.

Linsenman, Bob. *Michigan Trout Streams: A Fly-Angler's Guide.* Woodstock, VT: Backcountry Publications, 1993.

McMonagle, Pat. *Michigan Mountain Biking: A Guide to Mountain Trails in Michigan.* Boulder, CO: Broken Spoke Pub., 1994.

Modrzynski, Mike. *Hiking Michigan.* Helena, MT: Falcon Press, 1996.

Stovall, Pamela. *Short Bike Rides in Michigan.* Old Saybrook, CT: Globe Pequot Press, 1995.

Terrell, Mike. *Mountain Biking Michigan: The Best Trails in Northern Lower Michigan.* Holt, MI: Thunder Bay Press, 1996.

Terrell, Mike. *Northern Michigan's Best Cross Country Ski Trails.* Williamsburg, MI: Outdoor Recreation Press, 1995.

Van Valkenberg, Phil. *Mountain Biking the Great Lakes States.* Helena, MT: Falcon Press, 1995.

Voices of the Lakes: Shipwrecks and Our Maritime Heritage. St. Ignace, MI: Great Lakes Diving Council, 1996.

Appendix

Index

Index

Index